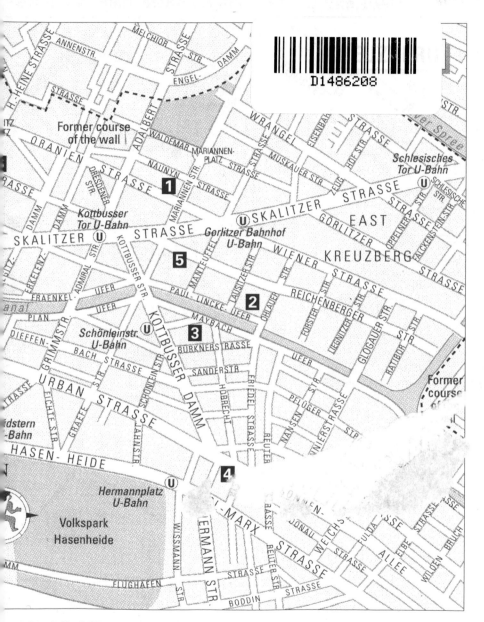

5 Tata, the Arndts' first nanny, sheltered Lina and sometimes Ruth here and in her cottage in Burig for two years.

6 Bruno had a room here and worked as an air-raid warden.

7 Ida Forbeck lived here and she took in Charlotte for several months.

8 Herr Mattul, a tailor in Spittelmarkt, hired Ellen. Through his son she met Colonel Wehlen, who lived in west Berlin and employed her and Ruth.

**Note:** Despite heavy bombing, most street names and locations remain the same as during the war. The area is about three kilometres (one and three-quarter miles) south of the Reichstag and Hitler's bunker. This map has been adapted with kind permission from *The Rough Guide to Berlin*, published January 2001 by Rough Guides Ltd, London.

# SURVIVAL IN THE SHADOWS

# SURVIVAL IN THE SHADOWS

## SEVEN HIDDEN JEWS IN HITLER'S BERLIN

Barbara Lovenheim

**Peter Owen**
London

PETER OWEN PUBLISHERS
73 Kenway Road, London SW5 0RE

First published in Great Britain 2002 by
Peter Owen Publishers

ISBN 0 7206 1141 5

A catalogue record for this book is available from
the British Library

Printed and bound in Great Britain by
MPG Books Ltd, Bodmin, Cornwall

# Contents

# Illustrations
*Between pages 124 and 125*

Dr Arthur Arndt with his wife Lina and their children Ruth and Erich, 1924

Ellen as a toddler; Bruno aged eight; Erich and Ruth on their first day of school

Ellen's mother, Charlotte Lewinsky, as a young woman

Dr Arndt as a young man during the First World War

Dr Arndt's 1922 Piccard car; Dr Arndt, Lina and Lina's oldest sister

Ellen photographed in 1940; Charlotte with Ellen's aunt, Johanna Kroner

Ellen and Erich at a party, Berlin, 1940; Ellen, Erich and a friend on the beach in 1940

Ruth's Star of David and Erich's identity card from Siemens

Ruth's state identity card, dated 1939, and her identity card from Ehrich & Graetz

Erich's friend, Bruno Gumpel, 1943; Ruth as a nurse in the Jewish Hospital, Berlin, 1941

Ruth in the *Judenhaus* before the family went into hiding

Portraits of Ellen, Erich, Ruth and Bruno, taken in 1940

Bruno's mother, Ella, his father, Gotthold, and his older brother, Günther

Erich working in Max Köhler's factory; Max's son, Hans, at his lathe

Floor plan of Köhler's factory, where the members of the group lived and worked

Dr Arndt's special transport permit enabling him to visit patients

Klara and Max Köhler; Anni Gehre with her grandson; Anni Harm and her young daughter

Anni and Max Gehre after the war in the USA; Uschi Treptow with her husband, 1947; Uschi's parents, Ernst and Marie

Gretchen Dübler and her daughter Annalee with Ellen and Erich in Berlin, 1990; Max and Klara Köhler as featured in a German newspaper after the war

Purzel Lefèbre and Charlotte with two German soldiers during the war; Ruth with the Santaella family in the Harz mountains after D-Day

José and Carmen Santaella with their Yad Vashem award citing them as Righteous Gentiles in 1991

Charlotte photographed in Berlin, 1946

Dr Arndt's passport photograph and Lina's 'Victim of Fascism' card

Ruth and Bruno in Berlin on their wedding day, 29 September 1945

The portraits of Ellen and Erich and Ruth and Bruno, given to Arthur and Lina Arndt in 1946 by the two couples

Celebratory New Year party held at the Arndts' on 31 December 1945 for friends and survivors

Ruth, Bruno, Ellen, Erich and Charlotte on board the *Marine Flasher* taking them to the USA; the ship approaching New York Harbor, 20 May 1946, with around eight hundred passengers from Europe

Ellen, Erich, Charlotte, Bruno and Ruth on the pier of New York Harbor after disembarking

Ellen and Ruth featured in the *New York Post* enjoying ice-cream sodas before going up to the top of the Empire State Building

Erich, Ellen, Ruth and Bruno at the Arndts' and Gumpels' fiftieth wedding anniversary celebration in 1993; the two couples with the family celebrating Erich's seventieth birthday

Ellen and Erich in 2001 revisiting the factory on Oranienstrasse, Berlin, where they hid for two years

The Santaellas' daughter, Teti, and Teti's daughter visiting the Yad Vashem Museum in Israel in 1999 where the Santaellas are listed as Righteous Gentiles; Ellen, Erich and Ruth on a trip to Berlin, 1999

7

*Whoever saves a single life is as one who has saved an entire world.*
– Inscription on the medal awarded to Righteous Gentiles
by Yad Vashem

# Introduction

I stumbled on the extraordinary saga of the Arndt, Lewinsky and
Gumpel families quite accidentally in my home town, Rochester,
New York. During the course of a visit there my friend and col-
league Barbara Appelbaum, who directs the Center for Holocaust
Awareness and Information, asked me to edit a book with her pro-
filing Holocaust survivors from Germany and Austria living in the
Rochester area. When I read a transcript describing how Ellen and
Erich Arndt and five other Jews hid together from the Nazis for
over two and a half years in Berlin, I was stunned.

Like many other American Jews, I subscribed to the theory that
all Germans were overtly or covertly anti-Semitic. While I knew
stories of Jews who had been protected by non-Jews in countries
such as Holland, France and Belgium, where most ordinary civilians were fiercely opposed to Hitler, I could not imagine that a
group of seven Jews could have survived in the heart of Berlin –
under Hitler's nose, so to speak.

I decided to meet the Arndts and propose writing a full-length
book on their life underground. They were receptive but wary. Not
surprisingly, several journalists had approached them through the
years, but, for one reason or another, a book had not materialized.
They were also understandably nervous about entrusting intimate
details about this important part of their life stories to another person.

We decided to proceed with the proviso that we work closely as
a team. The book we envisaged would not be a typical 'as told to'
memoir, because there were three people and three voices
involved: Ellen and Erich Arndt and Ruth Arndt Gumpel. Instead,
it would be a narrative based on the group's collective memories
and transcripts of their journals and other documents.

The Arndts' primary motive was to thank the more than fifty
non-Jewish Germans who risked their lives to save them during

their perilous struggle to escape the Nazis during the war. While five of these protectors – the Gehres, the Köhlers, the Schulzes, the Treptows and the Santaellas – have been officially honoured by Yad Vashem, the Holocaust memorial in Israel, as 'righteous Gentiles', there were many others who played minor but equally important roles. As Ellen often reminds me, the people who knew their true identities and did not say anything to the German authorities were as important as the people who actively provided them with food and shelter. A chain is only as strong as its weakest link.

Ruth's husband, Bruno, whom she met during her years in the underground, died several years ago from cancer. Ellen, Erich and Ruth, however, are very much alive. I have been working with them for over two years, and I have come to know them all very well. What I have come to value most about them is their openness and their lack of rancour and bitterness. Despite the deprivations and human losses they suffered as a result of Hitler's barbarous policies against the Jews, they vowed that they would not allow him to rule their lives. Defying Hitler and the Nazis, to them, meant cultivating a zest for life and, ultimately, telling their story to the world.

Ellen and Erich live in an airy two-bedroom apartment in a suburb of Rochester in a building next to my mother's apartment house. The Arndts moved to Rochester about forty years ago from Hempstead, New York, where they settled after emigrating to the USA in 1946. If it were not for their heavy German accents you would assume they were typical upper-middle-class Americans. Ellen is slim with short grey hair. She usually dresses in trousers, sporting a gold chain with a Star of David inlaid with tiny blue stones around her neck. She is incredibly bright and funny, with a dry, ironic sense of humour; outspoken when she feels the occasion merits it and extremely generous to her friends and family. Erich has a full head of thick grey hair and wears glasses. Several years ago he retired from his job as a division manager with the Alliance Tool and Die Company; now he tunes pianos in his spare time. He suffers from diabetes and sometimes has to use a walking-stick. Less outgoing than Ellen, Erich is the decision-maker in the family, and he has a similarly understated, wry sense of humour.

After moving to Rochester, the Arndts joined a Reform synagogue, where Erich was president of the congregation for several years. Ellen held a leadership role in the sisterhood. They are no longer so active in their temple, but Ellen continues to give talks to schoolchildren and college students about her experiences during the war. Erich tends to shy away from public appearances; he prefers to read and listen to music.

The Arndts have two daughters, six grandchildren and two great-granddaughters. Their younger daughter, Renée, who has five children, also lives in Rochester with her husband, a psychiatrist, and two adopted Korean teenagers. Renée's eldest daughter, Timna, from an earlier marriage, has two small daughters, Sarah and Sophie. The Arndts' eldest daughter, Marion, lives in Michigan; she and her husband have one son in his twenties. Ellen and Erich are very family-minded these days: they frequently take their teenage grandchildren to lessons and concerts and take care of them after school; they also help Timna, who works as a nurse, with babysitting and chores. They often put up their other grandchildren when they come to town for a visit, host holiday dinners and mediate in family crises.

Erich's sister, Ruth Arndt Gumpel, is also extremely family-oriented. She has two sons: Larry, an audio supervisor for CBS, and Stanley, a technical specialist for pre-press. Ruth and her husband, Bruno Gumpel, moved to Petaluma, California, from their home in Queens, New York, to be near Stanley and his son Alex after Bruno – who passed away several years after the move – retired from his position as a technical supervisor with CBS.

Ruth, who worked in New York as a paediatric nurse, is lively and irreverent, with a wicked sense of humour. She has a penchant for stylish hats and colourful scarves. She belongs to a poetry-reading group in Petaluma, where she has made a number of new friends. She also volunteers in a local hospital as well as an animal shelter. But her chief focus is helping out with her teenage grandson, Alex.

Ellen and Erich are still extremely close to Ruth. They speak to each other on the telephone every Saturday – promptly at noon – and they visit often. They have all participated actively in the creation of this book. They want the world to know that there were some 'good' Germans who were more responsive to their conscience than to Hitler. In a society where everyone is guilty, it is sometimes argued, no one is responsible. That was not the case in Nazi Germany.

Of the 1,400 German Jews who reportedly survived the war hiding in Berlin, the Arndt–Lewinsky–Gumpel group was the largest to have survived as a unit. Perhaps owing to the anti-German sentiment that prevailed in the USA after the war and the persistence of anti-Semitism in post-war Germany, it was not until 1980 that scholars took note of the Arndts' incredible story and the help they received from German Gentiles. In that year, Ellen and Erich Arndt and Ruth and Bruno Gumpel were flown to Germany by the Berlin Senate; there they were honoured together with other former Berliners who were forced to leave Germany because of the Nazis. In 1987 Larry Gumpel taped a two-hour video on their underground years that was donated to the Holocaust Center of the Jewish Community Federation of Rochester. In 1990 the two couples were again flown to Berlin and interviewed for an exhibition, 'The Jews of Kreuzberg', that was displayed in a house on Adalbertstrasse in Kreuzberg. In January 1991 Ruth and Bruno were interviewed by the Museum of Jewish Heritage in New York City.

In 1997 Ellen and Ruth were each independently taped by the Spielberg Shoah Foundation. During the summer of 1999 Channel 4 television in Britain aired an hour-long documentary, *The Hidden Jews of Berlin*, which featured Ellen and Erich Arndt together with three other German Jews who lived in the Berlin underground. Ruth and Bruno Gumpel have also written private memoirs.

In preparing this book I have drawn on all of these sources. But primarily I have relied on my own interviews, conducted over the course of two years. I have interviewed the Arndts many times, sometimes individually, sometimes as a group. After writing a draft, they would each read it and edit it, and we would discuss it together. Then I would rework it accordingly until we could establish the right tone and details in order to render anecdotes as authentically as possible.

Barbara Schieb, a historian in Berlin who specializes in the Holocaust, has also worked closely with me on the manuscript. Barbara has consulted for the Wannsee International Memorial, the Berlin Museum and the Shoah Foundation. She interviewed Ellen, Erich, Ruth and Bruno ten years ago in the course of doing research for the Gedenkstätte Deutscher Widerstand, a memorial honouring the German resistance that is located on Stauffenbergstrasse. She has checked my narrative against her taped interviews, making suggestions and sometimes revisions. Equally important, she has read the manuscript for historical accuracy and supplied me with data on deportations and bombing raids from credible German sources. She has kept a sharp watch on such details as the correct spelling of German names and addresses, the distances between various places and whether the details remembered by the Arndts were historically logical.

In October 1999 I travelled to Berlin with Ellen, Erich and Ruth to retrace their footsteps. We travelled on the same train and bus route that the Arndts used during the war to cross Berlin and visited the sites of their original homes and hiding places. Many of these buildings were destroyed by bombs and have been replaced by new, colourful structures; others managed to survive the war. Amazingly, the façade of the factory at Oranienstrasse 20, which functioned as the headquarters and shelter for the group, has not been altered, even though the interior has been remodelled as a studio for artists. Together we stood in the courtyard and looked up at the windows of the factory; we also walked up the stairwell and looked at the doorway, where workmen some years ago found remnants of the warning device rigged up by Erich and Hans Köhler to protect the group.

We also saw two other buildings that survived the war intact: Erich's five-storey brick elementary school on Paul Lincke Ufer (formerly Kottbusser Ufer), and the small annexe of the synagogue on Paul Lincke Ufer where Erich had his bar mitzvah and where the two couples were married after the war. Since the main sanctuary of the synagogue was destroyed during Kristallnacht, the annexe was remodelled for services. Most current members of the congregation are recent émigrés from the Soviet Union.

In recounting this tale of astonishing ingenuity and daring I have relied on the documents and interviews mentioned above. The Arndts are loath to fictionalize their story, but we agreed to dramatize certain anecdotes so that they would come alive for the reader. In most cases this meant supplying connective material and adding dialogue.

Despite the fact that their underground years were long ago, this period of their lives was so traumatic that they can still remember many small details. For example, Ellen can recall clearly the outrageously eye-turning hat and silver fox furs that her mother took into hiding with her. Ruth remembers such details as the interior of her family's last home on Oranienstrasse and her meeting with José Santaella at the Hotel Adlon. Ellen and Ruth both recall vividly their escapades at Frau Liebold's, while Erich remembers how he masqueraded as a German officer.

Sometimes it took some detective work and negotiation on all our parts to verify important details. For example, Erich recalled that his father gave him a cyanide pill as a precautionary measure before he went into hiding; Ruth is quite sure that she never received a pill. We decided that Dr Arndt must have handed a pill to Erich (who, as a circumcised male, would be in the most peril if he were captured by the police) but did not give a pill to Ruth, who might have found it too upsetting to handle at the time and who bore no physical signs of Judaism.

We also agreed that using dialogue would give the narrative a greater sense of immediacy. But since it is impossible accurately to recall conversations that occurred so long ago – most people cannot remember what they said two days ago – we decided that I would recreate conversations to flesh out an incident, then we would work on the dialogue until it felt right to the Arndts and they were happy that we had captured the tone and spirit of the original exchanges.

Working out the timing of occurrences was also problematic, even though everyone could usually recall the time of year and whether the incident happened early on or later during their period in hiding. Erich and Ellen are not sure when they went to the Berlin Opera to see *Madame Butterfly*, but they know it was a Saturday night in the autumn of 1943.

Similarly, Ellen, Erich and Ruth all vividly remember the huge bombing raid on Prinzenstrasse that occurred in the autumn of 1944. We know it was after Ruth returned from Diedersdorf, and Ellen remembers that it was still warm outdoors. Erich knows it was a Saturday night, because Bruno – who was working nearby as an air-raid warden at weekends – was not with Erich when it occurred. Looking through Erich's personal diary of bombing raids, we discovered that a massive raid had occurred on Saturday night, 16 September 1944, and we agreed that this was probably the one. In most cases we could not be that specific about dates, even though we could approximate the season and the year, often by recalling a tell-tale detail such as a coat or a hat.

While there were other groups of German Jews who were hidden by Germans, the Arndt–Lewinsky–Gumpel group is the largest one known to have survived in Berlin intact. What accounts for their incredible tale of survival against all odds? There is no simple answer to this question. Undoubtedly there were numerous occasions when one person could have been detected by the authorities, and that would have led to the exposure and death of all the others. Miraculously, this never happened. And since it was risky for them to go to air-raid shelters because they might have been recognized by neighbours, they were also in great danger of being hit by bombs. The threat of starvation was severe, particularly during the last months of the war. They could have died from any one of these factors, but they didn't.

Undoubtedly they were incredibly lucky. However, luck was not the only component and perhaps it was not the chief element. They were extremely clever, courageous and, above all, determined to survive. They had contempt for the Nazis and never questioned their ability to outsmart them. As Erich often remarks, you could tell a Nazi any lie as long as you did so brazenly; anyone gullible enough to believe Nazi dogma would believe absolutely anything.

They were also extremely careful. Dr Arndt went out only late at night and only every few weeks, for fear of being identified by neighbours. Ruth frequently disguised herself as a widow, wearing heavy veils, when she went outside. They did not reveal their last names to most of the people who protected them, and they never revealed the location of the factory.

They also took the precaution of establishing strict codes of behaviour to be adhered to in the factory at all times. In doing so, their stoical and disciplined natures served them well, allowing them to carry on without falling apart, without becoming obsessed about their dire situation or turning against one another. They focused on the necessities of daily living, instead of becoming pre-occupied by the mortal danger faced by them and other Jews, a typical but remarkable survival mechanism. While they all at various times felt frightened, helpless and depressed, they did not allow these feelings to master them. Doing so would have made them too vulnerable. Instead of crying, they tried to laugh, at times finding humour in the most terrifying and painful situations.

Their strong ties to each other and the reassurance they gained from being part of a group also contributed significantly to their morale, shielding them from feelings of isolation that could have weakened their ability to get through particularly tough times. Even when they felt desperate they did not feel alone. But, ultimately, it was their fierce will to survive that was their chief weapon, prompting them to spend their days planning survival strategies: where to sleep that night; how to steal food or ration cards; what areas of the city to avoid; how to recognize Jewish traitors; where to find jobs; and how to recognize a 'good' German. Without this will to live they would have likely perished.

They are mostly dry-eyed when they retell the story of these traumatic years. Sometimes they laugh at how they managed to outwit the Nazis. Less frequently their pain surfaces. For example, when Erich recalls his emotional reunion with a Russian Jewish soldier at the end of the war, tears come to his eyes and he walks on to the terrace of his apartment, where he stands and stares into the open sky.

It has been extremely difficult for the Arndts to talk evenly or at length about these terrible happenings. Neither Ellen nor Erich will today watch films about the Holocaust. Ellen shies away from looking at photographs of concentration camp victims, fearing that she will recognize someone she knew. It has been difficult as well for me to ask them about such details. No one, after all, likes to remember pain and loss: we prefer to recall pleasant or funny incidents.

I have tried to report their story as honestly as possible. I hope that it will endure as a reminder that not even the most despicable tyrant can fully eradicate goodness.

*Barbara Lovenheim*
*New York*

# 1
# INTO THE SHADOWS

The most powerful antipode to the Aryan is the Jew . . . He is and remains the typical parasite, a sponger who, like a malign bacillus, spreads more and more as long as he will find some favourable feeding ground. And the consequences of his existence, too, resemble those of the parasite: where he appears, the host nation will sooner or later die.
– Adolf Hitler, *Mein Kampf*, 1925

A cold December wind swept through Kreuzberg, a largely working-class district of Berlin, rattling windowpanes and swirling snow and debris through the streets. Labourers returning home wrapped their scarves tightly around their faces and dug their hands deep into their pockets, keeping their heads down as they hurried along. It was December 1942, and to average Germans – those who were counting on Hitler winning the war – the reports from the eastern front were disturbing. The Sixth Army of General Friedrich Paulus was cut off in Stalingrad, surrounded on all sides by Soviet troops. A recent effort to break through and relieve the worn-out garrison had failed, leaving the Germans without adequate food or medicine or ammunition to take on either the fierce Red Army or the brutal Russian winter. General Kurt Zeitzler, the chief of the Army General Staff, knew that the Germans were doomed unless Hitler authorized a retreat. But when he implored him to yield, the Führer lost his temper. He would sacrifice his troops rather than give in. His embattled soldiers would defend the Volga to their death. Germany would never surrender.

Nor was this the first major upset. Early in November Field Marshall Erwin Rommel – the celebrated Desert Fox of the German army – had been routed by the Eighth Army of British General

Sir Bernard Law Montgomery. A week later British and American troops led by General Dwight D. Eisenhower had landed on the beaches of Morocco and Algeria to launch Operation Torch, a tactic designed to threaten German forces in Tunisia with a giant pincer movement and thus secure the Mediterranean.

It was clear to all but the most naïve Germans that a major – perhaps decisive – defeat was in the making in Stalingrad.

For the 33,000 Jews trapped in Berlin at this time, reports of the Soviet advances in Stalingrad ignited the first real flicker of hope that the Nazis might be defeated before they could exterminate the entire Jewish population. Few Jews who had survived this far into the war believed they faced anything but death: rumours had seeped into the community that the Nazis planned to annihilate all the Jews in Europe. Terrifying reports were circulating daily that seemed to verify this: stories of mass murders in the concentration camps; of Russian Jews being stripped, shot in the back and dumped in large burial pits piled with other dead Jews; of families torn asunder on arrival at the camps; of children perishing in mysterious ways.

And now those Jews who were working twelve hours a day in armaments factories knew that their time was running out. At Siemens the Jewish rumour mill known as the *Mundfunk* ('mouth radio' – a play on *Rundfunk*, the German word for radio) was carrying warnings that a massive factory raid was being planned, a raid that would purge all German factories of their Jewish workers and deport them to camps. Paul Josef Goebbels, Hitler's Minister of Propaganda, was probably the initiator. He had vowed publicly to make Berlin *judenrein* (free of Jews) and he would stop at nothing to carry out this threat.

Erich Joachim Arndt, the slim nineteen-year-old son of a respected Jewish doctor and First World War veteran, knew that he and his family and friends would be swept up in the coming raid. Since 1940 Erich had been working as a slave labourer at Siemens-Schuckert-Bohrwerk, a huge armaments factory in Spandau, a north-western suburb of Berlin, that employed about five thousand Jews during the course of the war. There he had watched helplessly as his co-workers were beaten and brutalized. Each day brought more reports of friends and relatives who had been rounded up and shipped to the camps, of arbitrary raids on *Juden-häuser* and day-care centres, of covered vans rumbling ominously through city streets.

Emigration from Germany was now illegal for Jews – the borders had been shut in October 1941. Escape to neighbouring countries was extremely difficult and dangerous. Erich could no longer count on his youth, physical health and employment skills to protect him. Nor would Dr Arndt's Iron Cross save the family. Every Jew, rich or poor, able-bodied or frail, male or female, was vulnerable.

Erich saw one solution: he and his family had to go into hiding to survive. Every day co-workers from Siemens were disappearing. The factory *Mundfunk* reported that some of these Jews were being sheltered by non-Jewish friends. Some had taken on Aryan identi-ties while working quietly in nondescript jobs. Others were hiding in sheds, back rooms and ditches.

When Erich discussed his idea with his older sister, Ruth, and his girlfriend, Ellen Lewinsky, they agreed that it was a good plan. Ruth and Ellen were also employed as slave labourers in munitions factories, and they had each witnessed the brutality of the Nazi *Vorarbeiter* (supervisors). All three young people had had close calls, and on several occasions the Arndts had hidden overnight in the living-rooms of their Lutheran friends Anni and Max Gehre and Martha Maske, alerted by rumours that the Gestapo would sweep through Kreuzberg that evening, ferreting out any Jews they could find and herding them into vans.

Ellen had already lost many close relatives – her father, David Lewinsky, her beloved great-aunt, Johanna Kroner, with whom Ellen and her mother had been living in Berlin, her cousin Ulla and Ulla's mother, Selma, and her cousin, Meta and Meta's parents. Ruth and Erich had lost their aunt Paula and many classmates and friends.

Like Erich, Ellen and Ruth had been counting on their value as slave labourers to keep them alive. But with the news of an impending purge they realized that the factories were no longer refuges from deportation. Now it was only a matter of time before they, too, would be sent to a labour camp in Poland where, they feared, they would be overworked and starved until they dropped dead. Their youth, health and ability to work would not keep them alive for long. They agreed wholeheartedly with Erich that they had one option: to stay alive they had to go underground.

Now Erich had to persuade his father, a task he knew would not be easy.

Arthur Arndt, a handsome bespectacled man with a penchant for cigars, had grown up proud to be German. As far back as anyone could remember his family had prospered in Germany; one of his great-uncles had been a Royal Escort for Frederick the Great. Arthur was the only surviving son of an Orthodox Jewish glazier from Kolberg, a small but well-known seaside resort on the Baltic. In 1913 Arthur had entered the prestigious Friedrich Wilhelms Universität in Berlin to study medicine. But after the First World War broke out the following year he interrupted his studies to serve for his country as a medic in the army. When the war ended on 11 November 1918 he volunteered to serve in a field hospital in France for a year, caring for wounded soldiers.

On Arthur's return to Berlin the German government awarded him an Iron Cross for his outstanding war performance. A year later he was accepted as an intern at the world-renowned Charité Hospital. There he specialized in obstetrics and gynaecology. In 1921 he married the daughter of a kosher butcher, Lina Arnoldi, whom he met while attending the university. Lina, red-haired and petite – she was less than 1.52 metres (five feet tall) – was energetic and spirited, with a wicked sense of humour that contrasted with Arthur's straightforward manner. He was attracted by her warmth and her good nature, while she admired her husband's idealism and shared his passion to serve their country. They were exactly the kind of high-minded, industrious people that were needed in Germany after the devastation of the First World War.

The Arndts settled in Kreuzberg, a district in south-east Berlin populated by a mixture of working-class labourers and middle-class entrepreneurs, many of whom ran small and medium-sized firms in the area. Of the more than 340,000 Germans who lived in Kreuzberg in 1933, only 6,000 – less than 2 per cent – were Jews. While most residents (both Jews and Gentiles) were moderate Social Democrats, the area around the Görlitzer train station at the intersection of Skalitzer Strasse and Oranienstrasse became a hub for Communist activity. Eventually it became a centre for working-class opposition to Hitler.

Arthur Arndt was one of the few doctors in the area. He soon attracted a large clientele of both Jewish and non-Jewish patients, developing a reputation as a thorough and compassionate physician who would tend to the needy even if they did not have enough money to pay his fees. On 16 May 1922 Lina bore him a daughter, Ruth Anni Thea. A year and a half later, on 30 November 1923, the Arndts had a son, Erich Joachim.

Soon Dr Arndt was doing so well that he was able to afford a nanny, a non-Jewish woman named Anni Schultz ('Tata'), to help Lina. In 1925 he bought a motor car – a 1922 Piccard, a Swiss-made open touring car – and he even hired a chauffeur to take him on his rounds, becoming one of the few men in the neighbourhood with his own motorized vehicle.

In 1928 the family moved into a large, seven-room apartment on Skalitzer Strasse, a big, busy thoroughfare dominated by an elevated railway and two trams and crowded during the daytime with delivery boys, shoppers and garment workers carrying newly made coats and suits on their backs.

Lina and Arthur were proud of their Jewish heritage, but, like so many other young German Jews raised in Orthodox homes, they were progressive about their religion. While they observed the major Jewish holidays and planned to introduce their children to the history and language of the ancient Hebrews, they did not keep a strictly kosher home nor did they observe Jewish rituals to the letter. They would send their children to secular schools and cultivate friendships with their non-Jewish neighbours.

Eventually Arthur and Lina decided to join a temple; the closest one was a handsome Orthodox synagogue on Kottbusser Ufer, a quiet street along the Landwehrkanal lined with magnificent chestnut trees. While most of the 2,000 congregants were Orthodox Jews, many were like the Arndts – liberal Jews who would, in today's world, be similar to conservative or reform Jews. Next door to the main building was a small annexe referred to casually as 'the little temple', where youth services were held. When Erich turned thirteen in 1936 he had his bar mitzvah there.

Despite the increasing anti-Semitic regulations which by then had stripped Jews of many of their rights – including the right to marry non-Jews, the right to work as civil servants and the right to hire female domestic workers under the age of forty-five – the Arndts were well liked and respected by their Gentile neighbours. Dr Arndt's patients continued to seek his services. Many of them hoped that Hitler would soon be overthrown, that the German people would not tolerate such a despot for long.

Then at the end of July 1938 Dr Arndt received a letter from the government informing him that as of 30 September Jewish doctors would be taken off the Medical Register and could no longer call themselves physicians. Thereafter all Jewish doctors would be known as *Krankenbehandler* (healers for the Jewish infirm) and could not treat Aryan patients. A few weeks later, on 15 August, Erich received a letter dismissing him from the Leibnitz Gymnasium on Mariannenplatz, a top school where he had distinguished himself as an outstanding student and athlete. He went to work as a bicycle delivery boy.

After these blows Dr Arndt began aggressively making plans to emigrate. He managed to locate a distant cousin in the USA – the son of his father's second cousin – and wrote to him requesting four affidavits, which would enable the family to apply for exit visas to America. Early in the autumn of 1938 Dr Arndt received the affidavits and Lina called her sisters to relay the good news. A few days later Dr Arndt received an urgent call from his 26-year-old nephew, Heinz Paul, the son of Lina's oldest sister. Someone had reported to the Gestapo that Heinz was having an affair with an Aryan woman. Heinz was sent to Sachsenhausen, a concentration camp, for violating the law. He was given forty-eight hours to obtain a visa and leave Germany, otherwise he would be interned there for good.

Heinz appealed to Uncle Arthur. Could he have one of the affidavits? Dr Arndt felt that he had little choice: he could always get another affidavit, he assumed, and Heinz's life was in danger. He could not commit his nephew to a life of internment when he had the power to save him. So he gave the affidavit to Heinz, who promptly left Germany.

The next month, in the middle of the night of 9 November, Nazi Brownshirts swept through Germany. They smashed and looted more than 7,000 Jewish-owned businesses and shops, set fire to more than 250 synagogues, including the one where Erich had had his bar mitzvah, and rounded up 30,000 Jewish men, many of them prominent citizens, and sent them to concentration camps.

The massive pogrom raised Nazi discrimination against the Jews to a new and terrifying level, and from now on the Nazis would use force and brutality to enforce their policies. Dr Arndt knew he had no time to waste. He wrote to his cousin requesting another affidavit. Throughout the cold winter he stood in long queues at consulates, trying to obtain an appointment with an official who could give him exit papers. He also appealed to everyone he knew for help. He pleaded with the Jewish official in charge of emigration. All to no avail.

In the months following the November pogrom, which came to be known as Kristallnacht, panic and rage swept through the Jewish community as everyone clamoured to leave the country. There were at least 1,000 applicants for every available visa; even countries opposed to Hitler's terrible policies now curtailed their quotas, arguing that they could not accommodate more German Jewish refugees. But Dr Arndt kept looking for ways to leave, and he enrolled in a workshop to study fumigation so that he would be able to support the family by working as an exterminator when they emigrated if he wasn't allowed to practise as a doctor. He also enrolled Erich as an apprentice at a special workshop on Holz-marktstrasse run by the Jewish Council of Berlin. There Erich

27

learned locksmithing, welding and how to operate metal-working machines.

As countries began curtailing the flow of German refugees, bribery and connections became the only way to obtain the few available visas. Even people with these could not always book passage on ships, all of which were now overloaded. Dr Arndt was well off, but he was not wealthy. He had many friends, but he did not have the right connections.

Early in April 1939, when it seemed as though things could not get any worse for the Jews, Dr Arndt received notification that he had to move to a more 'suitable' apartment. Ruth watched heartbroken as her father sold most of his medical equipment and handsome furniture. Then the family moved into a tiny and shabby two-room apartment at Oranienstrasse 206 – into a five-storey building in a drab commercial street that had been designated by the authorities as a *Judenhaus*.

The apartment was cramped and dismal, a far cry from the Arndts' previous home. A short, narrow hallway, where Erich kept his two bikes, led from the door to the kitchen. Next to that was a room with a lavatory. Bathing was done from a basin in the kitchen. The large room that tripled as a living-room, dining area and bedroom for Dr Arndt and Lina opened off the left side of the hallway. It was stuffed with furniture, some of it salvaged from their former home. Dr Arndt slept on a single bed on one side of the room, and Lina slept on a chaise-longue that stood against the other wall. A plain rectangular wooden table with half-a-dozen straight chairs around it occupied the middle of the room. There Dr Arndt would sometimes sit after dinner, smoking a cigar.

Ruth and Erich slept in a room that opened to the right of the hall. It contained a single bed on each side of the room, a table and a chair. The Arndts missed the space and comfort of their former home, where they could receive guests, where they each had their own rooms and as much or as little privacy as they wanted.

Shortly after the family moved to its new quarters, France and Holland closed their borders to Jews. Sweden, Denmark and Switzerland began sending back Jews who arrived without proper papers. Moreover, after a White Paper was issued by the British on 17 May 1939, Jews could no longer emigrate to Palestine. And there was huge competition for a limited number of visas to Britain and the USA.

By the time that war erupted in September 1939, 225,000 German Jews – about half the country's Jewish population – had managed to leave the Third Reich. For those who remained, the difficulties of everyday life grew increasingly intolerable. Jews had to turn in their radios and, shortly after, their pets. They received special ration cards stamped with the word *Jude;* they could shop for only two hours each day, and they were allowed less meat and butter than Aryans. By January 1940 Jews were denied legumes and most fruit and meat. (Only Jews who did heavy labour were permitted to buy 200 grams of meat a week, compared with Christian labourers who received 1,000 grams.) Jews were also prohibited from purchasing new clothes, shoes and underwear; they could not even buy the materials needed to mend clothes and shoes.

By early 1941 they could not legally obtain canned food, fish, poultry, eggs, milk, apples, tomatoes, coffee or cigarettes. Most had to make do with subsistence diets consisting of watery soup, cabbage, turnips, potatoes, noodles and bread. Those with money or connections bought an occasional egg or a chicken on the black market for exorbitant sums of money; others depended on the mercy of non-Jewish neighbours and family butchers for handouts. The threat of dying from malnutrition and disease was ominous and omnipresent.

As the restrictions against Jews escalated, emigration grew to a virtual standstill. Britain would no longer accept Jewish refugees, fearing they might be Fourth Columnists. And in the USA Congress would not raise quotas to accommodate more Jews, and existing quotas were going unfilled. Qualified Jewish candidates were often rejected for technical reasons. Some Jews, in desperation, set out for China, India, Africa and other far-away nations carrying only the cash and jewellery they could hide inside their clothing. Others were like Dr Arndt – they would not consider relocating to countries where they could not speak the language or understand the customs, where the prospect of supporting their families was poor.

In the autumn of 1941 the Nazis imposed even more restrictions on the Jews trapped within its boundaries. On 19 September 1941 all Jews in Germany were required to wear a large yellow star with the word *Jude* in the centre in black letters. The star had to be worn on the left side of their jackets or coats or dresses. On 15 October Germans began deporting German Jews for 'resettlement' in what they called work camps in Poland and Latvia. Most of these early deportees were elderly men and women. On 23 October the final blow came when the government closed its borders to Jews, officially banning emigration. Not even major bribes could buy one freedom. Hitler wanted no more news travelling to foreign ports. He determined, instead, to send all remaining Jews to concentration camps where he would implement the Final Solution.

A year later sealed supply trains with locked doors were transporting between 1,000 and 1,500 Jews from Berlin each month to concentration camps. Elderly deportees, war veterans and their families and Jewish religious leaders and administrators were first sent to Theresienstadt, a ghetto-like transit camp in Bohemia that the Nazis kept in moderately good condition so it could be used as a showcase for Red Cross inspectors. But the majority of Berlin deportees were sent straight away to Auschwitz-Birkenau, where the gas chambers were by this time fully operational, killing up to 10,000 Jews a day. Healthy men and some fit women were assigned immediately to work duty; elderly and infirm men, the majority of women and almost all children were sent directly to the showers. As soon as the doors were locked, crystals of Zyklon B, a cyanide gas originally manufactured as a potent disinfectant, was leaked into the rooms from small openings in the ceiling, killing those inside within minutes.

News of these gassings was carefully guarded by German officials. But, even early on, some soldiers and railway workers were spreading sinister stories about deaths and strange smells in the camps, stories that trickled into the Jewish communities, setting off even more panic and causing the suicide rate among Jews to soar.

(It is estimated that one in every ten German Jews committed suicide on receiving a deportation notice.) Then, in November 1942, Rabbi Stephen Wise of New York confirmed the rumours. Acting on information provided by a German industrialist, he publicly reported that 2 million European and Soviet Jews had been murdered by the Nazis and that Hitler had plans to annihilate the entire Jewish population. The report was carried by the BBC and heard by Germans who monitored foreign broadcasts. Although the Arndts do not recall hearing the broadcast, rumours of mass atrocities intensified and spread quickly through the *Mundfunk*, particularly in factories such as Siemens.

Dr Arndt, like many middle-aged and elderly Jews, however, believed that the camps were truly work camps and that people with skills could survive in them. And now the impending defeat of the Germans at Stalingrad gave him hope that the worst had come and gone. He knew that he could no longer count on his war record to protect his family from the wrath of the Nazi government, but he hoped that as valuable workers he and his children might be spared. Deep in his heart he believed that right and the supremacy of moral law would ultimately triumph.

But Erich disagreed, passionately and persistently. He was convinced that holding out for better times, or trusting to God or to an imminent Allied victory, were no longer viable options. Perhaps they never had been. So even though Erich was not by nature a rebel or a defiant son, he took it on himself to do whatever was needed to save his family. He began to unfold a plan to his father. They talked about it early in the morning, when Erich returned home from Siemens, or on Sundays, when Erich did not work.

Dr Arndt initially resisted Erich's proposals. He believed in German law. If the government planned to 'resettle' the Jews, he would obey. After all, he was a veteran of the last war and a law-abiding citizen. 'I will not turn you and your sister and your mother into outlaws,' he protested when Erich introduced the topic. 'If we are summoned to the camps, we will obey the law. There at least we will also have food and shelter.'

'If we go to the camps, we will probably die,' Erich challenged.

'Maybe not right away, but soon. Tante Paula has been deported. If she is still alive, why haven't we heard from her? She is Mother's closest sister. Ellen's father and her aunt and several of her cousins were sent away. She has not heard a word from any of them. If they are still alive, why aren't they writing to us? Why haven't they asked us to send them anything? Do you seriously think they are still alive?'

Erich brought up the subject every day for weeks. Dr Arndt's response was always the same: '*Nein, nein, nein.*'

Finally, Erich sensed that his father might be weakening. 'Even if I agreed, how would we live?' Dr Arndt asked one evening. 'Maybe a single man or even two could make it. But how could a family of four expect to manage? Who would be foolish enough to hide and feed four people?'

'Six people,' Erich corrected. 'Ellen and her mother plan to go with us.'

'That is even more preposterous!' responded Dr Arndt, promptly retreating to his former position. 'Who will possibly hide and feed six Jews? Who would take that risk?'

Erich suggested Anni and Max Gehre and Martha Maske.

'But the Gehres have only a small one-bedroom apartment,' argued Dr Arndt. 'And Tante Martha doesn't have room either. It's one thing to hide us for one night in their living-rooms. It's another to hide us for months or weeks or even days. They will be killed if anyone finds out. We will all be killed.'

Erich kept pressing, and Dr Arndt kept objecting. How would they get enough ration cards to feed six people? Why would anyone risk sheltering them? 'If we don't die from the Nazis, we'll die from starvation,' he said, over and over. 'It's impossible. Absolutely impossible.'

'We barely have enough to eat now,' Erich continued to argue. 'We cannot buy new soles for our shoes. We cannot ride on the trains. We must wear this star – being branded as though we are cattle. How much worse can it be in the underground? At least there we will have control of our lives!'

Dr Arndt refused to yield. Finally, on a Saturday night in late

December, Erich delivered an ultimatum. 'We cannot keep talking for another month,' he told his father. 'We might not be here in another month. We are running out of time and, even if you and Mother don't join us, Ruth and Ellen and I are going. We would rather die on the streets of Berlin than starve to death in a Nazi work camp!'

Erich knew that an ultimatum might be effective. Under no circumstances would his father split up the family. After all, his parents had refused to send Erich and Ruth to Britain on a *Kinder-transport* – a children's transport – a trip that would have ensured their safety.

Dr Arndt had never seen his son so firm, so impassioned. On one level he admired his determination. It was a trait that Erich had inherited from him but until now it had never surfaced. Finally, faced with the prospect of Ruth and Ellen leaving on their own, Dr Arndt gave in. The Arndts would either survive as a family or perish as a family.

The next day, Dr Arndt set up a meeting with Max and Anni Gehre. They lived a short distance away at Kottbusser Ufer 25A, between Lausitzer Strasse and what is today Ohlauer Strasse, in a small one-bedroom apartment. It had a tiny pantry behind the kitchen that they had converted into a small bedroom for their teenage daughter. Max Gehre had a loud laugh and a direct manner. He had not attended high school, but he was a hard, conscientious worker; after serving in the First World War he got a job as a toolmaker in a factory that made pots and pans. Soon he was promoted to foreman of his division.

Max had heard through his neighbours that Dr Arndt was a thorough and conscientious physician. When Max went to him to receive help for a stomach ailment, the two men hit it off right away. They traded stories about their experiences in the army.

Anni Gehre also went to Dr Arndt when she needed medicine. She, too, had been born into a working-class family, and she was even more outspoken than Max, with a deep, hearty laugh.

Two years after Erich was born Anni gave birth to a daughter. When she contracted diphtheria, a deadly disease in those days that was not easily treated, Dr Arndt restored her to health. The Gehres never forgot this. As far as Anni was concerned, Dr Arndt had saved her only child and she would be indebted to the Arndts for ever.

So when the strict laws against Jews were passed and Gentiles were prohibited from going to Jewish physicians, the Gehres had maintained their relationship with the Arndts. They would invite them to dinner now and then or obtain for them extra meat from their butcher. Dr Arndt was optimistic that Max and Anni would be sympathetic when he went to see them. But he was not at all sure that the couple – however generous – would be able to help him.

Anni invited him in immediately, Dr Arndt later told his family, and insisted on giving him a hot drink. But before Anni could even ask what was on his mind, the doctor got right to the point. He told them that Erich had heard rumours that a massive factory raid was being planned. 'All the Jewish workers will be sent to camps. That means that we are no longer safe. When we are sent to a camp, I may live, because I'm a doctor, and Erich may survive, because he is a machinist, and even Ruth may make it, because she is a nurse. But what kind of work could Lina do there? She may not have the same chance as we.'

He paused, then continued: 'We have decided to look for places where we can hide, just until this war is over, which should not be long now. Perhaps you can help us.' He was not comfortable in this new role of a supplicant. Proud and self-reliant, he took his responsibility as a provider seriously and he did not like asking others for assistance.

The Gehres, however, did not hesitate. They would do whatever was required to protect their friends. 'You will stay with us,' said Max.

Anni immediately agreed, offering to shelter Dr Arndt in her daughter's tiny bedroom. 'She will sleep on the couch in the living-room,' she told him.

Dr Arndt, touched by their gesture, quickly protested. 'If you insist on hiding someone, I prefer that it be either Lina or Ruth,' he said. 'If it comes to the worst, Erich and I will manage on our own.'

But Anni would have none of this. 'No,' she insisted, waving her hand. 'You will stay here. It is easier to find places for Jewish women. They are not as difficult to hide as Jewish men. They are not potential candidates for the army, and they are not circum-cised. You know very well that if the police find a man out of uniform they will immediately ask him for papers. And what hap-pens when you don't have papers and they bring you in for questioning?'

Dr Arndt knew she was right. 'But what about Erich? He is even more vulnerable than I am.'

'I will find places for everyone,' said Anni. 'Don't worry.' She saw in this an opportunity to repay the doctor for all he had done for her. And she would not be deterred. In her own way she was as stubborn as he. 'I have friends who will help. You saved our daugh-ter's life. Now it is our chance to save yours.'

Anni and Max went on to discuss how they would share their food rations with Dr Arndt and, to the extent it was possible, with his family. As for more hiding places, Anni had many friends near by – some of them former patients of the doctor's – who were opposed to Hitler. She would begin by asking them. If they did not volunteer, she would use her powers of persuasion to bring them around.

When Dr Arndt gave the news to Erich and Ruth, they were immensely relieved. Lina tried to be be pleased as well, but anxiety was etched in her face. However, she knew she had no choice but to go along with the plans. Arthur Arndt then turned to his son. 'I've made the first step. You are now in charge.' Thereupon he took out one of his cherished cigars from his leather cigar pouch, sat down in a chair, lit a match and inhaled. After savouring the sensation, he exhaled and watched as the smoke slowly drifted up towards the ceiling.

# 2
# WITHOUT A TRACE

Anyone who still maintains social relations with the Jew is one of them and must be considered a Jew himself and treated as such. He deserves the contempt of the entire nation, which he has deserted in its gravest hour to join the side of those who hate it. – Joseph Goebbels, 'The Jews Are to Blame!'; *Das Reich*, 16 November 1941

Anni Gehre wasted no time. Almost immediately she called on Max Köhler, a short, squint-eyed man in his late sixties who was another of Dr Arndt's former patients. The Gehres had met the Köhlers when they lived next door to them on Reichenberger Strasse in Kreuzberg and Anni had done some sewing for Max's wife, Klara. The families had become good friends, and Anni continued to see Klara after she and Max moved to Kottbusser Ufer, a short distance away.

Anni knew that Max, a pacifist and a member of the League of Human Rights, loathed Hitler and the Nazis. 'Hitler is going to get us into a war and we will be defeated, and that will be the end of Germany,' Max had said over and over, before the invasion of Poland. 'Hitler is a madman and should be hanged.' Anni knew that Max, strong-willed and independent, would be sympathetic to the Arndts' plight.

He owned a small factory located at Oranienstrasse 20 – at the other end of the street where the Arndts had been living for more than four years in the *Judenhaus* – about a twenty-minute walk from the Gehres' home. The factory made air-brushes for artists and subcontracted work from larger companies for small mechanical components, ranging from typewriter parts to small keys for desk tops and drawers. Max ran the factory with his son, Hans, a bachelor in his early forties, a self-schooled electronics wizard who shared his father's contempt for the Nazis.

Max suggested that Erich work in his shop as a journeyman and offered him the usual wage of sixty marks a week. Erich would call himself 'Walter Driese'. Max employed four other workers: an elderly cousin with white hair and a moustache – who was known simply as Uncle Willy – and three teenage apprentices, Manfred, Horst and Helmut. Only Helmut was a potential danger, since he was an outspoken Nazi loyalist. But this did not bother Max. After all, he was the boss. No one working for him would think to challenge his judgement.

Next, Anni went to see Martha Maske, a widow in her sixties and a close friend of Lina's who, despite Hitler's attempts to turn Jews into pariahs, had continued to visit Lina regularly in their shabby apartment on Oranienstrasse. Martha adored Lina and her family, and she went out of her way to help her with household chores and bring them meat and eggs from her small supply of rations. She had warned the family when she heard rumours that a Gestapo raid was to take place in Kreuzberg and insisted on sheltering them overnight in her small apartment. But when Anni went to her and asked if she could shelter one of the family, Martha broke down in tears.

'Please don't ask,' she said, weeping. 'You know I would do anything for the family. But I can't do this. Maybe I am a coward. I will give you food for them, but I cannot take them into my house. I am too afraid.'

Anni's meeting with her neighbour Frieda Lefèbre was more encouraging. Frieda – known to everyone as 'Purzel' – was a widow in her mid-forties and a close friend of Anni's as well as a patient of Dr Arndt's. She and her teenage daughter, Ilse, lived in a pleasant, two-room apartment on the second floor of the Gehres' apartment complex, on the other side of the courtyard. Purzel agreed to shelter Lina, Erich and Ruth. She and her daughter, she said, would share the living-room, while the Arndts could sleep in the large bedroom facing the courtyard. There were two very serviceable single beds in the room, as well as a comfortable chaise-longue.

Ruth, however, had already gone off and made other plans. She had arranged to stay with the parents of a male friend – a *Mischling* (a child with one Jewish parent and one Gentile parent) – who lived across the Landwehrkanal.

'That is much too dangerous,' protested her father when Ruth told him her plan. 'These families are not safe. They can be arrested at any time.'

'No,' she told him. 'The father is Christian; the mother is Jewish. They are "privileged". The authorities are not arresting Christian men who are married to Jewish women. Everyone knows that.'

'That may be the policy right now,' said Dr Arndt. 'But it could change at any time. I won't permit it.'

Ruth tried to reassure him. 'It'll be fine. We'll all have more room this way and more food, and I really don't think it is dangerous.'

'But if anything happens, we could all be in danger. I beg you to reconsider.'

But Ruth refused to listen. She had inherited her father's stubbornness and she was certain that she was helping out by giving her brother and mother more space. Finally the doctor backed down. He knew that he could not change her mind.

Anni then extended Purzel's offer to Ellen Lewinsky, Erich's blonde, fair-skinned girlfriend who looked more Aryan than Jewish. Ellen and Erich, who had met at a family party, had been dating one another for more than three years. They planned to marry when the war ended. Lina now treated Ellen as a daughter and her mother, Charlotte, as a relative.

Ellen realized that Purzel could not possibly shelter them all, so she set out to find a hiding place for Charlotte. Anni knew that Ellen was bright, plucky and extremely resourceful; she was optimistic that she would succeed. First, Ellen began making subtle inquiries among people she trusted. One of those was Herr Bukin, a short, stocky, balding White Russian who was married to a tall, fair-haired, outspoken Jewish woman. The Bukins rented a room in the apartment in which Ellen and her mother lived; they had been there when Ellen's Aunt Johanna had been arrested by the

Gestapo. The Bukins knew that Ellen and Charlotte could be next, and Herr Bukin offered to help Ellen find a safe refuge for her mother. After several days of deliberation he talked to Anni Harm, a young married woman who worked alongside him in a leather factory. Anni had a passion for hand-rolled cigarettes from the Ukraine, and each month Herr Bukin managed to get her a supply through his connections on the black market. She lived in the Neukölln section of Berlin, south-east of Kreuzberg, with her two-year-old daughter, Evelyn. Her husband, a soldier, was fighting on the eastern front.

Anni had a pleasant, two-bedroom apartment. Since her husband was gone most of the time, she was amenable to having company and an additional income. More important, she was fervently opposed to the anti-Semitic policies of the Third Reich and resented the fact that her husband had been conscripted to fight in the army. She said that she would shelter Charlotte for a hundred marks a month – just enough to pay for Charlotte's food and household expenses – as long as her husband consented. She would have to wait until he came home on leave to finalize the plans.

With hiding places secured for the Arndts and a provisional one lined up for Ellen and her mother, the Arndts made plans to move. Throughout December they packed many of their belongings in boxes and suitcases leaving out just enough clothing to see them through the coming months. The Gehres agreed to take all their possessions and give them to friends for safekeeping. Tata, the Arndts' first nanny, offered to bury Dr Arndt's expensive medical books and equipment and the family's silver and other prized possessions in the grounds around her small summer shack in the village of Burig. Then they decided on the date for their disappearance – Monday 9 January 1943.

As the day approached, everyone was jittery, not knowing from hour to hour if one of them would be arrested by the Gestapo. Erich, fearful of being picked up by the officials while working at Siemens, developed a stomach ulcer. He used it as an opportunity to stay at home, afraid that he could be seized any day. The day before he was due to be examined by doctors at the company Dr Arndt fed Erich a large chunk of hot salami provided by the Gehres, since red meat eaten the evening before a physical examination would show up the next day as blood in the stool. The ruse worked, and Erich was deemed too ill to work. He never again returned to Siemens.

In the last week of December and the first week of January the Arndts dispersed their belongings. Each night Erich and his father would put a carton or suitcase on a sled. It was a bitterly cold winter, one of the coldest recorded in Berlin; the dark streets, lit only by the moon, were caked with ice and snow. Heavy black-out curtains covered every window, so there was little danger of being spotted by neighbours. Erich and Ruth would bundle up in their warmest coats and scarves and pull the sled through Oranienstrasse, cross Skalitzer Strasse and turn right on to Manteuffelstrasse. Then they turned left on to Kottbusser Ufer, thus avoiding going along Skalitzer Strasse – a major thoroughfare which was more likely to have policemen on it than the smaller side streets.

When they reached the Gehres' tenement at Kottbusser Ufer they would haul the sled quietly through the darkened courtyard, walk upstairs and ring the bell twice to alert the Gehres that they had arrived. Max would come down and help Erich carry a carton or suitcase up the steps. Then Anni would serve them a cup of hot ersatz coffee – a tasteless brew made from roasted barley seeds – before they returned home.

Toward the last week of December Erich and Ruth were outside loading a carton on the sled. As they prepared to take the sled through the snow, Bruno Gumpel, one of Erich's closest friends from the Holzmarktstrasse workshop, unexpectedly showed up. Even though the two boys had both worked at Siemens, they had rarely seen each other there. When Bruno arrived and saw Erich and Ruth loading cartons on to a sled, he knew immediately what was going on, but he asked no questions. Instead, he offered to help Erich pull the sled.

Ruth let him take over and went inside to help her mother prepare another carton for delivery. When Erich and Bruno returned, they talked briefly with Dr Arndt, and Bruno told him that his mother and his aunt had recently been deported.

'Let us hope the war is over soon and they will return by the spring,' said the doctor.

'I pray that you're right,' said Bruno, 'but I don't think so. I don't know if I will see them again.' Then, his eyes filling with tears, he quickly picked up a carton and went outside with Erich. Together, they delivered the second package to the Gehres.

It turned out to be a lucky meeting. A year later, when Bruno was also in hiding, he decided to look up Erich and, remembering the Gehres' apartment, went straight there to find out where he was.

On 31 December Erich and Ellen were invited to a friend's house. There a small group of Jewish boys and girls – mostly factory workers from Siemens and Schubert Flugzeug, the munitions factory in which Ellen worked – had gathered to celebrate the New Year. Seated on a couch was Stella Goldschlag, a shapely blonde with a dazzling smile who waved at Ellen. They had been classmates at Feige & Strassburger Schule on Nürnberger Strasse, a fashion design school where Ellen had briefly studied pattern-making before being drafted to work in the munitions factory. Shortly afterwards Stella had been recruited to work in the drill department at Siemens, and she was working as a slave labourer there at the time of the party. Everyone at the gathering was talking about the pending defeat of the Germans at Stalingrad and the likelihood of an Allied landing in Europe. When would they come? When would the war be over? Before the next New Year? Before June?

No one said a word about the rumours of an impending factory raid and what they might encounter in the concentration camps. Nor did Ellen or Erich mention their plans to go into hiding. The fewer people who knew what one was planning to do, the more likely one would be able to do it. 'Trust no one, tell no one – not even your friends, not even your relatives' was the maxim. It saved lives. And, although no one could have guessed at the time, Stella would later become a notorious informer for the Nazis.

In preparation for their disappearance Lina sewed her family's identification papers into the seams of their winter coats. Early in the evening of 9 January Dr Arndt left a suicide note on the table in the living-room. Such a note, he believed, would stop the police from searching for the family. Then Lina and Ruth donned their winter coats, boots, mittens, scarves and hats. Ruth hugged her father and her brother and promised to be careful. She and her father planned to meet the following Monday evening at 9 p.m. across from the Gehres' tenement, in a secluded dark spot along the Landwehrkanal. Lina hugged her husband and her son, and she and Ruth picked up their small suitcases and walked silently out the door. Ruth accompanied her mother to Purzel's. Then she carried on to her hiding place across the canal.

As soon as they left, the doctor and Erich looked carefully around the apartment to make certain they had left nothing of consequence. Bereft of all their most cherished possessions that had made it habitable, the rooms looked drabber and shabbier than ever. As they went to leave, Dr Arndt turned to his son. 'I'm giving you a capsule of cyanide in case of an emergency. I hope you will never have to use it. But if you need to, do not hesitate.'

Erich nodded and tucked the pill inside his shirt pocket. Then the two men hugged each other, trying to avoid tears. As he closed the door Dr Arndt locked it for the last time and threw the keys into the snow. Then the two men set off in the chilly darkness, each of them carrying a small suitcase. When they arrived at the Gehres' tenement building Erich turned and walked up the one flight of stairs to Purzel's apartment, where his mother was now waiting for him. Dr Arndt meanwhile walked across the courtyard and climbed another set of stairs. As he reached the third floor he could see a sliver of light escaping from beneath the door. There Anni and Max were waiting for him.

The doctor woke up the next morning without the reassuring presence of his wife, his son or his daughter for the first time in over twenty years. From his room he could hear Anni pattering around in the next room; in the background was the muffled sound of a radio. He lay on the bed, staring at the ceiling, as a feeling of profound anxiety overwhelmed him. Had he done the right thing? Was his family safe? Why hadn't he emigrated when it was still possible to do so? How had it happened that he, Arthur Arndt, a law-abiding citizen, had been turned into a fugitive in the country he loved simply because he was born Jewish? He felt deeply betrayed – betrayed by the country he had fought to preserve, betrayed by the leaders who had allowed this situation to arise and, most of all, betrayed by the ideals and the system of law in which he had believed all his life.

Dr Arndt, a man who was used to being in charge, was now completely dependent on Max and Anni Gehre for food, for news about his family, even for conversation. He would not be able to go outside without worrying about getting caught. He could not make any telephone calls, since the Gehres did not have a phone. Worst of all, he would not know from minute to minute whether his wife and son and daughter were free or being tortured by the Gestapo. Was Anni's a safe haven or a prison?

But he had agreed to the plan. Now was not the time to let his doubts get the better of him. He was still the head of the family and a physician; he alone could restore his family to health if they got sick. As Jews in hiding none of them could go to a doctor or hospital for medical care, since to do so required identity papers. He had prepared for this aspect of his life underground, taking with him as much medicine as possible – bottles of vitamin B, cough syrup with codeine, different kinds of ointment and pain medications – as well as bandages and the basic medical instruments he would need to diagnose and treat illnesses and accidents.

He had also managed to bring about 20,000 marks with him. Even though it seemed like a large sum – seven times what Erich would earn in a year at Max's factory – he knew it would not go far. So he planned to use it sparingly, saving most of it for bribes if anyone was caught. Meanwhile he tried to comfort himself with the knowledge that Lina and Erich were just minutes away. Anni had promised him that she would visit Purzel frequently to make sure that they were all right. Dr Arndt could get to them quickly, and he trusted Purzel to do her best to protect his family. Meanwhile he would try not to worry; it would do no good to reveal his anxieties to the others, least of all to Anni and Max who had extended themselves so generously.

A knock on the door interrupted his musings. 'Arthur,' he heard Anni saying, 'Would you like breakfast? I have just visited Purzel and everyone is all right. Ruth is also there. They asked me to let you know that they all slept well and said you should not worry.'

Arthur Arndt sat up, relief flooding through him. He looked at his watch; it was already 10 a.m. and he was suddenly hungry for breakfast.

It had been decided that Erich would begin working for Max Köhler the following Monday. Early in the morning Erich took off on his bike for Köhler's factory, wearing a woollen cap on his head and, with a scarf wrapped securely around his face to cover everything but his eyes, he pedalled quickly up Kottbusser Ufer to Mariannenstrasse. There he turned right, crossed Skalitzer Strasse and, when he reached Heinrichplatz, turned left until he reached Oranienstrasse 20. This was not the most direct route from the Gehres, but Erich did not want to ride past the family's previous home on Oranienstrasse 206 for fear that someone might recognize him.

As Erich approached Köhler's factory he passed many tiny shops, delicatessens, restaurants and other small businesses. To the right of Oranienstrasse 20 was a tobacco shop; to the left was a small grocery. Up the block was a small restaurant – Max & Moritz – where forced labourers from France, Belgium, Holland and other occupied countries gathered at noon for lunch.

When Erich arrived – the trip from the Gehres' took less than ten minutes – he opened the large wooden door on the street and walked through a narrow cobbled entranceway and into a small courtyard flanked on two sides by an L-shaped building. Tenants lived in the left wing of the building, the longer part of the 'L'; the building in the back across the courtyard was reserved for commercial properties. Max Köhler's factory was located on the third storey of the building. A sheet-metal shop took up the ground floor, while the floors just below and above Max were occupied by a couple called the Kleists who ran a leather company, making bags, wallets and other goods.

Across from the door leading upstairs to Max's factory (the door was located in the left wing near the corner of the 'L') was an open space with stairs leading down to a large storage cellar that had been converted into an air-raid shelter for the building's tenants and workers. In front of the residential wing was another small storage cellar. It was here that Erich locked his bike when he arrived.

Max's factory was a large rectangular space measuring about 140 square metres (1,500 square feet). A heavy metal door opened into a vestibule. On the left was a lavatory that was used by the workers; directly across to the right of the vestibule entrance was another for the exclusive use of Klara Köhler, Max's wife. Frosted glass doors separated the vestibule from the main factory space. After coming through these doors, one passed a double sink on the left. On the right there were several small enclosed workspaces with windows that overlooked a courtyard. The first was used by Max Köhler and his wife Klara. It had a large desk, several cabinets and a stove. The second was used by Max's son, Hans. It had a long workbench, a small lathe, several cabinets and another stove. Just outside the workroom were storage lockers.

On the factory floor near Hans's shop was a large wooden work-table, where the employees gathered to eat lunch, another stove, a dozen or so lathes of varying sizes, several milling machines, a large grinder and a press. Work benches were set along the four large-paned windows that looked out on to a courtyard at the back of the building. In the rear of the factory floor was a small, windowless storage room containing materials and supplies. Opposite this were narrow circular iron stairs leading down to the courtyard beneath.

At this point Erich had no idea of the major role the factory would play in saving all of their lives; what concerned him that day was making a good impression on the other workers. Shortly after he arrived Max introduced him to Klara, a large, good-natured woman, and Hans, his son from his first marriage , who ran the factory with him. Both Klara and Hans knew Erich's true identity, but Hans was much more comfortable with the idea than Klara, who

46

was frightened that someone would find out and they would all be endangered. However, she felt she had to go along with her husband's decision to help the family.

Then Max took Erich to meet the other labourers, introducing him as their new foreman, Walter Driese. They nodded and carried on working, taking little notice of the new person assigned to them. Max was their boss. They trusted him.

Within a week Erich had settled in and was enjoying his new job. Each morning, promptly at 7 a.m., he arrived with the other labourers wearing dark-blue work clothes. Then he checked in with Max or Hans and began his work for the day.

After working at Siemens for more than two years, Erich felt as though he had been let out of prison. At Siemens, Erich had been assigned to work twelve-hour shifts in the lathe department. Usually he worked overnight, and he had to travel two hours by train each way to the company, located on the other side of Berlin from Kreuzberg. Despite this gruelling work schedule he received no benefits or time off, and he was paid just twenty-six marks a week – roughly half of what an Aryan worker received for working eight hours a day. The supervisors were crude and ill-tempered; they humiliated Erich and the other Jewish workers with insulting remarks and beat those workers who could not work fast enough or who dared to protest to them. But Erich learned how to make the best of a terrible situation: he did his work quietly and well, kept to himself and did not talk back to the guards.

Compared with his arduous routine at Siemens, working at Köhler's was almost like a vacation. Hired as a journeyman to supervise the other labourers, Erich now earned more than twice the sum he had made at Siemens. He worked only nine hours a day. And, not least, he had responsibility and, perhaps most important, the respect of his fellow workers. He turned out to be extremely competent. His primary role was making tools to run production jobs and supervising the work of the apprentices. He quickly gained the confidence of the workers, who did not even think of questioning his religion or his politics.

Erich's main challenge was protecting his true identity. He had to remember to lock the door of the lavatory, so that no one would accidentally walk in on him and discover that he was circumcised. He also had to be sure to bring food with him for lunch, so that he could eat with the others. And he had to be discreet in terms of discussing the Nazi regime and make appropriate remarks when people talked about the war.

Within a short time Erich had sized up the other workers. Uncle Willy, Max's cousin, was the other journeyman in the group. Elderly, quiet and gentle, Willy was courteous to Erich from the beginning, immediately deferring to him – despite his youth – as his new supervisor. Of the three apprentices, Manfred, just sixteen, was the youngest. Like most other young German boys he was a member of the Hitler Youth, but he rarely talked about politics. Horst, seventeen, was similarly polite, without strong opinions about the war. Helmut, also seventeen, was another matter. A passionate Nazi loyalist, Helmut was arrogant and outspoken. From their first meeting he tried to impress Erich by boasting about his accomplishments and his fanatical attachment to the Führer. Erich knew that he would have to be on guard around Helmut, saying as little as possible that could trigger suspicion. One remark to the Gestapo would bring officers to the plant immediately.

By the end of the second week, everyone had adjusted relatively well to their new routine – that is, everyone but Ruth. She had discovered that travelling every day to and from Purzel's was more arduous than she had anticipated, but, having decided that the best strategy was to stay with her friend's parents, she was loath to move at this late stage.

Although she was only a year and a half older than Erich, her position in the family as the firstborn child had imbued her with a certain responsibility. From their earliest childhood days Ruth had looked out for Erich, playing games with him on the beach near their grandparents' home in Kolberg and holding his hand when they crossed the street outside their home on Admiralstrasse. In 1936 the Arndts had transferred Ruth to the Jewish middle school on Grosse Hamburger Strasse to insulate her from the anti-Semitic slurs she had experienced in her German gymnasium for girls on Frankfurter Allee. At the Jewish middle school Ruth excelled in writing poetry and was a good student. Witty, outgoing and very determined, she soon became a class leader.

She had also inherited her father's passion for medicine. When she graduated in April 1939 Jewish girls had only three options for job training: dressmaking, hairdressing and nursing. Ruth quickly opted for nursing, hoping to work with children and babies. In April 1940, after a year working in a Jewish household as a domestic (a requirement imposed by the Third Reich on all young women – Jews as well as Christians – to train them for their future duties as wives and mothers), Ruth enrolled as a student nurse at the Jewish Hospital, a course that cost her parents around twenty marks a month. She began by taking care of young children at a Jewish orphanage in Niederschoenhausen, a northern suburb of Berlin. During air raids she and the other student nurses would carry the children and their cribs downstairs into the cellar. From the orphanage she went to work at a hospital run by the Jewish Council of Berlin in Iranische Strasse, a hospital for Jewish patients.

In September 1941 Ruth graduated in what turned out to be the last nursing course for Jewish girls in Berlin. The next month she was drafted to work as a slave labourer at Ehrich & Graetz, a well-known electrical manufacturing company that built radios for the German military. There she soldered and operated drill presses, usually working twelve-hour day shifts and walking more than two and a half kilometres (a mile and a half) to and from work, since Jews were not permitted to ride on trains when such short distances were involved.

It was at Ehrich & Graetz that Ruth had been reunited with the young man she had met briefly before. Although *Mischlinge* were not governed by the same Nazi restrictions as full-blooded Jews, the Germans recruited many to work as forced labourers. When Ruth's friend heard of her plan, his family offered to shelter her in their apartment. It was pleasant and sunny, located on Bürknerstrasse, a small street south of the Landwehrkanal, approximately a ten-minute walk from the Gehres' tenement building. Each morning before the sun rose, she would wrap a large scarf around her head and walk to Purzel's to spend the day with her mother. Shortly after sundown Ruth would return to her hiding place.

Finally, after two weeks of this, Ruth realized that it made more sense to stay with her mother and brother. 'Thank God,' said Lina, when Ruth told her she had decided to move. 'You have finally come to your senses.'

The doctor, too, was relieved at her decision, as was Purzel. She had felt strongly that Ruth – who was known in the area – would be safer staying with her mother and brother than moving about unnecessarily. Purzel, a widow, small and fragile-looking with short brown hair and a pleasant smile, was blessed with common sense as well as generosity. She and Anni Gehre had been friends for more than twenty years, brought together partly because they both had daughters who were almost the same age. Purzel's daughter, Ilse, was beautiful and blond – the epitome of the ideal Aryan female. She and Anni's daughter had played together in the park and attended the same schools. After graduating from vocational school, they had both trained as secretaries. They were still good friends, and their mothers, as so often happens, were even better friends. Anni had sent Purzel to Dr Arndt when Purzel had needed medical treatment for her hip, which bothered her periodically (she limped slightly as a result of a birth defect). He took good care of her and helped her to walk without a stick; in return she said he was the finest doctor she had ever met.

Therefore, when Anni asked Purzel if she would shelter the Arndts, Purzel immediately said yes. She did not stop to consider the risks; her response was instinctive. What, after all, had Hitler done for her? Black-outs, curfews, food rationing, air raids. And now her trusted doctor was in danger. She would do her best to help.

'There is only one problem,' Purzel had confided to Anni. 'Ilse's boyfriend sometimes comes to visit. He is a soldier in the army. I do not think he is a Nazi. But he is a soldier.'

Both women knew this was less than ideal. 'He brings us extra food ration cards,' added Purzel, realizing that once she had mentioned Ilse's boyfriend it could complicate matters considerably. 'I'll put a heavy blanket on the bedroom door, so he won't hear anything when he's in the front room. And I will tell Lina and Erich to sit quietly on the bed when he's there.'

'Yes, and if he hears a noise, you can tell him it's your cousin,' offered Anni, anxious to solve the problem.

'Good. I'll do that. Besides, he does not come here looking for hidden Jews. He comes to see Ilse. If he's not looking for Jews, he won't find them.'

After a long pause Anni agreed. She did not like the idea of a German soldier visiting, but she had no other place to hide the family. Besides, they could use the extra ration cards. She and Purzel would make it work.

To reduce the possibility of neighbours finding out that the Arndts were staying with her, Purzel suggested that while they were in the apartment they should walk around in their socks. Meanwhile she set about securing a blanket on the inside of the bedroom door to muffle extraneous sounds.

After Lina and Erich moved in, the issue of Ilse's boyfriend became more of a diversion than a terror. During his visits (never unexpected ones), Erich would use electrical wires to make contact with the metal base of a lamp in the room. This would create static in Purzel's radio, thereby making it impossible for the soldier to listen in to the war news. Once the soldier had left, Ruth and Erich would double over with suppressed laughter.

Laughing helped relieve the tension – and the tedium – of staying put in one room day after day. Soon after Ruth joined her mother Erich brought them a bag full of hundreds of small, flat keys from the factory, the edges of which needed to be filed. Lina and Ruth spent their days filing these, while they listened to war reports on the radio and read the German newspapers that Purzel brought them. Ruth also passed the time composing poems about their plight in her head and reciting out loud the addresses of friends and relatives who had emigrated abroad. (It was too dangerous to write them down, so she had memorized them and would recite them daily so as not to forget.)

Often she would lull herself to sleep at night remembering the good times they had experienced growing up; she could hear in her head the gentle clippity-clop of the horse-drawn wagon that used to go along the street early in the morning outside her bedroom window. Then, often, she and Erich and Lina would wake up suddenly as the whistle of a shrill air-raid siren shook the room. In the rooms below and above them they would hear activity as tenants hurried out of the apartments and down the stairs to the air-raid shelter near by. Purzel usually knocked before she and Ilse left, asking if anyone wanted to go with her. 'No,' Lina would always say. 'It's too dangerous. We'll see you later.' Then Erich, Lina and Ruth would move into a corner of the room where they would be less likely to be hit by glass if a window should break. They would sit there – sometimes for over an hour – feeling the room vibrate when the large anti-aircraft guns on the corner of Skalitzer Strasse went off. Ruth and Lina would hug each other waiting for the buzz of bombers flying overhead. Then they would hold their breath while they heard the crash of bombs exploding like thunder in the distance.

When the all-clear siren sounded they would go back to bed, hearing the voices and footsteps of other tenants returning to their apartments. Ruth would usually fall asleep quickly, relieved that the crisis had passed. But often she would dream that she was at the bottom of a steep hill. On the top were two large lions, pawing the ground and growling. When Ruth turned around to look at them, they would run down the hill and chase her. Ruth ran and ran while they pursued her. And then she would wake up, shaking and petrified, and she would see her mother lying there, and she would move closer to her, hoping that Lina would make the lions go away. But the lions never left. They haunted her subconscious for many years. Even when she was safe and settled in America, the lions taunted her at night.

# 3

# UNRAVELLING LIVES

Troops without ammunition or food . . . Effective command no longer possible . . . 18,000 wounded without any supplies or dressings or drugs . . . Further defence senseless. Collapse inevitable. Army requests immediate permission in order to save lives of remaining troops. – Radio wire from General Friedrich Paulus to Hitler, 24 January 1943

By mid-January Paulus had lost two-thirds of his original army of almost 300,000 men on the Eastern Front. His remaining troops – numbering about 91,000 – were starving and frostbitten from the extreme cold. Paulus had been urging Hitler for some time to withdraw, so that he could save what remained of his men, but Hitler had consistently refused, instead issuing orders for the men to push on, dying if necessary for the sake of the Third Reich and promoting Paulus to Field Marshall as an incentive for him to resist surrender. Finally, on 30 January, the Soviets broke into the headquarters of the Sixth Army, demanding surrender. The chief of staff, General Schmidt, agreed to the terms. Paulus, exhausted, sat quietly on his bed in a darkened corner of the bunker, too depressed to deal with the situation.

Three days later Hitler and the German High Command broadcast the news to the German people, praising the heroic efforts of the troops of the Sixth Army, who had fought to their last breath defending the Fatherland. The reading was preceded by the roll of muffled drums and followed by the playing of the soul-stirring second movement of Beethoven's Fifth Symphony. Throughout the next four days of national mourning, all cinemas and theatres were closed and the radio played dirges from morning to night. Fears that Germany would once again be brought to its knees by the

Allies swept through Berlin as darkness and an eerie stillness engulfed the city.

It was around this time that Anni Harm's husband, a soldier in the Wehrmacht, returned from the Eastern Front. Anni was immensely relieved to see that he was safe. After dinner she wasted no time asking him for permission to hide Ellen's mother, Charlotte, in their apartment. 'Herr Bukin has asked me to shelter a Jewish woman,' she told him. 'She will pay us a hundred marks a month – enough to pay for her food and help out with household expenses.'

'Hide a Jewish woman?' protested Herr Harm. He was neither a Nazi nor anti-Semitic, but he was predictably alarmed about the wisdom of such an act. The neighbours, he warned, might find out and report Anni to the Gestapo. 'You know I don't agree with Hitler's policies towards the Jews. But can we endanger our daughter? I do not want to hear that you've been arrested for hiding a Jew.'

Anni told him that Herr Bukin had recommended Charlotte highly and pointed out that she was well dressed, well spoken and quiet. 'She looks like a typical German,' said Anni. 'How will anyone know she is Jewish? Besides, we could use the extra money. And I would like the company. It's the right thing to do.'

'It may be the right thing to do. But is it the safe thing to do? The Nazis have no mercy for Germans who help Jews.'

'We'll be fine. God is on our side.'

'God is not on anyone's side these days,' her husband countered.

'It is the right thing to do,' Anni insisted. 'I want to help.'

Herr Harm finally agreed. When Anni relayed the news to Herr Bukin he immediately told Ellen. The news reassured her, as she had become increasingly anxious about finding a safe place for Charlotte. Arrests and transports had picked up sharply in recent weeks – some 2,900 Berlin Jews had been deported in January – and the population of remaining Jews was rapidly diminishing. She and Charlotte had watched helplessly as young co-workers were arrested every day; they both knew their time was running out. It was only a matter of days – or even minutes – before they too would be arrested.

Ellen Lewinsky and Charlotte had moved to Berlin in May 1939 from Blesen, a farming community of about 2,000 inhabitants located on the Obra River, a tributary of the Warthe River about 160 kilometres (100 miles) east of Berlin. In Berlin Charlotte hoped to get exit visas to Brazil so that she could join her brother, Heinz, who had fled there in 1933 after Hitler came to power. Charlotte, a pretty, dark-haired young woman who liked to travel and socialize, had been married off by her father to a young Jew, David Lewinsky, when she was in her early twenties. They moved north to David's home town, Deutsch-Krone, where in 1923 Charlotte had a blonde, grey-eyed daughter and named her Ellen. David, a good-hearted man, doted on Charlotte and his beautiful daughter, but he had almost no business sense. After his father died he and his two brothers quickly plundered Charlotte's dowry in an effort to run their father's business.

When Ellen was two years old Charlotte could no longer tolerate the marriage. She decided to leave David. She took Ellen and moved back to Blesen to stay with her parents, Siegfried and Henriette Gurau. Siegfried, a successful grain merchant, was a cheerful man with blond hair and a reddish beard, who owned a large house set on several acres of land with pear trees and fruit bushes. Ellen soon became the centre of the Guraus' lives. Since the Guraus were the only Jewish family in the tiny hamlet, Ellen first attended a Catholic nursery school, then entered the same one-room Protestant elementary school that her mother and grandfather had attended. Once or twice a year Charlotte took Ellen to Berlin, where they stayed with Siegfried's younger sister, Johanna Kroner, a widow who lived in Charlottenburg near the Municipal Opera House.

In spite of their Jewish origins, the Guraus were popular and well liked by the other villagers in Blesen, most of whom were solid, middle-class Catholics – proud and God-fearing Germans. Siegfried was generous to the poor craftsmen in the town, often selling them merchandise from his general store for very low prices or extending them credit. He was popular as well with the middle-class farmers who sold their grain to him. They often gathered in Siegfried's shop at the end of the day to catch up on the news while Siegfried gave them his favourite schnapps.

When Hitler was made Chancellor in January 1933 the villagers did not connect the Guraus with the Jews the Führer was targeting in his virulent anti-Semitic speeches. Then, gradually, things began to change as the farmers sought distributors who were less politically controversial. They were family men, and they felt that associating with a known Jew could hurt their business and their income.

The next autumn Charlotte had to cancel plans to send Ellen to a private school in a larger town because it would not accept Jewish students. Charlotte's younger brother, Heinz, returned to Blesen, hoping to persuade Siegfried and the family to emigrate to Brazil while it was still possible to get visas. 'It's going to be terrible,' he argued. 'You won't be safe here. Hitler is going to make it impossible for all the Jews, or kill them, or both.'

Grandpa Gurau, then in his late sixties, would not listen. 'I'm an old man. Where should an old man like me go? What would I do in a country where I don't speak the language? My business is here and my friends are here. We are staying.'

Heinz returned to Brazil and found a cigar manufacturer who was willing to marry Charlotte by proxy. Charlotte refused to consider it. 'I was married once, and that was enough!' she protested when she received the letter. 'Nothing will ever make me marry again. My place is here, taking care of my parents.'

Ellen, still too young to understand the complexities of either the new political situation or a bad marriage, knew only that things were getting worse: neighbours began spying on her grandparents; at school she had fewer and fewer friends; boys would often chase her home, yelling, 'Jew girl, you don't belong here. Go to Palestine.'

However, the worst humiliation was to come. Her teacher, Herr Conrad, was forced to teach racist theory to thirteen-year-old Ellen and her classmates. Unhappy at this, he urged Charlotte to take

Ellen out of school to protect her from further embarrassment. Charlotte promptly did so and looked for a boarding-school that would accept her daughter. She finally found one outside Berlin. Six months later Charlotte could no longer afford to pay the tuition fees, since the family business was failing owing to Nazi pressures, and Ellen had to return home. It was 1936. Grandma Gurau was now ill and confined to bed most of the time. Since Nazi restrictions had forced the Guraus to dismiss their trusted housekeeper, Ellen tried to help with the household chores, but she was too young and not strong enough to be of much help. Sometimes she managed to see her Christian friends, who would climb over the Guraus' fence in the evening to visit. Several months later her grandmother died, whispering on her deathbed, 'Horrible things are going to happen.'

After her death the isolation in Blesen became intolerable. Ellen persuaded her mother to let her work as an au pair with a Jewish family in Berlin. Ellen would live with Aunt Johanna. In 1937 the Gestapo ransacked the Guraus' home and took all of Siegfried's valuables. A year later, during Kristallnacht, Siegfried was arrested and placed in gaol. But the chief of police was so mortified that he transported Siegfried's bed to the prison and asked Charlotte to bring home-cooked meals to him there. Several months later Siegfried was ordered to sell his businesses for less than a quarter of their value.

His spirit broken and his health weak, he developed pneumonia. As soon as Ellen found out, she rushed home and stayed with him until he died. Shortly after his death Charlotte wrote to Aunt Johanna and told her that she and Ellen were moving to Berlin and wished to stay with her.

Early in May 1939 – not long after Ellen's sixteenth birthday – Charlotte and Ellen boarded the train for Berlin, taking with them two folding cots, an oriental rug, a Meissen coffee service and several suitcases full of clothing. As the train pulled out of the station they were resolute and dry-eyed. The village that for so long had been their home had turned against them. They were happy to leave.

\*

Aunt Johanna was a widow in her sixties whose daughter had emigrated to Palestine to escape the Nazis. Her son had set off in the opposite direction, for California, and Johanna never heard from him again. She earned a modest living as a seamstress and let out rooms in her Krummestrasse apartment to three non-Jewish tenants – Herr Bukin and his wife and Elizabeth Bodemann, a young German secretary intent on finding a wealthy husband.

On 3 June Charlotte's first cousin, Else Goldstein, hosted a small Saturday-night party to introduce Ellen to other Jewish teenagers. It was at this party that Ellen met Erich Arndt. According to Erich, Ellen, dressed in a red chiffon blouse, a white pleated skirt and red high-heeled sandals, seemed to illuminate the room. Erich, not yet sixteen, had been invited to the gathering through a friend. Like many teenage boys, he was more interested in cars and bikes than girls. But he was immediately attracted to Ellen, sensing in her at once a combination of vulnerability and strength. Before leaving, he asked her to spend the next afternoon with him in the park. Elizabeth Bodemann went along as a chaperone; she brought a book to read under a tree so that Erich and Ellen could talk privately. Before the date ended Erich had proposed. 'We'll go to America,' he told Ellen. 'We'll have two children, a boy and a girl, and we'll name then Philip and Marion. And we'll buy a large American car – perhaps a Buick.'

'You must be crazy,' laughed Ellen. 'We don't even know each other. Besides, my mother and I are only here for a short time. We're learning Portuguese. We're going to get visas to Brazil to join my Uncle Heinz.'

But Erich persisted. He had decided to marry Ellen, and he would not be swayed.

By the time that war broke out in September Ellen and Erich were seeing each other regularly. Charlotte, who was still spending most of her time standing in long queues at embassies, had enrolled Ellen in a nearby dressmaking workshop so that she would have a skill when they emigrated. Despite her initial reservations about the work, Ellen discovered that she was a talented seamstress, and her teacher – Frau Strelitz – asked her to stay on as an assistant.

Erich, meanwhile, became an outstanding student in the Holz-marktstrasse workshop. They continued to see each other at house parties on Sunday afternoons and whenever they could find any free time. Despite the severe limitations imposed on them by anti-Jewish legislation, they thrived together. They still had good friends and supportive families. Britain opposed Hitler, and they were convinced that Churchill would rescue them. Young and idealistic, they were sure they would survive. They could not conceive that times would get worse instead of better.

But as the war escalated, the borders of countries that were hostile to Germany closed down, and even Jews could not break the barriers. By the spring of 1940 Charlotte had given up all hope of obtaining an exit visa. Dr Arndt had already resigned himself to waiting out the war in Berlin. The following autumn Erich was recruited to work as a slave labourer at Siemens.

In March of 1941 Ellen was recruited to work the evening shift – 3 p.m. to midnight – at Schubert Flugzeug, a medium-sized munitions factory in Reinickendorf, a suburb in northern Berlin next to Spandau. She was assigned to the lathe department, where she quickly excelled: She was so good at measuring and performing exacting tasks that she was assigned to work with more complex machines. Soon after Ellen went to work at Schubert Charlotte was recruited to work the day shift in another large factory. As a result they almost never saw one another, since they were working on opposite shifts. Ellen tried to spend Sundays with Erich and his family. Charlotte spent her free time with Johanna and other relatives.

Hitler seemed invincible and his popularity in Germany soared. The Arndts realized now the war would continue and there would be no easy resolution. But they vowed to endure whatever was to come. They had no other choice but to live each day and trust in their ability to survive.

As the deportations and restrictions against the Jews intensified, Ellen and Erich tried to control their anxiety, focusing instead on devising strategies that would give them more freedom. When in March 1942 Hitler passed a new law prohibiting Jews from riding on public trains and buses, Ellen felt this was the last straw in terms of restrictions. She knew she had to find a way of travelling to see Erich, who lived around thirteen kilometres (eight miles) away.

At first she considered pinning her Star of David on to her jacket and taking it off when she arrived at the railway station. But she knew that this was highly dangerous. The star had to be sewn on tightly, and the Gestapo would not hesitate to stop a Jew at random and tug at the star to make sure that it was attached securely. If it was not, one could be arrested. Nor could she leave her home without the star, since the woman on the ground floor was a fierce Nazi loyalist who knew that Ellen was Jewish. She constantly kept on eye on her to make sure that she was obeying the regulations.

Soon the weather grew warmer and Ellen reached into her wardrobe for her spring coat – a shadow plaid of grey and beige with a yellowish overweave. When she laid it on the bed she recalled that it had two deep pockets sewn on the front. An idea took hold of her. She removed the pockets and sewed the star on to one of them. Then she sewed press studs on to the back of each pocket and on to the left side of her coat, lining the pockets up carefully to match the pattern.

When she visited Erich, she left her house wearing the pocket with the star. As soon she was safely out of her neighbourhood she darted into an alley or dark doorway and switched pockets before getting on the train. Before arriving at Erich's she switched the pockets back. Lina and Dr Arndt were sticklers for following Nazi regulations. Ellen did not want to invite their wrath, and Lina had already chastised her for stitching the star on too loosely; she could only imagine what would happen if they discovered that she was not wearing it at all. Erich, however, admired Ellen's bravery and decided to try the same trick in order to travel on public transport. He managed to detach the star from his jacket and got a seat on the train to Ellen's home. But after arriving at the station he had to duck into an alley to reattach the star, and it took him so long to sew it on securely that he decided that it was too risky to try again. In the end he endured this particular restriction, although he managed to defy the Nazis in other ways.

60

At Siemens there were hundreds of small anti-Nazi resistance cells composed of slave labourers who were secretly developing tactics to undermine the Third Reich. Some of these resistance workers focused on getting others to sabotage the war effort by producing faulty components. Erich, for example, would sometimes drill holes that were too big or too small, thereby rendering the parts useless. At other times he diverted fluid into the wrong machines. Once he helped several workers dismantle and smuggle a small lathe out of the factory. After taking the lathe apart a few boys strapped pieces across their backs and on to their legs and covered the bulges with their winter coats. Then they walked into the factory yard with fellow workers who staged a fight to distract the guards. When the guards came over to see what was going on Erich and the other workers walked through the gate to a pre-arranged place where they deposited the parts. Erich never found out who had ordered the lathe or what it was to be used for. He did not need to know. He would do whatever he could to undermine the Nazi regime.

Ellen was equally defiant. After working at Schubert for several months she formed a friendship with one of her Jewish supervisors, Heinz Birnbaum. Heinz lived near Aunt Johanna's, and he frequently walked Ellen home at night. After gaining her confidence, Heinz told Ellen he needed materials smuggled out of the factory for a secret project. Ellen asked no questions and did what he asked. Once she carried out a cone-shaped device for him in her bra and only later realized that it was a detonator for a firebomb.

Unbeknown to Ellen, Heinz was a key member of what became known after the war as the Baum Gruppe – a controversial group of Jewish leftists who were intent on sabotaging the Third Reich. On 19 May Ellen learned that the previous evening several firebombs had exploded in the Lustgarten, a large park in the middle of Berlin, nearly destroying an elaborate anti-Soviet open-air exhibit that Goebbels had mounted to dampen public outrage about the growing Soviet victories. The authorities had managed to extinguish the fire before any real damage was done and were trying to find the saboteurs.

When Ellen first heard about the bombing she did not immediately associate it with Heinz, even though he was absent from work the day after it occurred. There were so many communists and anti-Nazis working underground in Berlin that it could have been set off by anyone. Heinz continued to be absent for several days. One morning she returned from shopping for groceries to find him hiding in the stairwell of her aunt's building. His face tense and drawn, he told her that the Gestapo were after him and pleaded with her to help him.

He asked Ellen to go to his room on Wilmersdorfer Strasse to remove the pamphlets and papers that were stashed there and deliver them to an apartment on the other side of Berlin. 'I cannot go,' he told her, 'because they're looking for me. If I go, all will be lost. You're not on the list. You'll be safe.'

Ellen did not hesitate. Heinz was a friend in need. She could not refuse to help him. As she walked quickly to his apartment she ducked into an alley and stuffed her jacket with the yellow star into her large black bag. When she arrived at his house she went to Heinz's room. There she gathered up all the leaflets she could find and put them into her bag. Then she boarded a train for Kurfurstendamm. From there she walked a few blocks and delivered the papers to a young, bespectacled, dark-haired man.

A week later Ellen learned that seven Jewish saboteurs suspected of being linked to the strike against the Lustgarten exposition had been arrested. Heinz was not on the list. In retribution for their action the SS arrested 404 Berlin Jews who had nothing to do with the bomb and sent them to Sachsenhausen. One hundred and fifty-four were shot on arrival; the others were killed later or deported to Auschwitz. At the same time the SS selected ninety-six Jews from those already interned at Sachenhausen and shot them.

Ellen was horrified when she found out that so many Jews had been arrested for nothing, although it wasn't until much later that she found out they had all been killed. When she returned to work at Schubert the following day she tried to remain calm. Her supervisors were already concerned about Heinz's absence, and she knew it was only a matter of time before they would connect him with the bombs. A week later Heinz was arrested and sent to Plötzensee Prison to await trial with the other saboteurs.

Soon after the arrests Ellen's father phoned Frau Hanisch, the tenant who lived beneath Aunt Johanna and who had offered to let Charlotte use her telephone, to tell her and her mother that he was being deported. Less than a month later the Gestapo arrived at Johanna's home to pick her up. Ellen and her mother let the men in. Johanna was shopping at the time, but when she returned and found the Gestapo waiting for her she moved swiftly into the bedroom, ostensibly to pack her suitcase. When Ellen and Charlotte heard Johanna opening the window, they ran into the room to see her preparing to jump out in a suicide attempt. They grabbed her and pulled her back inside. Ellen persuaded the Gestapo to let her ride with Johanna to the Levetzowstrasse Synagogue, a large house of worship in the Moabit section of Berlin that had been converted into a transit centre for Jews *en route* to concentration camps.

By the time they arrived at the synagogue Johanna was paralysed with fear. Her cheeks, usually rosy, were white. Her eyes were listless. There Ellen saw groups of elderly men and women walking solemnly together, staring blankly into space. Many were holding a small bag in one hand and a loaf of bread under their arms. Ellen said afterwards that they wore the look of death on their faces. Ellen kissed her aunt goodbye and watched as Johanna walked into the synagogue, clutching her small suitcase and talking to no one. Tears streamed down Ellen's face and she fled, feeling sick to her stomach and trying to erase from her memory what she had seen and especially her last glimpse of her aunt. She wanted to recall her as the vibrant person she had always known, and she knew that was how Johanna would wish to be remembered. Ellen never saw her again.

All that summer she was haunted by the look of terror on Heinz's face when he had appeared in her stairwell, the choking sounds of her father saying goodbye on the phone and the expression of fear on her aunt's face when she arrived at Levetzowstrasse. She vowed that she would never allow the Nazis to take her mother, Erich or herself. She would do whatever she had to do to help them all survive.

So when Erich suggested going underground Ellen did not hesitate. Already skilful at defying the German regulations and taking risks, she did not doubt her ability to live by her wits. Her instincts, she felt, would guide her; her love for Erich would sustain her. And her Aryan looks would help protect her.

Ellen soon learned to her surprise that her mother was as ready for the coming adventure as she was. In preparation for their disappearance Ellen had taken a large basket of possessions to one of her foremen from Schubert, Herr Hayden, telling him that she and her mother were relocating to a smaller apartment and did not have room for all their clothes. Herr Hayden was not surprised, since Jews were always being reassigned to smaller houses. In fact, his wife, Frau Hayden, who knew from her husband that Ellen had trained as a seamstress, asked her if she would be willing to come by once a week and help her with alterations. Ellen agreed.

Charlotte gave their two camel-hair blankets to Herr Bukin and asked him if he would sell on their behalf their valuable oriental rug and Meissen coffee service on the black market. A few days later Ellen and Charlotte packed their remaining clothes. Fortunately, because of Ellen's sewing skills, most of the garments were in good shape. Even so, Ellen packed only the clothes she was likely to need that winter – two navy-blue dresses, a couple of skirts and sweaters, two pair of low-heeled shoes and as many blouses, slips, bras, underpants, socks and rayon stockings that she could stuff into a small case. She planned to wear one of her winter coats – a deep-red one with pockets and a belt – and carry her other plain black coat over her arm.

But when Ellen walked into the bedroom that she shared with her mother, she gasped. Charlotte had a totally different idea about how to dress in hiding. On top of her suitcase was her latest dress, made of an elaborate floral-patterned silky fabric that didn't crease and an attention-grabbing hat tiered like a wedding cake, with flowing veils and chicken feathers on top. Next to these were were two huge silver fox boas that hung to the floor when Charlotte wore them. 'Mother,' Ellen protested. 'Are you mad? You can't wear those where we are going! You'll be too conspicuous. We're supposed to be in hiding!'

'That's just the point,' Charlotte responded, unperturbed. 'Who will think I'm a Jew in hiding, wearing these clothes? It's the perfect disguise.'

After several more attempts, Ellen saw that trying to pursuade her mother to change her mind was useless. And so the two women said goodbye to Herr Bukin and thanked him for his help in locating Anni Harm and taking care of their possessions. Elizabeth Bodemann was now living downstairs with Frau Hanisch. Ellen wanted to say farewell to them, but since Elizabeth was going out with an SS officer she decided against the idea. She knew that neither Frau Hanisch nor Elizabeth would voluntarily put her or her mother in jeopardy, but the latter might inadvertently say something to the officer. So Ellen played it safe and said nothing.

Shortly before they left Charlotte wrote a suicide note and placed it on the dining-room table. Next to the note they left their yellow stars and Jewish ID cards; they did not want to be found with their identity papers on them if they were stopped on the street or arrested by the Gestapo. Late at night, when the streets were quiet and dark, shielded from light by heavy black-out curtains on all the windows, Ellen and Charlotte calmly walked to the Charlottenburg underground station, each carrying a small suitcase. There they boarded the train for Neukölln where Anni Harm lived. Ellen went with her mother to Anni's; then she travelled back to Purzel's. From now on they would all take their chances together.

# 4

# JUST IN TIME

We have failed to lay our hands on about 4,000 Jews. They are now wandering about Berlin without homes, are not registered with police and are naturally quite a public danger. I ordered the police, the Wehrmacht and the Party to do everything possible to round these Jews up as quickly as possible. – Excerpt from the diary of Dr Paul Josef Goebbels, dated 27 February 1943

Early in March a truck with Gestapo officers parked in front of the Krummestrasse building looking for Ellen and her mother. They had been reported missing from work, and the Gestapo was sent to pick them up. An officer with a rifle rapped at the door. As Herr Bukin opened it he said that they had been sent to collect the Lewinskys.

'They killed themselves,' Herr Bukin told him calmly. 'There's a note on the table.' The officers pushed him aside and entered the room. Herr Bukin, his neck moist with sweat, invited them to search the apartment. 'See for yourselves. They're not here.'

The officers began lifting pillows from the couch; they looked behind doors and peered into cupboards. When they could not find any sign of anyone hiding they left.

Herr Bukin went into his room, poured himself a large glass of vodka and gulped it down. Then he slumped into a chair, head in his hands and sat there for at least an hour until he felt sure the officers would not return. He did not see himself as a brave or particularly selfless man, but in circumstances such as these how could he behave any differently?

Shortly after Erich and Ellen saw Stella Goldschlag at the New Year's Eve party before they went into hiding, Stella was transferred to the drill department of Erich & Graetz where her mother was also working. On the morning of Saturday, 27 February, Stella heard the ominous rumble of trucks outside. Peering through the window, she saw heavily armed men SS men garbed in black tunics jump from the trucks and approach the factory. Workers panicked as a Gentile supervisor rounded them up and herded them to the stairwell. Most were scantily clad and had no time to grab their coats or their lunch-boxes. Stella, who had been forewarned that an *Aktion* of some sort was going to occur, quietly pulled her mother aside and cautioned her to dawdle, so as to be at the end of the line. Once they were on the stairway she took her mother's hand and the two women slipped quietly into the cellar. There they hid behind a pile of construction materials until the trucks disappeared. When the shift changed several hours later they walked outside, flashing the wrong side of their ID cards to the guards – the side without the 'J' for *Jude* – who took no notice of the two blonde-haired women strolling casually through the gate.

Most Jewish slave labourers were not so lucky. During the course of that massive raid on munitions factories, which came to be known as the *Fabrikaktion* or 'Factory Action', the Gestapo arrested about 7,000 Jewish workers and their families, seizing young children from their beds and hurling them into vans as they screamed for their mothers and fathers. Then they were driven to either one of the Jewish collection centres or large entertainment halls, which had been converted into centres to accommodate the crush of people. There they were forced to stand for hours without food or water, with no choice but to urinate on the floor, and whipped and beaten when they tried to resist or flee.

The *Fabrikaktion* was the largest single raid to occur in Berlin, but Goebbels, who had been instrumental in orchestrating it, was enraged to discover that he had not achieved his goal: He had intended to arrest 11,000 Jews. The Germans had rounded up only 7,000. Four thousand Jews had managed to elude the Gestapo and were on the loose. In fact, most of these workers had gone into hiding just days before the raid took place, alerted by rumours that an *Aktion* was imminent. Some labourers were tipped off by their Gentile supervisors, who had been told by their bosses that forced labourers from occupied countries would soon be replacing their Jewish workers. Most of these workers, therefore, had no time to prepare; they left their homes hurriedly, packed a few clothes, valuables and some food into a small bag and walked quickly out of their homes at night, knocking on neighbours' doors and pleading for help, often asking only if they would hide them for a night or two while they looked for more permanent shelter. Some workers – like Stella and her mother – escaped while the raid was in progress, running into back rooms and cellars or scrambling out of windows and into ditches when they heard the sinister noise of the trucks or saw the SS approaching.

A small number managed to find immediate shelter with compassionate neighbours and friends. Stella and her parents, for example, hid with family friends, the Feilchenfelds, and they remained there until the following July, when their whereabouts were reported to the Nazis by a neighbour. Other Jews had to spend days or even weeks hiding in sheds and cellars before they could find a refuge. Then they had to struggle for month after month, moving from one room to another to avoid being detected and emerging in public only when absolutely necessary. Eventually the Germans created a name for the activity: they called it *flitzen* (flight). Those Jews who hid referred to their condition as *untergetaucht* (submerged) and to themselves as *getauchte Juden* (submerged Jews) because they lived underground, surfacing only to find new shelter or food. At some point the term *U-boote* or 'U-boats' was coined to describe them, because they behaved like submarines.

When Jews were arrested they were taken to one of several police headquarters, often the national Gestapo headquarters at Prinz Albrecht Strasse 8. From there they were often sent to the local Gestapo headquarters, Burgstrasse 26, a torture chamber where victims were brutally interrogated, often bludgeoned with sticks or whips, until they lay unconscious on the floor. Many did not survive.

'They kicked both of my shins to the breaking point and kept beating the same spot on my spine,' recalled Stella, who was confined there. 'I was bleeding from my mouth, ears and nose and couldn't eat for days. They wanted to throttle me. Three times they took the safety off a pistol and put it against my temple.'

Others were in such a bad way after this treatment that the Gestapo deemed them unfit for labour at a work camp and sent them to be 'healed' at the Jewish Hospital on Schulstrasse 79 in Wedding. Once rehabilitated, they were then deported to concentration camps. A few continued to feign illness or even injured themselves so that they would never be considered fit enough to merit deportation. Several managed to survive the war being confined in the hospital.

But some captured Jews were given a choice: the Gestapo would release them and even their families if they would cooperate with the SS and work as *Greifer* – 'catchers' – informers who would lead the Gestapo to other hidden Jews. *Greifer* did not have to wear a Star of David. As employees of the Third Reich they would receive food and shelter and they would carry identification cards to certify their legitimacy if they were stopped on the street. Sometimes the authorities promised to take one relative off the deportation lists every time a *Greifer* brought in a new catch.

In the months following the *Fabrikaktion* the Gestapo managed to recruit fifteen to twenty Jews who pledged their services as *Greifer*. Most survived as long as they were productive. When they failed to bring in new recruits they and the relatives they had allegedly saved were deported to concentration camps and killed. A few of the most ruthless *Greifer* managed to stay alive until the end of the war. Stella Goldschlag was to become the most notorious of these informers. After she and her parents were arrested in the summer of 1943, she went to work as a *Greifer*, parlaying her extensive contacts and not inconsiderable wiles to save her parents from deportation. She soon became the Nazi's chief informer, leading them to over 300 *U-boote*, most of them former classmates or co-workers. Eventually she became so hooked on her privileged lifestyle that, even after her parents were sent to Auschwitz, she continued working for the Germans and remained in their employ through the last year of the war.

The Arndts were sequestered in Kreuzberg when the raid occurred, and they did not learn of it until several months later, when Ellen ran into Herr Bukin at Anni Harm's and he told her that the Gestapo had been looking for her and Charlotte. Nor did Ellen or Erich learn of Stella's devious activities until the following autumn. None the less, Dr Arndt was increasingly anxious about Erich's bike ride to and from the factory each day. Erich was the ideal age for military service. As a young man not in uniform he could easily be stopped by the police and asked to produce identity papers. And, since he did not have any – not even fake ones – he could be taken to headquarters for questioning. There he would be strip-searched, and the officials would soon discover that he was circumcised. He would be taken to prison and tortured, possibly forced to reveal the whereabouts of everyone else in his family before he had a chance to kill himself. It was imperative that Erich disappear from the city streets before this happened.

When Arthur voiced his concerns to Anni Gehre, she agreed: it was too risky for Erich to continue to commute to work each day. She went to discuss the problem with Max Köhler. As soon as she explained the situation Max offered to shelter Erich at night in the factory. 'As long as he's already working there, he might as well sleep there,' Max said. 'If I am going to hire a Jew, then I am also going to make sure the Nazis don't find him.'

Erich went to the factory the next morning as usual, pedalling through the chilly air and watching the sun rise as it cast a warm yellow glow around the squat brown tenements. At the end of the working day he waited until the other labourers had left. Then he walked through the rear door and down the iron spiral staircase to the courtyard, leaving the door unlocked so that he could re-enter later that same evening. He left his bike in the cellar and walked to Purzel's.

Close to midnight he left her house, carrying with him a small suitcase filled with personal belongings – some shirts, soap, underwear, a razor and a torch. It was a clear, cold, starry night, and there was a full moon, causing the snow to reflect more light than Erich would have wished for. He walked inconspicuously back to the factory, hugging the shadows beneath the buildings. When he reached the courtyard he went round to the back and quietly climbed the spiral staircase to the workspace. Inside it was cold and eerie, almost pitch dark. He turned on his torch and stumbled around. Finding a pile of cleaning rags on the floor he spread them out, lay down on them and tried to rest.

He slept fitfully. Awakened by the morning light as it filtered in through the large windows, he went to the sink and splashed cold water on his face and smoothed his rumpled shirt. This time he left the factory through the front door, carefully locking it behind him. He brought his bike upstairs from the cellar and steered it carefully through the front courtyard and on to Oranienstrasse. Before mounting it he made sure there were no people on the street. He cycled west as far as Moritzplatz and waited there for about ten minutes. Then he hopped back on to his bike and rode back to the factory, arriving at his usual time. He went upstairs, opened his locker and changed into his work clothes, mingling nonchalantly with the other workers.

That evening Erich remained in the factory after the other workers left, telling them that he was working on a project that he wanted to finish. Max's son Hans, who often stayed late to work on his own projects, remained behind as well and offered Erich some food that he had brought with him. When Hans went home Erich piled the rags on the large work table, hoping that the stove near by would provide some warmth. He had never felt so alone. He lay awake for several hours, staring at the dark ceiling and watching his breath curl into a spiral from the cold. Finally he fell into a restless sleep.

The next evening Max brought him a pot of food from his home – leftovers from Sunday lunch – and said he would bring Erich food from their Sunday supper every Monday, so that Erich could have at least one dinner a week and save scraps of food for his lunch-box. It was important for him to have what seemed to be normal lunchtime provisions when eating with the other workers. Hans also offered to bring in whatever food he could share from his home on Sonnenallee, a large street in Neukölln, where he lived not far from his father. Hans, a slim, graceful-looking bachelor in his forties, was self-educated and brilliant, an independent thinker and iconoclast, who, like his father, despised the Nazis. Hitler, he warned, would destroy Germany. He also had little praise for the Allied industrial leaders, believing them to be in league with German munitions companies such as IG Farben and Siemens. 'Everyone', he said, 'wants the war to continue. Everyone is getting rich on the war. That's why the Americans are not stopping it. They are making money out of us.'

Despite the difference in their ages the two men soon became soul-mates. With Erich Hans could openly discuss his philosophy at length, something he could not do with other Germans. The two men also shared a passion for electronics and enjoyed inventing mechanical devices. They were able to try out ideas together.

By the end of the week Erich knew he would have to rig up a warning system so that Ellen and Ruth and his father could visit him at night. Ellen planned to see Erich in the evenings and bring him food, while Dr Arndt hoped to stop by the factory once every ten days, late at night, to check on his son's health. He was to do this throughout the next two and a half years, always appearing in a suit and a tie and carrying a small medical bag.

Since neither the Gehres nor Purzel had a telephone at home, when Ellen and Dr Arndt wanted to visit Erich they had to ring the factory in advance from a payphone on the street. They used the code word *Eisen* (iron). They would call only after working hours or at weekends. When Erich answered the phone and heard the caller ask for *Eisen* he would know it was one of the group. If it was safe to enter, he would answer '*Eisen.*' If it was not OK to visit, he would answer '*Nein!*' They were careful not to talk at length, since one could never tell who was listening on the phone call. Once they had got an all-clear signal, they would come to the factory and Erich would let them in. Each of them also had a key to the street door, which was locked after 8 p.m.

Hans agreed that a warning system was essential and offered to help Erich install it. They attached two thin wires to a small transformer and threaded one wire through a large hinge on the factory's steel door. They taped the other to the inside of the door. Then Erich rubbed the paint off a small area on the outside of the door, exposing the metal. Two more wires were run from the transformer to a buzzer in Hans's office. When anyone visited after 5 p.m. he or she could rub the wire on the exposed metal, thereby creating an electrical connection that triggered the buzzer, alerting Erich that one of the group were at the door. (The warning system was to survive the war and remained in place until construction workers renovated the building in the 1990s.)

After the system was in place, Ellen came to visit, bringing Erich food and cooking it for him over the Bunsen burner in Hans's office. By the end of the second week Ellen could see that Erich was exhausted from sleeping on a pile of rags. She decided to deliver a folding cot to the factory – one of the two that Charlotte had brought from Blesen and stored with the Gehres. She would bring it on a Saturday when there would be no workers around.

Cots were not lightweight; this one had a heavy wood frame that folded in two in accordion fashion and weighed about 13.5 kilograms (30 pounds). When Ellen came to collect it Anni gave her a canteen of hot pea soup for Erich. She attached the canteen to the side of the frame with a strong rope. After hauling the cot downstairs Ellen managed to drag it with difficulty to the Görlitzer Strasse tram station. When the tram arrived, the conductor looked at her askance. 'You can't get on with that thing! It's too big.'

'But I've got to, sir,' said Ellen, tears welling up. 'My family was bombed out of their house and I need to take it to them. Let me at least get on the open part in the back. Just one stop. Please?'

'It's against regulations,' the conductor insisted, but relented as Ellen started crying. 'Well, all right then, just one stop. But be quick.'

When Ellen got to the Skalitzer Strasse station –a five-minute ride away – she somehow managed to drag the cot off the tram and on to the street. There a worse problem confronted her: she had to walk several blocks to the factory and then climb three flights of stairs. She dragged the bed for ten steps and rested, dragged it again and rested. Finally, she made it to the courtyard and managed to haul the bed up one flight of stairs. When she got to the landing she sat down and cried. Her arms ached, her legs ached and she did not think she could keep going. But she was afraid to call out for Erich, because she did not know who might be in the building.

Finally she made it to the landing and rubbed the wire on the door to alert Erich. The buzzer sounded in Hans's office. Erich opened the heavy metal door to find Ellen standing there, tears streaming down her face and dirt all over her coat. They fell into each other's arms. He carried the cot – and the pea soup – inside, and in Hans's office they warmed up the soup and had a feast, Ellen crying and laughing with fatigue and relief.

The following morning Hans came in and cleared out a space in several large cabinets over the coat cupboard in the small vestibule. There Erich could store the cot. A few evenings later Ellen brought Erich a feather bed to lay on the base of the cot and use as a mattress, as well as a pillow and some blankets that Lina had hidden with the Gehres. The factory was becoming more like home.

Charlotte was by this time adjusting to life with Anni Harm. Anni had told her neighbours that Charlotte was her aunt from Hamburg who had come to Berlin for medical treatment. To support the story Charlotte would leave Anni's house every morning at exactly the same time. Usually she wore a silk scarf under her coat and a hat. She would walk slowly to the nearest underground station and take the first train that came along, getting out each day at a new stop. There she would walk the streets and look in shop windows. Sometimes she would sit in a restaurant for several hours and read a newspaper; other times she would go to a cinema to see a film. Then she would return to Anni's. They would spend the afternoon talking, taking tea and looking after Evelyn, Anni's toddler. The neighbours were not suspicious.

Ellen and Ruth usually visited once a week. Ellen would do some housework for Anni and Ruth would tend to Evelyn. Anni always gave the girls a treat, usually delicious vanilla pudding with raspberry sauce. Since Ellen was a stranger in the neighbourhood she had few qualms about travelling outside in daylight. But Ruth was well known: she had lived in the area all her life. So as a precaution she would travel only before the sun rose or in the evening after the sun set.

But Anni turned out to be helpful in other ways as well. Soon after Charlotte moved in, Anni's husband was reassigned to Schwerin, a small town in occupied Poland about 160 kilometres (100 miles) due east of Berlin.

'That is close to Blesen, where we grew up,' Charlotte told Herr Harm, when he came home on leave. 'We used to go to synagogue there.' Then she remembered the Düblers. Gretchen Dübler had grown up in the house across the road from Charlotte. Eventually Gretchen became a telephone operator and married Karl Dübler, a salesman from Schwerin who sold tractors and other farm equipment. After their marriage the couple moved to Schwerin.

Charlotte knew that Gretchen and Karl were good people – she could trust them with her secret. 'Would you contact them?' she asked Herr Harm. 'Tell them we are all right and in hiding. Maybe they can help us.'

'Of course he will contact them,' volunteered Anni before Herr Harm had a chance to object. By this time her husband was so disillusioned with Hitler and the course of the war that he was willing to comply. When he returned to Schwerin he immediately looked up the Düblers.

'Charlotte and Ellen are alive and in Berlin?' said Gretchen, tears coming into her eyes. 'What a miracle! I will talk to Karl. We will do something to help.'

The following day Gretchen handed Herr Harm two food ration cards. She had recently given birth to twin girls and did not need their cards. The Düblers grew their own vegetables and fruit in their large garden; they could supplement their meals with home-grown produce, and they could get milk from a local farmer. 'Tell them we will send two children's ration cards each month,' said Gretchen. 'We have plenty of food from the garden, and our babies do not eat much. This way at least they won't starve. Perhaps it will help.'

Herr Harm thanked her and sent the cards to his wife with a

note explaining that Charlotte could expect to receive them monthly. They would be sent to her care of the Gehres. Charlotte and Ellen were immensely grateful; even children's ration cards would make a difference to their diet.

But such good fortune as this was soon overwhelmed by news of the worst possible kind. Ellen was walking through the streets one day to buy some bread with ration coupons that Anni Gehre had given her. All of a sudden she found herself face to face with Elli Fuss, a Jewish co-worker from Schubert. Recovering their composure, the two women had a discreet conversation. Elli, it turns out, had left Schubert shortly before the *Fabrikaktion* occurred. She was hiding with a non-Jewish family, she told Ellen. Ellen told Elli that she, too, had gone underground. Neither woman told the other where she was staying.

'We need more ration coupons. Do you know where I can find some? I have money to pay for them,' said Ellen.

'I will get a few extra coupons from my protectors,' offered Elli. 'Meet me at Alexanderplatz tomorrow at noon at the south-east corner.'

The two women went their separate ways, and the following noon Ellen went to meet Elli. When Elli arrived she was crying. Wordlessly she led Ellen to a kiosk on the corner. On it was a large red poster listing the names of saboteurs who had recently been executed. The name of Heinz Birnbaum, Ellen's good friend from Schubert, was on the list. He and eight other saboteurs had been guillotined – a method of execution considered to befit traitors – on 4 March 1943 for 'acts of high treason'.

Ellen burst into tears when she saw the notice and began trembling. She had discovered at Schubert that Heinz had been arrested, and she had even tried to smuggle a pair of mittens to him in gaol. She had known deep down that he would never escape, but reading about his execution realized her worst fears. That evening Ellen cried herself to sleep. The next day she put a small picture of Heinz in her wallet to remember him by, but every time she took out the picture she found herself choking up with tears and grief.

Around two weeks later life at Purzel's also took a turn for the worst. The Allies had stepped up their bombing of German factories, railways and other military targets. The US Eighth Air Force struck in the daytime; the RAF sent out night raiders. Even though these raids were designed to disrupt the production and transport of munitions, the bombs hit homes as well, leaving thousands of civilians homeless throughout Germany. To find shelters for these bombed-out civilians the authorities began looking for people with large apartments. Childless couples or single parents with one-bedroom apartments were often required to give up their bedrooms to homeless families, since the authorities decided that such apartment-dwellers could sleep in their living-rooms. It was around this time that Purzel received a notice from the housing inspectors to say that they would be coming the next day to check the size of her home.

Purzel immediately went into the bedroom and told Lina, Ruth and Ellen about the inspectors. 'You cannot be here. It will be death for us all.' None of them had ever seen Purzel so frightened. They had only been with her for two months and already they had to leave. After a few moments' silence Lina, her face tight with anxiety, asked, 'But where can we go? Ruth and I can't go outside. It's too dangerous.'

'Then you must hide,' said Purzel, calming down and starting to think rationally. 'Over the bathtub there is a large shelf with a curtain in front of it. It is piled up with bedding and suitcases. We will empty it so that Lina and Ruth can hide there. Ellen will have to leave the house. Maybe she can stay with her mother for the day.'

Everyone swung into action, clearing the bedroom of any signs that might betray them. They all slept badly that night. In the morning Purzel brought a ladder to the bathroom so that Lina and Ruth could climb into the storage space. Ellen and Ruth held the ladder for Lina, who nervously climbed the rungs; then Ellen held the ladder for Ruth.

'Don't worry,' said Purzel. 'It will only be a couple of hours. I will open the door as soon as the inspectors have left. Stay still until then.'

Purzel gave Lina and Ruth some water, then shut the bathroom door. Ellen left for the day. That afternoon the housing inspectors arrived, and Purzel showed them her two main rooms.

'We will take the bedroom for a family,' said one of the inspectors. 'You can move into the living-room.'

'I need time to wash the bedlinen and clean the room,' said Purzel, hoping to delay them so that the Arndts could find a new place to hide.

'You can have one day,' said the inspector. 'We move them in the day after tomorrow.'

'I'll have it ready,' said Purzel, showing them to the door. 'Heil Hitler.'

'Heil Hitler, Frau Lefèbre,' the inspectors replied, saluting. They turned and walked down the stairs.

As soon as Purzel saw them leave the building she went straight to the bathroom and knocked on the door. She fetched the ladder and helped Lina and Ruth down. They went into the kitchen for a hot drink, while Purzel ran over to Anni Gehre's.

'An emergency,' said Purzel, knocking on Anni's door. 'Come over straight away.'

When the two women got to the kitchen Anni sat down and Purzel told her the news – that Lina and the others had to move out in two days' time.

Anni's eyes began to fill with tears, but she tried to be strong. Neither she nor Purzel knew what they could do, particularly at such short notice. Finally Anni came up with a plan. She would speak to Marie Wüstrach, the owner of a small family-run grocery shop on the ground floor of the Gehres' building. She had a small storage room in the rear of the shop. The room was dark and dirty and piled with boxes, but it had a small single bed. And there was a toilet in the hallway. It was a possible hiding place, at least for a few days.

However, Frau Wüstrach, a married woman in her fifties, was not known for her reckless or generous nature. When she washed her clothes, it was said that she washed only the most soiled areas, so as to use as little soap and water as possible. But she was not a Nazi and, more important, she was dependent on people such as

Anni and Purzel to buy her goods. Besides, she knew Lina, who sometimes shopped in her store, and she might be persuaded to shelter her and Ruth.

Anni entered the shop. 'Frau Wüstrach, you know Frau Dr Arndt who shops here.' (The wife of a doctor was always referred to as 'Frau Dr'.)

'Yes, of course.'

'She and her daughter need a place to sleep for a few days. Can they stay in your back room?'

'No, it is too dangerous. You know I like Frau Dr Arndt, but I do not think it is safe for her to stay here. What if a customer sees her?'

'We will close the door and she will stay inside,' said Anni. 'It's an emergency.'

'But I do not hide Jews. It is too dangerous.'

'You have no trouble taking their money,' said Anni. 'If you are willing to sell food to Jews, you should be willing to hide them. Otherwise, how can they buy food from you?'

Frau Wüstrach relented. She did not want to alienate Anni, who shopped there often. A bad word from her to the other neighbours could ruin her business.

When Ellen came home that night Purzel explained the situation. Frau Wüstrach would hide Lina and Ruth, but there was no room for Ellen. Anni went to the street and telephoned Max Köhler to see if he could help out. He in turn spoke to Hans, who offered to put up Ellen in a small shack that he kept in the country, about an hour's train ride from Berlin. He often went there at weekends, and in the spring and summer he grew vegetables there.

The next day Lina and Ruth moved into Frau Wüstrach's back room. It was a far cry from Purzel's pleasant bedroom, but they were immensely relieved to have shelter at all. Once there, Lina offered to buy food from Frau Wüstrach with some of the money Dr Arndt had given her for emergencies.

Ellen was not nearly as stoical about staying in Hans's one-room shack, furnished simply with a couch and a small table. It was March, and the weather was still extremely cold. The room had a big fireplace, but she was afraid to light a fire for fear that smoke from the chimney would create suspicion. Neighbours might visit to see who was there during the week. So, instead, she took all the blankets and quilts she could find and piled them on top of her to stay warm. She was cold and hungry. She missed Erich, Ruth and Lina. She told herself that it made no sense to stay there all by herself when she might be able to stay with them. At the very least, she could sleep on the factory floor. So, after a few days, she travelled back to Berlin and knocked on Anni's door. Anni volunteered to see if Frau Wüstrach would help out.

But when Anni asked Frau Wüstrach if Ellen could share the room, the shopkeeper spoke her mind. 'You said Lina and Ruth would only be here two days. Now it is three days and you want someone else to stay here, too. What do you think this is? A hotel for Jews?'

'Of course not,' said Anni quickly. 'I am looking for another place. They will be gone soon. Besides, the war will probably be over in a few months and Hitler's goose will be cooked. Anyone who helps a Jew will be treated well by the Allies.'

'Even if the Allies win, Hitler is still the boss here,' said Frau Wüstrach. 'They are shooting traitors. My husband wants them out!'

Anni knew that Frau Wüstrach meant business. The only solution was to find a new place for all of them. Ellen could certainly stay there for one or two nights, but that was it. Anni hurried upstairs to discuss the matter with Purzel. She did not want to worry Dr Arndt. He was anxious enough already. Purzel poured Anni some ersatz coffee, then they sat in the kitchen and stared at each other.

Anni had planned everything so carefully; she was sure she could find refuge for the family. Now there were three women without any place to sleep. 'There has to be a solution,' she said. 'It's too soon to give up.'

Purzel sat there, drumming her fingers on the table. Suddenly she had an idea. 'What about Tata?'

'Tata? Yes, of course! Tata will help,' said Anni. 'I'll go and see her.'

Tata had stayed in touch with the Arndts after Lina no longer needed her to take care of Ruth and Erich. A warm, practical and maternal woman, she had married Gustav Schulz, a retired janitor, late in life. She and Gustav lived in a small apartment on Reichenberger Strasse in Kreuzberg – not far from Max Köhler's factory – and they had a simple cottage in Burig, a rural suburb at the edge of Berlin near Erkner, where they spent long weekends in the spring and summer. This was where Tata had buried the Arndts' silver and Dr Arndt's medical equipment. She had also offered to help out in any other way she could.

Anni went to see her and told her that Lina needed a place to hide.

'Of course I'll shelter Frau Dr Arndt,' said Tata straight away. 'She can stay here in Berlin with us. When we go to the country, she will have the apartment to herself. She can also stay in Burig. No one will ever look there. It's too remote. And it's far away from bombs.'

Anni was relieved that she had found a partial solution. At least Lina would have a safe place to stay, and Tata could share her food with her. She and Gustav grew vegetables in the country and had chickens that provided eggs. Lina would not starve. But where could Ellen and Ruth go? She had run out of ideas.

# 5
# IN THE LION'S MOUTH

On 5 March 1943, 1,128 Jews arrived in Auschwitz from Berlin; 389 men and 96 women were assigned for work; 151 men and 492 women and children received special treatment. On 7 March, 690 Jews including 25 prisoners in protective custody arrived; 153 men and 25 prisoners and 65 women were assigned for work; 30 men and 417 women and children received special treatment. – Telephone message from SS First Lieutenant Schwarz to the Main Office for the Economy and Administration pertaining to the fate of Jewish deportees from Berlin, 8 March 1943

As the Gestapo scoured Berlin for Jews in hiding and raided remaining *Judenhäuser* in the middle of the night, Anni Gehre began to panic. She had exhausted all her contacts. Then her mind seized on Frau Liebold. A long shot – a very long shot – but a possibility. Frau Liebold, a large, bony, middle-aged widow who wore her dark hair in a knot at the nape of her neck, worked as a cleaning lady at the Berlin Opera House on Unter den Linden. She lived in a one-room apartment on the ground floor of the Gehres' tenement building, almost directly under Purzel. The apartment had a living-room and a small kitchen with a pantry that overlooked the back courtyard. There was only one drawback: Frau Liebold was a fanatical Nazi loyalist who worshipped Hitler. She believed without question every lie printed in the German papers or announced over the German radio.

'Are you crazy?' said Purzel when Anni outlined her plan. 'Why would Liebold hide two Jews? She'll turn us all in.'

'No, listen,' replied Anni calmly. 'Frau Liebold is the most stupid woman I know. She is also vain and gullible. She'll believe any lie, as long as it is a Nazi lie.'

'But hide two Jewish girls?'

'No. Of course she won't hide two Jews. But she will hide two special agents for Hitler.'

With that, Anni headed off to pay Frau Liebold a visit, with the intention of exploiting the widow's gullibility and her passion to serve the Third Reich. On arriving she knocked at the door.

'Frau Liebold, I must speak with you. Now.'

Once inside, Anni began. 'Frau Liebold, I have recently met two young women who have come to Berlin to work on a special assignment for the Führer.' At this Frau Liebold's eyes opened wide. 'They need to stay in this area and are looking for a room. As you know, rooms are now hard to find – so many homeless.'

'Yes, these are hard times,' nodded Frau Liebold.

'They will only be out at night. I cannot say what the mission is,' said Anni, lowering her voice, 'only that it is so important that the girls cannot even register with the police.'

'I see,' said Frau Liebold, nodding again.

'And they are willing to pay a hundred marks a month.'

'One hundred marks?' Frau Liebold gasped. She told Anni she would be honoured to help, although she did not have room in her tiny apartment for two women.

'There's your pantry,' pointed out Anni. 'Doesn't it have a bed?'

It was only a single bed, protested Frau Liebold. How could such important women consider sharing one small bed? And why would they even consider living in a pantry?

'But if they are willing, would it suit you?' Anni pressed.

'Yes, for a hundred marks a month, to help the Führer. Yes, I would do it.'

Anni knew she had won and, before the widow could change her mind, she assured her that she would talk to the women and recommend her highly. 'Max and I would of course put them up,' she said as she was leaving, 'but, as you know, we have no extra room at all. Not even a spare pantry. I promised to help find a place for them. We must all do what we can.'

'Yes, yes, of course,' agreed Frau Liebold, nodding her head furiously. 'Don't worry. I'll be happy to do it.'

Two days later Ellen and Ruth moved in with Frau Liebold. In the beginning, staying in their new digs appealed to their sense of adventure. There were, after all, two of them. If the worst came to the worst and Frau Liebold showed signs of suspecting them of duplicity, they reasoned that they could probably knock her out and flee. The main difficulty was sleeping in a tiny single bed and being confined to the pantry all day.

Before long Ellen and Ruth persuaded Frau Liebold to put another cot in the kitchen, while Ellen devised a way to while away the hours: she and Ruth would rip apart one of their old dresses and recut and fashion it into a new garment. For Ruth, who could not sew two stitches straight, this was such a challenge that it kept her mind occupied. Ellen also taught Ruth how to make small cloth bags that would fit inside their handbags. In these they could hide illicit items, including food filched from Frau Liebold's cupboards.

At weekends Ruth would style Frau Liebold's hair and Ellen would manicure her nails, fussing over her with a slew of compliments, a process that soon endeared both of them to their hostess. Obviously, she had not the slightest inkling that anything at all was amiss. On Sunday night, after Frau Liebold had cooked her meals for the week and gone to bed, Ruth and Ellen would carefully skim off as much food as was prudent from every pot, eat it and then replace the loss of a potato or a tiny piece of meat with tap water. Other food they bought with the ration cards sent by the Düblers, while Purzel and Anni also tried to give them whatever food or ration cards they could spare.

At night they would visit Erich in the factory, sometimes bringing him scraps of food they had managed to gather. They were all adjusting to the new routine when Erich came down with a sore throat and a fever. 'I've got to see Father,' he told them when they visited that evening. 'I need medicine.' He said he could probably cycle to Frau Liebold's early in the morning without being detected, but he was worried about going through the courtyard and up the stairs to the Gehres', where he might be recognized.

Ruth and Ellen came up with a solution. When Erich arrived the next morning, shortly after Frau Liebold had left for work for the day, Ruth took him into the pantry where he undressed, and

Ellen helped him into a girdle, bra and one of her dresses. Ruth combed his hair, applied makeup to his face and placed on his head a hat with a veil. Then they borrowed a pair of shoes from Frau Liebold's wardrobe, as Ruth's and Ellen's were too small for his feet.

Erich then staggered across the courtyard to the Gehres', weaving unsteadily on his high heels. As he climbed up the stairs, holding on to the banister for support, a workman passed him and stared. Erich, undeterred, kept climbing. When the man reached the landing below, he stopped and gazed up, as if to look under Erich's skirt. Erich reached the Gehres' apartment where Dr Arndt – who was expecting his son – opened the door. 'For heaven's sake!' he exclaimed. 'Have you lost your mind?'

'Close the door, Father,' Erich hissed. 'There's a workman down there looking up my skirt.'

The spectacle of his son in a dress, wearing bright-red lipstick, was so ludicrous that it made even Dr Arndt see the funny side of the situation. After examining Erich's throat and spraying it with medicine, he gave him a bottle of cough syrup and told him to gargle twice a day. The two embraced and, as Erich left, the doctor told him to take care.

Erich staggered back across the courtyard to Frau Liebold's. 'These heels are ridiculous,' he said, kicking them off across the room and wriggling out of his girdle and bra. 'How do women torture themselves with such things?' He got back into his usual clothes, hopped on his bike and pedalled back to the factory, arriving promptly at 7 a.m. to start work.

Inspired by Erich's successful disguise, Ellen and Ruth had a closer look at the widow's wardrobe to see what other clothes they could put to use. Rummaging through the shelves, Ellen pulled out a large black widow's hat with a heavy, old-fashioned veil, which she tried on.

'Look,' she said. 'What do you see?'

'I see a silly girl in an ugly black hat,' answered Ruth.

'Ah. But I see a widow,' said Ellen, twirling around in the hat.

'Why do you want to be a widow?' inquired Ruth. 'What a terrible thought!'

'It's not me who's the widow,' continued Ellen, placing the hat on Ruth's head. 'You are!'

'Why me?' said Ruth, bewildered.

'So we can go outside during the day. I'm going to die of bore-dom if I have to stay here one more day, and I want you to go with me. No one knows me round here, but they do know you, so you need a disguise.'

'As a widow?'

'Yes, why not? No one will recognize you under that hat and veil, and you can wear my black coat.'

That afternoon the two ventured outside, Ruth dressed in black and holding a handkerchief under her veil and leaning on Ellen's arm. They walked slowly to the station. When they boarded the train, solicitous fellow passengers enquired what was wrong.

'She has just lost her husband,' explained Ellen quietly, as Ruth pretended to weep into the handkerchief. 'He fell on the Eastern Front.' The passengers moved out of the way to allow the two young women to sit down.

Several stops later the two got off the train and emerged on to the street. There they ducked into the nearest doorway and stuffed Ruth's hat and veil into a large bag. Then they went to watch a film, the first they had seen in months; they enjoyed it so much that they sat through it twice.

After they left the cinema they once again disappeared into an alleyway so that Ruth could shroud herself in veils once more. By the time they returned home it was early evening. For an afternoon, at least, they had managed to forget the fear and boredom of the daily grind.

But anxiety soon returned. Not long after this adventure they were sitting together in the apartment taking apart a blouse so that they could remake it into another garment. Suddenly there was a knock on the front door. 'It's the Gestapo,' Ruth whispered. 'I knew this couldn't last. You go out the window. I can't go outside. I'll hide here,' she said, diving under the bedsheets. Ellen grabbed her black coat and climbed out of the pantry window.

Almost immediately Ruth heard a voice – one she recognized.

'My darling? Are you here? I came for the jacket.'

It was Frau Liebold's boyfriend, a middle-aged widower with a key to the apartment. He had left his jacket when he had last visited and had stopped by to collect it. Ruth heard him walk into the kitchen. He opened the door to the pantry, looked quickly at the mound of bedsheets on the cot and closed the door. Ruth's heart thumped so loudly she was sure he would hear it. Then, at last, he went back out the front door of the apartment, slamming the door as he went. Ruth emerged, still shaking with fright, and leaned out the window and called softly to Ellen to tell her it was safe to come back inside.

Ellen relaxed and walked to the front door. As she did so, she felt a tap on her shoulder. Her body tensed and she stopped breathing. As she stood there, stiff with fear, an unknown female voice said, 'Excuse me, you have paint on your coat. Let me help you get it off.'

Ellen looked down at her coat. There was a large smear of white powdery paint, which she had evidently brushed against as she climbed out of the window. She forced herself to remain calm. 'Many thanks,' she said, as the stranger insisted on brushing the paint off for her. 'Many thanks indeed.' Then she walked back inside the building as calmly as possible.

She and Ruth fell on the bed laughing with relief, as the tension drained from them. Then they stopped and stared at each other: how much longer could they continue like this? Sooner or later someone was sure to find them out.

One weekend early in May Frau Liebold invited Ruth and Ellen to join her for afternoon coffee. She wanted to introduce them to her son, a military man, and his wife who were coming to visit. 'He is an SS Sturmführer,' announced Frau Liebold proudly. 'You will enjoy meeting him.' She had told her son that Ruth and Ellen were special Nazi agents working for the Führer, and she could not wait to introduce her son to them.

The two young women looked at each other blankly. They realized the game was up. They knew they had to go through with the meeting – they would never be able to find another hiding place before the weekend. They also knew that they would have to leave as soon as possible afterwards.

The following Saturday they put on their smartest dresses, combed their hair carefully, applied makeup and walked into their host's living-room. 'Heil Hitler,' they said, raising their right arms as they entered.

'Heil Hitler, ladies,' saluted the officer, standing up and snapping his heels together. 'Do take a seat,' he insisted politely, before returning to his own chair.

Ruth and Ellen sipped their ersatz coffee slowly and chatted, trying to select neutral topics, ones not related to the war. After an hour of conversation – an hour which seemed like six – they excused themselves, explaining that they had to attend an important meeting and could not be late.

'Heil Hitler,' they saluted, as they took their leave.

'Of course, I understand. Duty calls,' said the son, once again standing up and snapping his heels together. 'Next time we will have a longer talk, I hope. Heil Hitler.'

They left the house and headed for the factory. Ruth draped a veil around her head and hung on to Ellen's arm apparently for support. When they reached the loft they had great fun recreating the scene in the apartment for Erich's enjoyment. After that they made themselves a hot drink. Gradually they became sombre. They knew that it was all up: they could not stay in the apartment any longer. Frau Liebold's son could not be as gullible and stupid as his mother, and they did not trust their ability to lie their way through another encounter. The next day they went up to Anni's to tell her that it was time for them to move again.

Several days later Ruth and Ellen told Frau Liebold that they were being reassigned and could not stay with her any longer. They thanked her for her hospitality and left. Ruth managed to move in temporarily with her mother at Tata's. Ellen, however, was stuck. There was no room at Tata's – there was barely room there for Lina and Ruth, who had to share a small double bed. Although anxious at the prospect of Ellen being homeless, Erich tried to calm her down. Eventually he decided to ask Max if Ellen could stay at the factory, too.

'Yes, of course,' said Max, to Erich's relief. 'If the Nazis are going to kill me for hiding one Jew, they might as well kill me for hiding two.'

'Thank you,' said Erich as relief flooded through him. 'Thank you very much.'

That next day Ellen left Frau Liebold's carrying a small suitcase of her personal possessions and went up to Anni's to tell her and Dr Arndt the good news. Anni was relieved that Ellen had somewhere to stay, but the doctor was appalled at the idea of her living alone with Erich.

'It is unseemly!' he told Ellen. 'You are not yet married, and I cannot agree to it. We will have to find another place for you.'

'But there isn't anywhere else,' she told him, tears welling up. 'There is no other place. Anni doesn't know anywhere, and neither do I. There's no room at Tata's or at Anni Harm's or here. Besides, in the factory I can take care of Erich and make sure that he doesn't sleep through an air raid. It will be better for him as well.'

'It's not right,' repeated Dr Arndt. 'You are not married. Ellen, you know that Lina and I love you as our own daughter. We know that you and Erich are committed to each other. But nature is a very powerful thing and – excuse me for saying this – what if you accidentally got pregnant? We can't take that risk, not in the underground.'

'We will not allow that to happen,' Ellen reassured him.

'All right,' conceded the doctor at last. 'But watch it!'

The following day Ellen moved into the loft. Soon it became apparent that the real challenge was not keeping the couple's natural impulses in check but in finding something for Ellen to do during the day. She could not be around while the other workers were there. And they were not the only problem: Klara Köhler was already nervous about having Erich hide in the loft. Her husband knew that she would protest vehemently if he told her that Ellen was going to live there as well. So Max and Hans took the easy way out: they decided not to tell her. But the situation imposed more stress on Ellen. Not only did she have to make sure the other workers did not find out about her, she had to make sure that Max's wife did not know.

Ellen would rise with Erich early in the morning and hustle to make sure everything was put away. Then they would leave the factory together. While Anni tried to find Ellen a job Ellen would return to the factory at 7 a.m. Max had told the crew that she was temporary help for the lathe department – after all, she had been trained to operate a lathe at Schubert. But while she was working on the machine, chips of magnesium were prone to burst into flames which alarmed her considerably. She knew she would not last in the job for long.

Soon Max came up with some alternative employment for her. Sometimes he would arrange for her to travel to the country to help his sister, who was ill and suffering from colitis. The trip took about two hours each way, and, while there, Ellen would help Max's sister chop up her food finely so that she could digest it more easily. Other days she continued to help Frau Hayden, the wife of her former supervisor from Schubert, with dressmaking alterations. Herr Hayden might have assumed that Ellen was in hiding, since she had disappeared from Schubert suddenly about three months earlier, but he never spoke of it to Ellen. And it did not stop him or his wife from using Ellen's services as a seamstress.

On Saturdays Ellen would wash clothing in the factory in an oil drum heated by a Bunsen burner. Erich would help out by wringing the clothes and hanging them up to dry on lines tied between the machines. On Sundays Ellen would iron his shirts and her blouses and fold them neatly so they could be stored in the shelf in the hallway. Once a month she would take sheets and towels to Anni Gehre, who would wash them in the laundry room on the top floor of her building and hang them in the attic to dry.

Ellen also mended clothes at the weekend, to make sure that she and Erich looked as presentable as possible. Socks were a special problem; they wore out quickly and they did not have ration cards to buy new ones. To make them last longer Ellen cut the tops off old, worn socks and sewed them on to the bottoms of other ones to make them more durable.

Meanwhile Anni Gehre kept looking out for jobs for Ellen. She managed to get her hired as a kitchen helper in a nearby restaurant, a dark, dingy place that served plates of boiled vegetables and potatoes to the blue-collar workers in the area. Ellen told the owner that her name was 'Frau Lehnert'. Her husband, she explained, was a soldier fighting on the Eastern Front; her mother was taking care of her daughter. She needed to work to support them, and she would be willing to receive some of her payment in the form of food instead of money. The owner, a large woman with strong, hairy arms, agreed to this.

Ellen was assigned to kitchen duty, peeling mounds of potatoes covered with mud and grit. She also had to carry large pails filled with potatoes and water from one side of the room to the other, a chore that strained her back and shoulders. Sometimes she would see the owner throwing kitchen debris down the cellar stairs to a large St Bernard dog that was chained to a wall and which wolfed down any scraps that came his way.

The advantage of the job was that she could eat a plate of potatoes and vegetables for lunch, and in the evening she could take a pile of baked potatoes, spinach and cabbage to Erich in the factory.

Anni also found a job for Ruth cleaning counters and taking care of supplies in a tiny food shop where she could help herself to sugar and chocolate and other food from jars on the shelves. Ruth learned to do this when the owner was out of the room or had her back turned, and she would deftly put the food in the pocket of her shirt. Usually she would take it back to the factory at night, and she and Ellen would make cocoa – or something like it – on the Bunsen burner. Ruth, who had been raised to be honest, found stealing provisions difficult at first, but eventually she became adept at it.

It did not take long for Ellen and the others to realize that the first rule of staying alive was to adopt the same rules as the enemy: no lie was too ludicrous; no disguise too far-fetched; no behaviour too immoral as long as it contributed to one's survival. At first they found it strange to live as fugitives, answerable only to themselves. Within a short time they discovered a new sensation: they were free, freer than they had ever been living under Nazi restrictions before the war.

It became second nature to lie for self-protection, to look the enemy squarely in the eye without flinching, to ignore what was happening in the rest of the world, to behave as though they were the masters of their own fates because, in fact, they were. Anything was better than being sent away to a camp by the Nazis. If they were going to die, they would die on the streets of Berlin.

Ironically, it was Charlotte who demonstrated the most sang-froid. Several months after moving in with Anni Harm, she came up with a strategy for getting a good meal, a strategy so brazen that Ellen would probably have tried to dissuade her mother from even thinking about it had she known about it in advance.

One day when Ellen came to visit her mother at Anni's, Charlotte told her what she had been up to. In the course of her afternoon walks in Berlin she often passed restaurants packed with German officers. Peering into the windows, she would see plates of wonderful-looking food, much of it uneaten; the officers seemed too preoccupied with drinking beer to finish their dinner.

'Such good food,' said Charlotte. 'All I could think of is how I could get some for myself.' One morning she made up her mind to do something about it. She got dressed up in a silky dress, stockings and her best pair of shoes, arranged her hair more carefully than usual and applied makeup. Wearing her spring coat and her tiered hat with the veils and the chicken feathers she got on a subway bound for Charlottenburg. There she walked along the crowded streets, looking for a restaurant crowded with officers. When she found one, she confidently walked in and asked to be seated.

The head waiter asked her to wait a few minutes, during which time Charlotte spotted a German officer seated alone at a small table, heartily eating a meal consisting of goose and potatoes and reading a newspaper.

'What about there?' said Charlotte, pointing to the empty chair at the officer's table. The waiter promptly led her to the seat, hand-ing her a large menu. ('I nearly passed out from all the choice,' Charlotte told her daughter.)

When the waiter returned, she ordered roast goose with all the trimmings – the same meal the officer was eating. The officer, over-hearing, complimented Charlotte on her choice. 'I recommend it. It's a delicious goose.'

When the waiter asked for her ration cards she opened her black leather handbag and started fumbled around in it. Eventually she exclaimed, 'Oh no, how awkward! I seem to have left my cards at home in my other bag. How stupid of me! I'll have the soup instead.' Most restaurants served one dish that did not require ration coupons; this was usually plain soup.

The officer gallantly offered to help out, telling Charlotte that he had so many ration cards that he would be honoured to let her have some.

'If you insist,' she replied. 'But I would not like to impose.'

'No imposition at all,' the officer continued. 'I would consider it an honour to have the pleasure of your company. My wife is far away, and even soldiers become lonely.'

'In that case I would be most grateful to you,' said Charlotte. She introduced herself to the officer as 'Frau Schultz' and told him that her spouse was far away, too.

And so, Charlotte continued to Ellen, 'I ate my fill of goose, potatoes and sweet and sour red cabbage, and I listened while he talked on and on. He seemed very anxious to talk.' Then, when the officer excused himself to go to the men's lavatory, she discreetly swept the bread rolls and some slices of goose into her handkerchief and put them into her handbag to eat the next day.

The officer returned, no wiser than before. Before leaving, the two of them enjoyed a dessert of stewed apple followed by real coffee. When Charlotte thanked the officer, he asked her to meet him the next week for another meal.

'Did you agree?' asked Ellen aghast.

'Yes,' said Charlotte with a slight smile.

'Mother! Is that safe! I mean, do you think he'll find out?'

'No. And even if he did, do you think he'd dare tell his superiors that he'd been deceived by a Jew? After all, if a German officer can't recognize a Jew when he sees one, would he admit it to others?'

Ellen eventually decided that her mother was probably right. Why would any German officer risk telling his associates that he had been taken in by a Jewish woman? He would either be reprimanded or exposed as a fool. In fact, Ellen was so inspired by her mother's bravado that after she told Ruth about her mother's deception they decided to do something similar.

Several days later they put on their best dresses and went to a restaurant crowded with German officers. Ellen volunteered to stay on guard outside, while Ruth went inside to try her luck. Ruth soon found an officer and managed to trick him into providing her with ration cards for a meal. But, after they had finished eating, he insisted on taking her home.

'No, I'm sorry,' she said, quickly walking to the door. 'I cannot let you accompany me now. I have to go.'

The officer followed her on to the street and refused to let her leave without him. As they continued arguing about her going home alone, Ellen stood near by, trying to work out a way to help Ruth escape. Finally she heard Ruth tell the man that she had to use the toilet. Then she made a dash for a Turkish baths establishment on the other side of the street, giving Ellen a discreet sign as she disappeared.

Ellen silently thanked God. It had been a close call.

But the officer was not about to budge and stood there on the street, waiting patiently for Ruth to return. Ellen also stayed near the restaurant, pretending to read a newspaper. At least ten minutes passed and the soldier remained, his arms folded and his foot tapping on the pavement. After another ten minutes he was still there. Ellen felt a tiny bead of perspiration trickling down her forehead.

A further ten minutes went by and the man remained, a slight scowl on his face. Finally a fellow officer came by and, after a short chat, they went off together, the soldier apparently shaking his head in bewilderment or annoyance.

Ellen waited until they were out of sight, then she walked slowly across the road, climbed up the stairs to the baths and cautiously entered. She found Ruth half-dressed sitting anxiously on a bench outside one of the steam rooms. 'He's gone,' whispered Ellen.

'I did not know what to do,' said Ruth weakly. 'I thought he was going to call his whole regiment to break down the door!'

'Yes,' said Ellen. 'He was certainly very stubborn.'

'Oh well,' said Ruth with a sigh, putting on her clothes, 'no more goose dinners for us.'

Soon Charlotte also ran into problems with her assignations. As she told Ellen, the officer invited her to meet him in the park. 'And then he wanted to take me to his room to see his stamp collection!' said Charlotte. 'Can you imagine?'

'It had to happen,' Ellen consoled her.

But her mother had not considered the possibility of this. After all, she was a middle-aged woman. When she had hesitated out of surprise, the officer mistook this for coyness. 'But, Charlotte,' he insisted, 'I just want to show you my stamps. I have no other motive. I am a married man; you are a married woman. But in my room we can talk quietly and enjoy a bottle of wine. I shall see you next week.'

'Of course,' Charlotte replied. 'You have been so generous. I look forward to the meeting.'

The following week she stayed at home. Some Jewish women might have taken advantage of the opportunity to secure a safe hiding place for themselves. But Charlotte never considered doing this. She was resourceful and independent, and she decided to find other ways to keep herself fed.

# 6

# ON THE RUN

I did not take on the job as a senseless exercise. It gave me uncommon joy . . . to catch these enemies and transport them to their destination. To be frank with you, had we killed all of them, the 10.3 million [Jews], I would be happy and say, all right, we managed to destroy an enemy. – Testimony of Adolf Eichmann at his trial in Israel in 1956

By mid-June 1943 Goebbels had succeeded in deporting most of the remaining Jews in Berlin. Most were sent directly to Auschwitz and at least half were killed immediately on arrival there. The capital, Goebbels is rumoured to have declared, was finally *judenrein* (free of Jews). Officially there were still 6,700 Jews living legally in the city. Most of these were married to Christians and, theoretically, were not candidates for deportation, particularly if they had converted to Christianity and were raising their children as Christians. The government also closed down the Central Association of Jews and deported its last administrators, including the celebrated rabbi Leo Baeck, to Theresienstadt. (Of the top thirteen Jewish leaders, only Baeck and Moritz Henschel survived.) In its place they set up a rump Central Association in the still functioning Jewish Hospital, where a handful of Jewish doctors, nurses, patients, prisoners of the Gestapo and catchers were interned. A few Jewish leaders were also assigned to take care of the Jewish cemetery, Weissensee.

What rankled with Goebbels was not the existence of this small cadre of legal Jews, but the existence of a subterranean diaspora of some 4,000–6,000 hidden Jews (too fragmented to be considered a community). That so many had managed to evade the Gestapo infuriated him to such a degree that he refused to acknowledge their existence in official documents. Nor could he figure out a coherent strategy to find them.

Most Germans who protected these Jews acted on their own initiative, sometimes impulsively, without assistance or direction from the kind of anti-Fascist resistance cells that had operated in factories such as Siemens. As a result the majority of Jews in hiding were cut off from each other, and the majority of their protectors were isolated from other protectors. Therefore the Gestapo could not easily track them down. Instead, they followed up any reports filed by Germans who said they heard strange noises in neighbours' bedrooms or said they had sighted Jewish neighbours or colleagues on the street. The Gestapo also stepped up city-wide dragnets, during which all young men out of uniform were stopped and searched. And they continued to enlist catchers to act on their behalf.

None of the Arndts were ever aware how many Jews were living in hiding in Berlin. But they knew that they had to do whatever they could to remain as inconspicuous as possible. For Dr Arndt and Lina this meant staying indoors almost all of the time. Erich would go out only in the afternoon, his work clothes providing anonymity. Ruth would often drape veils around her face and go out dressed as a widow. Ellen and Charlotte had more freedom, since neither of them were known in the Kreuzberg area. And Ellen was so fair-haired that she looked like the quintessential Aryan.

Even so, she needed employment, since she could not remain in the factory during the day and she could not stay for long periods of time with anyone else in the group, since there was no room and it would create suspicion among the neighbours. Her job at the restaurant was far from ideal, but it kept her off the streets and provided her and Erich with food. Then, early in July, Ellen developed a bad infection on her hand. When she went to Dr Arndt for treatment he told her she had developed an allergy from peeling dirty potatoes. She had to stop working, he warned her. Otherwise she could become seriously ill.

To leave her job without causing suspicion Ellen went to work one day and started crying. 'My husband,' she told the owner, sniffling and wiping her eyes with a handkerchief, 'he has been killed. So my mother, my child and I are moving to the west of Germany where we will be safer from bombs than here in Berlin.'

She left the restaurant and spent the next few days visiting her mother at Anni Harm's and spending time with Ruth at Tata's, while waiting for her hand to heal. She could not sew or operate a lathe until it was better. Meanwhile Anni and Dr Arndt racked their brains to think of people who might be willing to employ her. Finally the doctor came up with a possibility: two former patients, sisters called Bachmann, ran a dressmaking shop on Prinzenstrasse, a large street several blocks away that was lined with old tenements, shops, small restaurants and bars. Dr Arndt had treated the sisters for many years, and he knew that they were not Nazi loyalists. In fact, when he told the sisters he could no longer treat them, because of the government's rules prohibiting Jews from treating non-Jews, the Bachmanns were outraged. They liked Dr Arndt; they had many Jewish colleagues and could see no reason for the punitive laws.

Anni later told Ellen about her visit to the Bachmanns. She got straight to the point, telling the sisters immediately that Dr Arndt had sent her there. 'I cannot tell you where he is,' Anni told them, 'but he is safe and living in Berlin.'

The sisters clasped each other's hands with relief. Anni told them that his son was engaged to a young woman who was a talented seamstress. 'She has trained with Frau Strelitz,' said Anni. 'She, too, is in hiding, and she needs a job. Dr Arndt thought you might be able to use someone with her skills. As you know, he thinks highly of you both.'

The sisters asked Anni to sit while they went into the back room to discuss the matter. They returned a few minutes later with disappointing news. 'We would like to help,' said one of them, 'but we cannot use her as a seamstress. We use only very experienced people in the salon.'

Anni sensed that the sisters were genuinely willing to help, so she asked if there was anything thing else that Ellen could do for them in terms of work that would not put their business at risk.

The sisters consulted together once more. 'We could use her to clean the salon once a week, if that would help,' one offered. 'It is not challenging work, but we could pay her five marks.'

'And we'll give her a hot meal.'

'Yes, and we can give her hot water to wash after the workers leave, if she wishes. It's not much, but we can do this for her.'

'Thank you,' said Anni graciously. 'I'll tell Dr Arndt the good news.'

Ellen went to the Bachmanns the next day. There she went to work, scrubbing the dust from the crevices of parquet floors with a small brush and cleaning up cuttings from the workroom floor. The atmosphere was formal and quiet. There were three or four workers, none of whom gossiped or wasted time. They took little notice of Ellen, who ate by herself in the kitchen during the lunch-hour. At the end of the day the sisters allowed her to heat water for a sponge bath once the other workers had left. It was a treat that Ellen never forgot. Although she took a sponge bath once a week at the factory, having two a week was truly luxurious.

The Bachmanns were strict, high-minded and proud of their heritage. They wore no makeup and wore their dark hair in a knot at the nape of their neck. Charitable individuals, they were also, in their own quiet way, activists against the Nazi regime. They would not openly demonstrate against Hitler, but they would extend themselves to help their Jewish colleagues and friends. Ellen soon felt confident enough to ask the Bachmanns if they knew of anyone else who might need her services on other days of the week.

'See the madam across the street,' one sister advised her.

'Oh no!' exclaimed Ellen, surprised that the Bachmanns would even acknowledge the existence of a brothel near by. 'Not that kind of work! I can't do that!'

'No, no,' replied Fraulein Bachmann, 'I did not mean *that* kind of work! Tell the madam you are working with us and that you have been trained as a seamstress. She might need you to help her with dress alterations. She always needs new dresses for her girls, and I don't think she will care if you are Jewish. Tell her we recommend you highly.'

The madam hired Ellen straight away as a seamstress. Ellen now had three part-time jobs – a sewing job with Frau Hayden, a cleaning job with the Bachmanns and a sewing job with the madam – enough to keep her fully occupied during the daytime. She continued to travel to Max's sister's home several times a month to help her prepare meals. Ruth, meanwhile, had found a new job through Anni, cleaning and ironing for a wealthy woman who lived in a spacious house in the suburbs of Berlin. Ruth suspected that the woman knew Ruth was Jewish, but she never asked her about her background. Instead, she fed her amply at noon with large sandwiches laden with meat and cheese. Sometimes Ruth could not finish the sandwiches, so she wrapped the uneaten ones in a napkin and took them home to share with Lina at the end of the day.

Working as cleaning women and in brothels were hardly the kind of occupations that Ruth or Ellen had ever expected to undertake, but at least they were not starving. They were still relatively safe, and no one in their group had been apprehended or taken ill.

By the end of July 1943 the Allies were extensively bombing Germany's industrial cities. Cologne, Mainz and Frankfurt were hit hard, and many German war plants were severely damaged. On 2 August planes attacked around the clock, dropping nearly 9,000 tons of bombs on Hamburg. Nearly a million people were left homeless, and between 25,000 and 50,000 civilians died.

News of the destruction spread throughout Germany, lowering morale and creating panic. Anticipating the beginning of serious air raids on Berlin, almost a quarter of the city's population – some 700,000 civilians – crammed themselves on to trains, seeking refuge in the countryside. Those who could not leave the city filled their cellars with tins of food, cots and gas masks.

The Arndts hoped that the onslaught would mean a quicker end to the war. But they had little time to rejoice. By the end of July Charlotte had to leave her refuge with Anni Harm. Anni's neighbours, many of them Nazi sympathizers, were beginning to ask questions as to why her aunt still was there. Anni did not think

101

they suspected the truth, but she could not take any chances. Charlotte understood.

When Ellen came to visit that week she told her the bad news. 'We cannot place Anni in danger,' Charlotte said. 'And she has a heart condition. We do not want to put additional stress on her.'

'Don't worry, Mother,' said Ellen. 'I'll find another place for you.'

When she returned to the factory that evening Ellen broke down in tears. She knew that Anni had no more places to shelter her mother. 'Who can I go to?' she blurted between sobs. 'I don't know anyone else. Anni doesn't know anyone. Purzel doesn't have room. And Tata doesn't have room either.'

'I'll ask Max if she can stay here,' offered Erich.

'No. What would she do here? It's difficult enough with just two of us. Where would she go during the day? There has to be another solution.'

For the next few days Ellen desperately tried to recall all the people she knew on the chance that she had overlooked someone. The Bachmanns had made it clear that they would not shelter anyone overnight. The Düblers were too far away. The Bukins were out of the question. The Gestapo could show up again. Hans's shack in the woods was too awkward to get to and from. There were, however, the Haydens.

If her former supervisor and his wife were willing to hire Ellen – a Jew – wouldn't they be willing to shelter her mother? Ellen travelled out to their home the next day. They certainly would not turn her in to the authorities. They could say no, but that was the worst that could happen.

'Ellen, I did not expect you until next week,' said Frau Hayden when she saw her on the doorstep.

'I need to see Herr Hayden,' Ellen told her nervously.

'Wait here. I'll get him.'

'Herr Hayden,' Ellen stammered when he arrived. 'My mother is in trouble. She has no place to stay. I thought that maybe you could help.'

'No, I'm sorry,' said Frau Hayden. 'It is too dangerous. We have to think of our daughter.'

'But, Herr Hayden, if we don't find a place for her to stay we might all be caught. Please,' she pleaded, 'we have money. We can pay you. She won't be any problem at all.'

'No. It is too dangerous,' he repeated firmly

Ellen stood there, tears streaming down her face. 'We can pay a hundred marks.'

'For how long?' asked Frau Hayden.

Herr Hayden took his wife aside. 'We can use the extra money. Besides, we have already broken the law and employed a Jewish woman to mend your dresses. What danger could there be in keeping Ellen's mother here for a week?'

Frau Hayden relented. 'For a week maybe. But only for a week. And only if we get the entire hundred marks.'

Herr Hayden went back to Ellen and explained the terms. Ellen knew that a hundred marks – the equivalent of two weeks' salary for a typical German factory worker – was a huge sum of money to pay for a room for only one week, but she was desperate. She had no choice. Charlotte still had money from the sale of her china and the Oriental rug. Now she needed the room more than she needed the hundred marks.

'All right,' Ellen agreed. 'I'll bring Mother around tomorrow.'

After settling her mother in with the Haydens Ellen went to the elder Fraulein Bachmann and asked if she knew anyone who could hide Charlotte. She advised Ellen to ask the madam who had given her work mending dresses. Ellen remembered having seen a young woman with a child in the kitchen of the brothel. Clearly the woman was not a prostitute: she wore no makeup, and her dress was plain. She spent most of her time holding a small child on her lap and playing games with her. Ellen had already begun to suspect that the woman and child were Jewish, since that was the most likely explanation for their presence in a brothel.

When Ellen told the madam that her mother needed a room to stay and could pay some money, the madam told her to go to a nearby bar and look for a small blonde woman wearing a print dress who might be able to help her.

Threading her way through the dark, smoky bar, Ellen tried to ignore the leers she was attracting. 'Hey, Fräulein,' some man called to her. 'Want a drink?'

Ellen spotted a small blonde not much older than she was. She was wearing a patterned dress with a lace collar and looked as though she belonged in a convent. 'Madam sent me here,' Ellen told her.

'Oh yes?' said the girl quizzically, looking Ellen up and down.

'My mother needs a place to stay. We have been bombed out. Madam said you might be able to help.'

'I have only one room, and that's in use a lot of the time.'

'We can pay you,' said Ellen quickly. 'My mother is very quiet, and she won't be there when you need the room. We would just use it when you are not there. We don't have anywhere else to go.'

'How much money?'

They settled on a small sum. A week later Charlotte moved into a small room on Kurfürstenstrasse, a wide street in the north-east corner of the Schöneberg district, roughly between Gleisdreieck and the zoo. The area – especially around the underground station – was a red-light district where prostitutes openly solicited officers of the Nazi High Command. Many of these came to visit Adolf Eichmann, chief administrator in the Reich Security Main Office who had his headquarters on Kurfürstenstrasse 115–16. It was inside the large stone walls of this building that Eichmann, by now a key member of the Nazi inner circle who had distinguished himself as one of Hitler's chief butchers, orchestrated the implementation of the 'final solution to the Jewish problem' which he and other top Nazis had outlined in Wannsee in January 1942.

Charlotte's new refuge was only a few blocks east of Eichmann's headquarters. The room was furnished spartanly with a bed and a banana-shaped sofa upholstered in beige. The arrangement was that during the daytime Charlotte slept on the sofa; in the evening she was to leave her hostess on her own to entertain clients. During these evening hours Charlotte either went to a nearby cinema or visited Ellen and Erich who were only about twenty minutes away.

After several weeks, the young woman decided that her new tenant deserved something better than a sofa to sleep on, so she rearranged her business hours. She would see clients during the daytime and Charlotte would leave in the afternoon. At night Charlotte could sleep in her comfortable bed, and the prostitute would go back to the bar and look for new customers. At weekends, when the room was busy all the time, the girl would contact one of her co-workers who was not busy and Charlotte would stay with her. The woman took a liking to Charlotte because she was quiet and good-natured, but by late summer her neighbours were looking at the older woman suspiciously. Why was a well-dressed, middle-aged woman coming and going from the room of a prostitute? Charlotte knew it was time to leave.

When Ellen brought Anni Gehre the news that her mother had to move again – after such a short time – Dr Arndt searched again through his former list of patients. He decided to send Anni to visit Ida Forbeck, who lived on Prinzenstrasse, at the other end of the street from the Bachmann sisters, in a much poorer district. Early in his practice Dr Arndt had taken on Ida as his patient for free and delivered the baby of her unmarried teenage niece. Lina had provided the young mother with feather beds and food. The doctor was reasonably sure that Ida would try to help them.

Ida immediately offered to take Charlotte in as a guest. 'Yes, of course I will help. For Dr Arndt I will do anything. Bring her here. She can stay with me.' Once again the Arndts were depending on the kindness of Gentiles, some of whom barely knew the family. They had been in hiding for just eight months and almost two dozen Germans had already helped shelter them, including the Gehres, the Köhlers, Anni Harm, Purzel, the Bachmann sisters, the Haydens, Marie Wüstrach, the Düblers and several prostitutes whose names Ellen would never know.

And now Ida Forbeck, a thin woman in her seventies who wore her white hair in a bun, would add her name to the list. Ida, a charitable woman with almost no financial resources, lived in a small room with two single beds, a large tile stove in one corner, several straight-backed chairs and a plain wooden table. Ida shared the room with the sister of the niece whom Dr Arndt had helped as a teenager. The niece now lived next door to Ida with her young son and a man who was probably not the father of the child. Charlotte was immensely grateful for Ida's gesture, but she soon discovered that she would have to make do in less than desirable circumstances. Unlike Anni Harm's clean, bright apartment Ida's room was stuffy and hot, infested with bedbugs that hid in the mattresses and crawled on to the ceiling at night and fell down in clumps on to whoever was below.

When Ellen went to visit her mother in the evening she found her sitting in the middle of the room having a cigarette, next to Ida who was smoking a corncob pipe. Both women were furiously puffing smoke into the stale air, trying to prevent the insects from landing on them.

'Mother,' said Ellen, alarmed when she saw her mother scratching her arm, 'what on earth are you doing?'

'The bugs are attacking,' said Charlotte gamely, rolling up her sleeve to show Ellen several rashes on her arms, the results of a night attack.

'Oh no,' said Ellen. 'What can I do to help?' Without waiting for a reply, she went to the sink, soaked a rag in cold water and pressed the cold compress to her mother's arms. 'I know this is very difficult, but we have no choice. This was the only place I could get.'

'Don't worry,' said Charlotte. 'I know you are doing your best. The hardest part is sitting here with nothing to do and thinking about Aunt Johanna and your father and the others we never hear from. I know there is something terribly wrong. Johanna would have written if things were all right. I don't dare think what I know to be true.'

'Yes,' said Ellen. 'We all feel that way. But we cannot allow ourselves to think about them right now. That will not help them or us. We have to remain strong so that we can find them when the war ends.'

'I don't think they'll be alive when the war ends,' Charlotte said quietly; then added briskly, 'You're right. Brooding will not help them or us. How are Ruth and Lina?'

Ellen told her mother that they were doing well. They were still staying in Berlin, since both Tata and her husband were in Burig, but occasionally Tata would come to the city and bring vegetables and eggs from the country. Ruth often spent weekends at the factory with Erich and Ellen. But Lina almost never went out. She was afraid that someone would recognize her. She barely ever saw Dr Arndt, so Ruth took messages back and forth since she was less fearful of going out. And Ruth met her father every couple of weeks at the canal. 'Ruth says that both her mother and her father are in pretty good spirits, mostly because they knew we are all still safe. They ask frequently about you.'

'Thank you,' said Charlotte. 'Tell them I think of them often. Now, what is happening with the war? I cannot listen to the BBC. I see only the lies printed in the Fascist newspaper that Ida brings home.'

'The Allies are advancing to Sicily and then they will enter Italy, and then it is a matter of time before they get here. Even Max says the Allies are determined now to end the war. And you know how cynical he is!'

'Good,' said Charlotte. 'Now go, before the bugs get to you!'

Max's instincts were sound. On the evening of 23 August seven hundred Allied bombers flew over the city, dropping 1,800 tons of explosives and tens of thousands of tons of incendiary material on the capital. It was the beginning of an almost non-stop bombing siege that would continue for an unprecedented year and a half, destroying 26 square kilometres (ten square miles) of central Berlin, wrecking around one and a half million structures, killing or seriously wounding about 150,000 civilians and rendering over a million Berliners homeless.

While the raids made it more dangerous for the Arndts to remain safely hidden, their fears were offset by renewed hopes in an imminent victory. Unlike other Berliners who sought refuge in their cellars or in bomb shelters (often underground tunnels or large basements equipped by the government with chairs and fire extinguishers), none of the Arndts dared to venture into these shelters, afraid that they would be recognized by former neighbours. Instead, they remained inside, usually sitting against a wall and shielding their heads and bodies with a pillow or blanket to protect themselves from the prospect of glass shattering or beams collapsing. Even if a bomb didn't explode in the immediate vicinity, the vibrations from an adjacent area could loosen timber beams or cause windows to break. Ellen and her mother, less well known in the area, went to whatever shelters they could find.

By mid-September night-time air raids – usually two or three a week – were becoming a way of life, and as prospects of a German victory seemed to pale even Goebbels was rent with anxieties. 'Sooner or later we shall have to face the question of inclining towards one enemy side or the other,' he wrote in his diary while visiting Hitler in Wolfsschanze, the Führer's underground bunker in Rastenburg in East Prussia. 'Germany has never yet had luck with a two-front war; it won't be able to stand this one in the long run either.'

Of course, Hitler would not entertain such thoughts; he was still intent on winning the war. Sooner or later, he figured, Churchill and Stalin would have a falling out, clearing the path for Germany to triumph. A plan to restore Mussolini to power was in the offing. Hitler was also developing his magic weapons of reprisal – the V-I (commonly known as the buzz bomb), a pilotless jet-propelled aircraft, and the V-2 rockets – and he had already set up over sixty launching sites for these weapons on the north coast of France. Meanwhile, he had stepped up armament production in munitions factories in the occupied countries, notably Czechoslovakia, France, Belgium and northern Italy, all of which had escaped bombing. As a result, the German munitions output was virtually unimpaired by the Allied raids.

While the German people were initially stunned by these fierce attacks, most soon adjusted to the bombings and, indeed, endured them stoically. After all, an enduring belief in German infallibility and superiority had led them into what Edward R. Murrow – the CBS correspondent who flew over Berlin with British bombers – described as 'orchestrated Hell'. These same qualities would continue to blind the majority of Germans until Hitler demanded that they sacrifice their lives and those of their children to avoid capitulation to the enemy. And by that time it would be too late to escape from the tragic consequences of their folly.

As for those few other Germans – those who from the early 1930s had spoken out against Hitler or who had defied his policies by continuing to do the right thing – many of these would perish in the coming fires. But if they were to die, they would at least die with dignity.

Herr Mattul, a tailor who lived on Alte Jakobstrasse, near the north end of Spittelmarkt in the heart of Berlin's garment district, was one of these high-minded individuals. Early in his life – years before the Nuremberg Laws made it a criminal offence for Christians to marry Jews or have sex with them – Herr Mattul had fallen in love with a Jew and married her. The Mattuls had two children, Bruno and Inge, and out of deference to her husband Frau Mattul had agreed to raise them as Christians. Many other Jews in mixed marriages had raised their children as Christians, some of them choosing to do so before Hitler came to power, some choosing to do so after the Nazi regulations stipulated that children brought up as Christians would be freer from persecution than Jews who adhered to their faith.

Even so, the Gestapo continued to pressurize Christians – particularly Christian men – to divorce their Jewish spouses. A year after the Nuremberg Laws were passed in 1935 Christians in mixed marriages who worked in civil service jobs were forced to resign. Other private employers imposed similar pressures on Christian employees married to Jews. When the deportations began in 1941 Jews in mixed marriages were unofficially viewed as 'privileged' and not subject to deportation – presumably to appease their Christian spouses – but if Jewish spouses were reported as having a 'hostile attitude' towards the German government they could be arrested.

While some Christians in mixed marriages caved in to these pressures, the record states that most were like Herr Mattul and refused to divorce their Jewish spouses. In retaliation, the Gestapo would often harass and intimate the Jewish husbands and wives until they spoke out against the Nazi regime, thereby giving authorities an excuse to arrest them. While Herr Mattul was away on business during the summer of 1943 Gestapo agents went to his home and arrested his wife, either responding to reports that she

had criticized the government or exorting a confession of miscon-
duct from her once they entered her home.

When he returned to find his wife gone he hastened to Nazi
headquarters and demanded her return. 'She is married to an
Aryan,' he insisted. 'We are raising our children as Christians. She
is a privileged Jew, and the government has made a mistake. I want
her back. She is a good woman.'

The authorities told him it was too late. She had already been
transported to Auschwitz. They could not possibly release her.
Besides, she had brought the deportation on herself by speaking
out against the Third Reich, they told him. The Gestapo did not
make mistakes.

'But she is my wife and the mother of my children. She is a law-
abiding citizen. You have no right to do this.'

'There is nothing to be done,' said the officer coldly. Then saluting 'Heil Hitler' he left the room.

The tragic loss of his wife made Herr Mattul even more defiant
against the Nazi regime. Shortly after this he employed and helped
to shelter a Jewish woman – a former directoress of a dressmaking
salon – so she could work in his salon preparing samples for the garment industry. The Bachmann sisters, who knew Herr Mattul as a
colleague and who had heard through the industry grapevine that
he had in his employ a talented Jewish directoress, called him to
find out if he could use a young, talented seamstress who was also
Jewish.

A recommendation from the Bachmann sisters was not to be
taken lightly. Herr Mattul hired Ellen straight away as an assistant
to sew buttons, bows, hooks and other details on to finished
samples. Mattul's son, Bruno, a young man in his late twenties who
ran the family business with his father and dabbled in the black
market, shared his father's political sympathies. He immediately
welcomed Ellen into the household. But Inge, Bruno's younger
sister, who managed the household and the kitchen, was not so
pleased to have her around.

Whether Inge was angry about her mother's abduction by the
Nazis or fearful of being arrested in the same way because of her

mixed heritage, or a combination of both, Inge clearly did not want Ellen in the house. But she could not openly defy her father, so she withheld food from her, hoping to pressurize her into leaving.

But Ellen had no intention of going. She liked Herr Mattul and Bruno, and she needed work and a warm, secure refuge. As for food, she worked out a way to thwart Inge. Each day she would swipe an apple or a tomato from a basket that sat on the kitchen table, hide it in her skirt and then put it into her bag. The next day she would enter, casually chewing on the apple she had stolen the previous day as though it belonged to her. In fact she did this to spite Inge; after all, she could have eaten the apple at home. And when Ruth came to visit they managed to steal spoonfuls of stewed apple behind Inge's back.

Bruno, however, went out of his way to protect Ellen and find new jobs for her. Some time around late September or early October he sent her to a nearby bar on Spittelmarkt. The manager, a middle-aged woman, required an assistant who would wash glasses and set up the bar so it would be ready when customers came in at the end of the working day. She gave Ellen the job straight away; she did not care that she was Jewish. Most labourers had been recruited to work in munitions factories, so employers of all sorts were hard up for help.

The bar on Spittelmarkt was a ten-minute bike ride north of Max's factory, just south of Unter den Linden, where many consulates were located. One morning before leaving the factory Ellen asked Erich to stop by the bar later that day to help her carry home a package. That afternoon Erich told Max he had to go on an errand. He went outside wearing his work clothes and hopped on his bike. As he raced through Oranienstrasse to Moritzplatz his bike wheel caught on a tram track. He was thrown from the bike and landed on his side. At first he was too stunned to know what had happened. When he began to regain his faculties and tried to get up, his leg buckled and he saw that he had deep gashes on his side.

Several pedestrians rushed to help him. One man offered to call the hospital. 'No,' Erich said quickly, knowing he would be in much greater danger in a German hospital than bleeding on the street. 'I am fine, thanks,' he said, trying to ignore the pain in his head and the ache in his side. He managed to get up and walk to the bar. As he got going, the people dispersed. Holding on to the bike handles for support, he walked slowly, trying to keep most of his weight on his uninjured side

'What happened?' Ellen gasped when Erich entered the bar limping, his side covered with grit and mud.

'I fell off my bike,' said Erich weakly. He slumped in a chair, exhausted. Ellen ran to the bar and brought him a glass of water. Later she helped him walk back to the factory. Hans was there. 'What happened?' he asked, alarmed to see Erich wounded.

'I fell off my bike,' repeated Erich.

'Did any police see you?'

'No. No police were there. But my leg hurts. We're going to see Father later tonight.' Then he lay down on the cot.

That evening, toward midnight, Ellen helped Erich hobble to Anni Gehre's so that he could see his father. To get up the stairs Erich had to lean heavily on Ellen's arm and on the banister on the other side.

Ellen knocked on the door until Anni came.

'Arthur, it's Erich,' Anni called out. 'He's hurt!'

The doctor helped his son into Max's and Anni's room, where he laid him on the bed and undressed him to examine the gashes on his side. 'Did the police see you?'

'No,' said Erich, wincing as his father began cleaning the wounds. Then he bandaged his son's hand, which had been sprained. 'At least no one saw you. It could have been worse. The wounds are bad, but they will heal. Tell Max you cannot use your hand on the lathe for a couple of days. I will check in on you a week from today at the factory.'

Dr Arndt gave Ellen some gauze and ointment to keep the wounds clean. Early the next morning Ellen left a note in Max's office telling him that Erich had had a slight accident and would not be able to work for several days. Then they left before the workers came in and went to the Spittelmarkt bar.

When the manager came in, Ellen told her that her boyfriend had had an accident and could not work. She asked if it would be all right if he spent the next few days there until his hand healed, to which the manager agreed. So Erich stayed with Ellen at the bar, spending most of his time reading through a huge stack of magazines that the manager kept on hand for her customers. A few days later he was well enough to return to work.

When he thanked the manager for her kindness in letting him stay there, she asked him if he could check the wiring of a large and very heavy chandelier that hung over the seating area of the bar. Erich duly climbed up a ladder to the top where he carefully dislodged the chandelier from its ceiling hook so that he could check the cables. Next he tried to replace the chandelier back on the hook. But he could not lift it sufficiently. After several more attempts he finally left it suspended from the wires, which were stretched to their limit. He scrambled down the ladder.

'We have to get out quickly,' he whispered to Ellen when he reached the ground. 'The chandelier's going to fall down!' He took her by the hand and pulled her through the back door and they fled. That night there was a major air raid. The chandelier indeed came crashing down – not because of Erich but as a result of a bomb.

# 7

# THE DEVIL HAS MANY FACES

I have just returned from a visit to Germany [and] have seen the
famous German Leader and also something of the great change he
has effected. [Germany] is now full of hope and confidence, and of
a renewed sense of determination to lead its own life without
interference. One man has accomplished this miracle. He is a
born leader of men. A magnetic, dynamic personality with a
single-minded purpose, a resolute will and dauntless heart. –
David Lloyd George, British Prime Minister, writing after a visit to
Berlin, *Daily Express*, 17 November 1936

By mid-October 1943 Charlotte had moved into a new room with
one of Ida Forbeck's neighbours, an elderly widow who had an
extra bed and wanted company, a woman known only to Ellen as
'Greta'. It was at Greta's that Ellen and Ruth met Co, a young, slim,
blond Dutchman in worn clothing.

Jacobus Spyker, known as Co, was one of the seven million
forced labourers who worked in the German munitions factories
throughout the war. Most were ordered to labour in factories in
their own countries; others, like Co, were drafted and sent to Germany. When Ellen and Ruth met Co he had been working in a
Berlin factory for almost two years. Forced labourers from occupied
countries were treated abysmally. They received minimal wages
and subsistence diets; they were harassed and often brutalized by
Nazi supervisors; and they were confined to shabby barracks.
Moreover, they were cut off from their friends and family.

Greta first encountered him as he was walking from his barracks
to his workplace. Taking pity on him, she offered him an apple.
They began talking, and Greta, who liked his forthright manner
and who welcomed company of any sort, invited him to share a
meal with her. Co immediately accepted, lured by the prospect of a

home-cooked meal, however spartan. Greta continued to invite Co for dinner now and then, and one day he met Charlotte there. During another of his visits Co met Ellen and Ruth, who sometimes visited Charlotte at the end of the working day. Co was delighted to meet young women his own age and asked if he could see them again. Ruth quickly agreed. She liked him and sensed that he was eager to develop a friendship.

They arranged to meet the following week at Greta's apartment. During their visit he told Ruth that he was from Vlaardingen, Holland. The Germans had forced him to work for them when they invaded the Netherlands in May 1940. He was lonely, and he was not afraid to talk about his background and voice his dislike of the Nazis with Ruth.

After several more meetings, Ruth trusted him enough to tell him her family's secret, although she was careful not to reveal their last names or the address of the factory. Co offered to introduce Ruth to Frau Meier, a woman in her late sixties whom he had also met on the street. Frau Meier, who did some trading on the black market, had offered to buy food for him if he could provide her with either money or any valuables that he might have smuggled into Germany.

Soon Co developed a friendship with Frau Meier and her husband, Paul, who would invite him to take meals with them. Now Paul Meier was recovering from the ravages of syphilis in a mental hospital nearly 100 kilometres (62 miles) away from Berlin. Frau Meier visited him about once a month, spending a week or so with him. Co had a hunch that she would be willing to share her apartment with Charlotte for a small sum of money. The apartment, he told Ruth and Charlotte, had two rooms and a separate kitchen; the bedroom had two good-sized single beds, and it was clean and sunny. It was also located just down the block on Prinzenstrasse.

Charlotte immediately agreed. She still had money. Indeed, money was never a problem for her or any of the Arndts: the doctor had spent few of the 20,000 marks he had taken with him into hiding, Erich was earning a respectable wage, and Ruth and Ellen also received modest amounts of money for their work. The problem was that cash could not necessarily buy them food or shelter. The vast majority of Germans were either anti-Semitic or indifferent to the fate of the Jews. They had watched silently as Hitler stripped Jews of their rights and assets, burning hundreds of their synagogues, smashing their stores and arresting thousands of the most prominent Jewish men. They had watched silently as the Gestapo rounded up their Jewish neighbours and herded them into covered vans. If these Germans had not protested when it might have been possible to prevent these events from occurring, why would they put themselves out now? And, as for the small group of Germans who had opposed Hitler from the beginning and who were sympathetic to the plight of the Jews, most were too frightened to do anything but not report them to the authorities. And no amount of money could allay their fears.

So whenever the Arndts found a German who was willing to go the extra mile and offer them temporary shelter or a meal or a few ration cards, they accepted with gratitude. Soon after Charlotte moved in with Frau Meier, Ruth trusted Co enough to bring him to visit Erich and Ellen at the factory at weekends. He often spent Saturdays with them, sometimes staying overnight and sleeping on a mattress on the floor near the stove in Max's workspace. Co also helped Erich with small chores and brought the group occasional packages of food that he received from his family in Holland. Eventually Hans Köhler and Dr Arndt met him, as well as Lina, who sometimes spent time at Frau Meier's and who met Co there when he visited. Soon he became a regular, friendly face.

By late October the Arndts had been in hiding for almost ten months – at least twice as long as they had anticipated. In the wake of the German defeat at Stalingrad, they had expected the Americans and British to invade the continent within months, bringing the war to a close by the summer of 1943. But the war was still not over and, despite Allied gains, there was still no sign of an imminent Allied landing in France. They were hungry and tired and restless. The confinement was particularly hard on Erich who longed to spend some time out of doors and, now that there seemed to be a lull in the air attacks, he was ready for an adventure.

One evening, as he flipped through a newspaper that Hans had left in the loft, his eye fastened on a large advertisement announcing a forthcoming production of *Madame Butterfly* at the Berlin Staadt Opera on the elegant Unter den Linden.

Impulsively he turned to Ellen. 'Let's go,' he said, pointing to the newspaper.

'The opera? Are you crazy? It's far too dangerous. There will be thousands of people there. And police. And maybe Hitler himself. He loves opera.'

'Only Wagner. Not Puccini.'

'I still think it's too dangerous.'

Erich suggested taking Manfred, the youngest apprentice and a member of a Hitler Youth Group. He would wear his Hitler Youth uniform, providing them with a cover, and they could also take Charlotte who could wear her silver fox boas. 'We will look like an average family! If there's a raid, we'll follow the crowd and go into a shelter. No one will recognize us there.'

Ellen finally agreed. She, too, needed a respite from the daily tension and boredom. And she was every bit as brave as Erich. When he proposed the idea to Manfred, he accepted right away, offering on his own initiative to wear his Hitler Youth uniform. They made plans to meet the following Saturday night at the underground station. Erich, who had managed to redeem a navy-blue suit from the trunk in Hans's office, combed his hair for the occasion and donned a tie. Ellen put on her favourite dress, stockings, high heels and her hat trimmed with mink. Charlotte, too, dressed in her best clothes, wearing her warm winter coat with the silver foxes and a large hat.

The following Saturday they met as planned and walked confidently toward the Opera House, where crowds were beginning to gather. As they approached the wide pavilion leading to the entrance, Erich recognized a young worker from Siemens whom he knew only as 'Tannenbaum'. Startled, the two boys stared at one other. Then Tannenbaum nodded his head, motioning Erich to one aside. The latter told Ellen to carry on towards the entrance with

Charlotte and Manfred and that he would join them shortly. As soon as Ellen and the others were out of hearing distance Tannenbaum and Erich began walking together.

'So you made it,' said Tannenbaum in a whisper. 'What are you doing here with a Hitler youth?'

'Going to the opera. We work together. What are you doing here?'

'Waiting for Stella.'

'Stella?'

'You remember: Stella Goldschlag from Siemens, Section 133, the sexy blonde who slept around.'

'Yes, I know Stella but not from Siemens. We met at a party. She went to art school with my girlfriend. Are you together?'

'My God, no.' And then, dropping his voice another level as he surreptitiously looked around, Tannenbaum said huskily, 'She's a *Greifer*. We call her the "Blonde Lorelei".'

'Are you sure?' said Erich, stopping suddenly. 'I can't believe it.'

'Yes, that's what she does.'

'But how do you know?' asked Erich.

Tannenbaum explained that he still kept in contact with a few friends from Siemens, all of whom had gone into hiding at the same time. One of them had heard from other friends that Stella visited restaurants and cruised round the Berlin streets looking for co-workers and acquaintances that she could lure into meeting her. She regularly went to the Opera House, knowing that Jews in hiding sometimes met there. 'She's usually with her sidekick Rolf Isaaksohn,' continued Tannenbaum. 'He's tall and dark and totally amoral. He turned in his uncle when the Gestapo first picked him up to prove himself to them.'

'I had no idea,' Erich whispered. 'We never see anyone from Siemens. We make it a point not to see anyone.'

'I've a gun.'

'A gun?'

'I'm going to kill her. She's worse than a Nazi. A Jew informer. Be careful. She wears a green hat with a green feather. Don't, under any circumstances, talk to her or let her follow you.'

Just then they spotted a policeman at the other end of the street and started talking loudly about the opera as they returned to the entrance, where Ellen was waiting impatiently.

'Where have you been? The opera is about to start! They won't let us in if we're late.'

'I'll explain later,' whispered Erich, casting his eyes around to see if Stella was near by. For a moment he was tempted to leave immediately. They walked up the stairs to their seats – located high in the balcony. Before the opera began, Erich took Ellen's hand and quickly told her about Stella. Ellen looked at him in disbelief. She remembered Stella. Bold, beautiful, and narcissistic, she had earned pocket money by posing in the nude for other students – most of them male. Ellen had never liked her or trusted her, even then. She was not sure she believed the story that Stella had been tortured, not because the Gestapo were not capable of such acts but because she did not think Stella would have allowed them to go that far: she would probably have offered to sell her services at the mere threat of a beating. But that was irrelevant now.

At least Stella did not know that Ellen and Erich were in hiding. She would not be looking for them. But they would now have to keep an eye out for her and warn the others. As the curtain rose, Ellen held Erich's hand tightly, trying to lose herself in the wonderful music resonating through the beautiful opera house. It was overwhelming, and she gave herself up to it completely. Some day, she vowed, she and Erich would be free to go to the opera every Saturday night. As the curtain fell on the last act, they found themselves standing, clapping wildly with the rest of the audience, caught up in the exhilaration.

Then they swiftly left their seats and merged into the crowds streaming out of the building. When they got outside the cold air stung their cheeks. Erich caught sight of Tannenbaum standing near the door. 'She did not show up,' he said quietly, slipping unobtrusively alongside Erich as he walked toward the street. 'Be careful. Good luck.' Then he disappeared into the darkness.

They had gone to the opera just in time. By the third week in November 1943 the bombings had intensified again. This time the bombs tore into central Berlin, demolishing the consulates near the Tiergarten and on Unter den Linden, as well as many office buildings and residences on Wilhelmstrasse and Friedrichstrasse. Even the magnificent Berlin Zoo went up in flames when a mine accidentally landed on the aquarium, destroying all the fish and snakes in it and damaging cages of wild animals, which had to be shot by guards to prevent their escaping into the city. When the crocodiles crawled into the River Spree, they, too, were hauled out and shot.

Erich now spent hours and hours in the evening listening intently to the wireless he had constructed; it could intercept military signals. Suddenly he heard 'Alabaster Taschenlampe' – the code the military used to indicate that bombers were headed for Berlin. 'Quick,' Erich said turning to Ellen and Charlotte, who was staying at the factory for a few days. 'The bombers are coming. Get going.'

The two went to the toilet, as they always did before air raids; then they dressed warmly in coats and scarves. By the time the sirens went off, both women were on their way to an official air-raid shelter located one block west of the factory on Oranienstrasse. The shelter held about three hundred people, and getting there ahead of everyone else assured them a seat on a bench. Erich still refused to go with them, since he was afraid of being recognized.

After Ellen and Charlotte left, Erich went to Hans's office and sat against the wall as usual, wearing a French army helmet that Hans had found in the street and given to him to wear during raids. This raid was particularly long and heavy. He could hear bombers flying overhead and explosions in the distance. After an hour the all-clear siren finally went off. Erich quickly got up and put a pot of water on the Bunsen burner, waiting for Ellen and Charlotte to return. When twenty minutes had elapsed he began to worry. Recent air raids had devastated areas of the city; the area north of Kreuzberg had been badly bombed. He did not think that Oranienstrasse had been blasted in this raid, but he could not be sure. Ellen usually returned within ten minutes of the all-clear siren. It was not like her to linger.

As fear took hold of him, he decided to investigate. He knew he could not risk going out into the street in his usual jacket and working trousers; he could too easily be stopped by the police, who often walked through areas after an air raid checking for fires and delayed explosions. So he donned his dark brown britches and black knee-high boots. Then he slipped into his father's leather coat from the First World War and put on a cap. In the darkness Erich could pass as a German officer.

He raced down the stairs and walked quickly but calmly to the large shelter where Ellen and Charlotte had gone. The area was clear of smoke, but standing in front of the shelter was a guard.

'Why aren't the people out?' Erich demanded to know.

'I have not yet received the order to evacuate,' the man answered.

'And why aren't you standing at attention?' asked Erich brusquely. 'Don't you know that when you address an officer you must stand at attention? If you don't show proper respect I'll report you to headquarters!'

'Heil Hitler,' said the guard, nervously adjusting his collar and standing up straight. 'Heil Hitler.'

'Now since you can't do your job I am going in to do it for you!' Erich marched brazenly into the shelter and gave the order to evacuate. Then he went outside and stood near the entrance as hundreds of Germans filed silently by. The cold seeped into his bones, and he felt a knot in his stomach. Where were Ellen and Charlotte? Maybe they had not made it to the shelter in time. Maybe they were lying somewhere in the street, wounded and unable to move. As his thoughts became more and more alarming, he glimpsed Ellen's blonde curls peeping out from behind the scarf she was wearing around her head. Charlotte was with her. Relief flooded through him and he cleared his throat loudly, hoping to attract their attention.

Ellen, startled, looked up and saw him; then looked away and continued walking forward with Charlotte, as though nothing had happened. Later she would find out why Erich was standing there.

It took at least half an hour for everyone to leave the shelter.

Some people were elderly and had difficulty walking up the stairs. When the shelter was finally cleared, Erich addressed the guard, who quickly stood to attention once again.

'At ease,' said Erich, saluting him. 'Heil Hitler.' Then he left and returned to the factory where Ellen and Charlotte were now anxiously awaiting his return. When he arrived he embraced Ellen, then sat down on a chair, overwhelmed by what he had done. He was used to masquerading during the day as a German journeyman; but disguising himself as a German officer and bluffing his way into an air-raid shelter where there were hundreds of German civilians was a different matter. Even he was impressed with his own nerve.

Not every German soldier could be so easily manipulated. For example, there was Colonel Wehlen. A slim and rather nondescript man, he was exactly the kind of man who could have made it to the top ranks – clever, calculating and ambitious. Instead, and possibly to his credit, he cared more about advancing himself than the Fascist cause.

Wehlen lived in an elegant apartment in Schöneberg near the Bayerischer Platz, a fashionable section of Berlin, with his wife and two young children, a girl and a boy both under five years old. Early in the war he had purchased a commission as an army officer, not only because he yearned for a military officer's status but because that status would give him access to privileged information about train schedules to and from the occupied countries. With this information, he figured, he would be able to buy food supplies – cheese from Holland and France, salami and coffee from Italy, chocolates from Belgium and whatever else the trains were carrying – and he could sell them on the black market for outrageous sums of money.

By the time Ellen and Ruth met Wehlen in the autumn of 1943 he had organized a network of at least a dozen high-ranking German officers who were involved in his black-market operation. While Bruno Mattul was never part of the major organization, he also dabbled in the black market, and through his dealings he had met and befriended Wehlen.

Wehlen knew that Bruno was half-Jewish, but he did not care.

The fate of the Jewish people was of no more consequence to him than the fate of the gypsies or the Germans or the Italians. So when Wehlen casually mentioned that his wife was having a hard time finding qualified household workers, Bruno offered to introduce Ruth and Ellen to him.

'But I have to warn you, they are Jewish,' said Bruno. 'Please be careful.'

'Of course,' replied Wehlen. 'Where did you find them? They are probably wonderful workers. I will be happy to meet them – and protect their identity.'

It was, in fact, the perfect arrangement: Wehlen could trust the women to be discreet about his clandestine activities. He, in turn, would be discreet about their background. As Bruno explained to Ruth and Ellen when he told them about the job, Wehlen had no interest in reporting them to the authorities. In exchange for their labours he was willing to pay them five marks a day and give them each a large hot meal at noon. Most important, Bruno stressed, they would have a safe, warm place to stay.

Frau Wehlen, a tall, slim brunette with a pleasant manner, employed the girls immediately. Ruth, trained as a nurse, would take care of her children; Ellen would clean the house and cook. Both would serve sandwiches and real coffee or whisky to the German officers who visited Wehlen to discuss with him where to store the goods and who would be potential buyers.

Ellen and Ruth quickly settled into a routine. The apartment had at least nine rooms, each of them elegantly furnished with deep pile rugs, mahogany furniture and velvet curtains. The kitchen was small but well supplied; the refrigerator was stocked with Dutch cheese, Belgian sausages, eggs, fresh apples and oranges and coffee beans. Frau Wehlen encouraged them to eat heartily and gave them extra food to take back to Erich, whom she knew about vaguely.

When she took her children to the country at weekends Ellen and Ruth discovered that selling contraband was not Wehlen's only indiscretion. During his wife's absence Wehlen would brazenly carry on with other women, and Ruth or Ellen would serve break-

Dr Arthur Arndt and Lina with Ruth aged two and Erich aged one, 1924

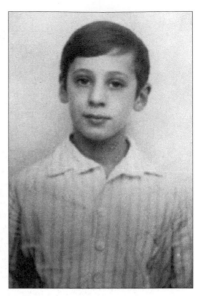

Ellen as a toddler in Blesen, where she lived with her mother and grandparents

Bruno aged eight

Erich and Ruth when they first entered school, with *Zukertüten* – cones filled with sweets and other small gifts

Ellen's mother, Charlotte Lewinsky, when she was a young woman living in Blesen

Above: Dr Arndt as a medic during the First World War

Left: Dr Arndt received a Cross of Honour citation for his outstanding service in the First World War on 16 August 1935, a month before the Nuremberg Laws were passed; the citation was signed by the police commissioner of Kreuzberg/Tempelhof.

Dr Arndt's 1922 model Piccard, which he bought in 1925, becoming one of the few men in the neighbourhood to own a car; his chauffeur, pictured, later joined the Nazi Party after leaving the Arndts.

Dr Arndt and Lina with Lina's oldest sister, Johanna Paul, who emigrated to South Africa after Hitler came to power

Above: Ellen in a fur hat she
made from scraps of mink her
aunt gave to her, 1940

Left: Charlotte (far left) and
Johanna Kroner (centre),
Ellen's aunt with whom she
and her mother lived in
Berlin; in 1942 Johanna was
deported to Riga and killed.

Ellen and Erich (second and third from left, top row) at a *Ringelpietz*, a Sunday party, Berlin, 1940; since German law forbade Jews from going to cultural events, Jewish parents often hosted these so that their teenage children could meet.

Despite laws forbidding Jews from going to beaches, Ellen (centre), Erich and a *Mischling* friend, Ruth Deutsch, brazenly defied them; this 1940 photograph was taken by a friend, even though Jews were not allowed to own cameras.

Ruth's Star of David, which was hidden in a box with family documents and buried in the ground during the war

Erich's identity card from Siemens, where he worked a a slave labourer from 1940 to the end of 1942

Ruth's state identity card that she was given in 1939 at the age of sixteen. All Jews were required to be photographed with their left ears exposed, since those of Jews were supposedly different from the left ears of Aryans.

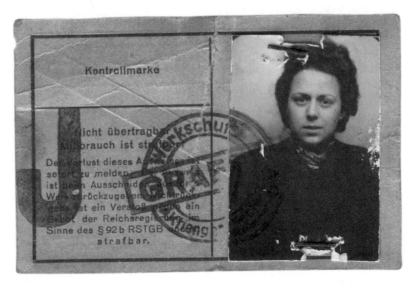

Ruth's identity card from Ehrich & Graetz, a munitions factory where she worked from 1941 to the beginning of 1943

Bruno Gumpel, a friend of Erich's, joined the Arndt group in May 1944. In 1943 he acquired a Czech passport and went to a forger, who replaced the original photograph with one of Bruno.

Ruth (second from left) with her classmates in the student nursing programme in the Jewish Hospital, on graduation day, 12 September 1941; it was to be the last student nursing programme for Jewish women until after the war ended.

Ruth posing in the family's small, two-room *Judenhaus* on Oranienstrasse, where they lived from 1938 until they went into hiding in 1943

Clockwise from top: Ellen, Erich, Ruth and Bruno, 1940

Bruno's mother, Ella Gumpel, who died in Auschwitz

Bruno's father, Gotthold, was experimented on in Auschwitz but survived and returned to Berlin after the war, where he was reunited with Bruno and Bruno's brother, Günther

Günther Gumpel, Bruno's older brother, who emigrated to London in 1939 and enrolled in the Royal Army Service Corps. He requested a transfer to Berlin after receiving a letter from Bruno at the end of the war.

Erich (far left) working in Max Köhler's factory. Seated at the window is 'Uncle Willy', the other journeyman; in the background is one of the apprentices.

Max's son, Hans, working at his lathe in the factory

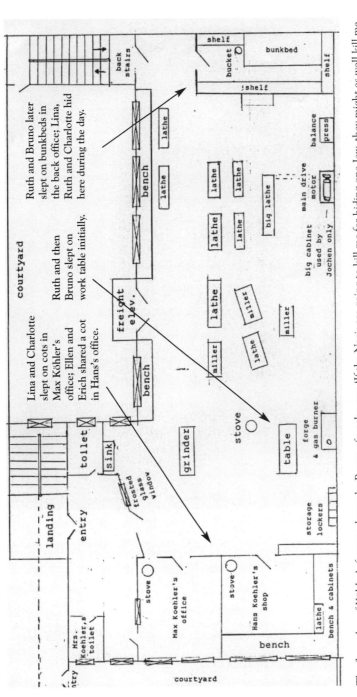

The floor plan of Köhler's factory, drawn by Bruno after the war. 'If the Nazis are going to kill me for hiding one Jew, they might as well kill me for hiding six Jews,' said Max Köhler, who employed Erich and Bruno as journeymen. Erich and Ellen lived in the factory soon after they went into hiding; eventually Ruth, Charlotte, Bruno and Lina moved in with them.

Text within the floor plan:

courtyard

back stairs

shelf
bucket
bunkbed
!shelf
shelf

balance
press

lathe

lathe
lathe
lathe
lathe

big lathe

main drive motor

big cabinet used by Jochen only

Ruth and Bruno later slept on bunkbeds in the back office; Lina, Ruth and Charlotte hid here during the day.

bench
bench
lathe

lathe
miller
lathe
miller

miller

Ruth and then Bruno slept on work table initially.

freight elev.

bench

stove

table

forge & gas burner

Lina and Charlotte slept on cots in Max Köhler's office; Ellen and Erich shared a cot in Hans's office.

toilet
sink

entry

grinder

frosted glass window

landing

Mrs. Koehler's toilet

entry

stove

Max Koehler's office

stove

Hans Koehler's shop

storage lockers

bench

lathe
bench & cabinets

courtyard

Polizeiamt Mitte

Dieser Erlaubnisschein ist nur gültig in Verbindung mit einem amtlichen Lichtbildausweis

Dienststelle

Berlin, den

Ort

B. Nr.

Nur gültig innerhalb von

Berlin

Wohngemeinde

**Polizeiliche Erlaubnis**

Dem Juden — Der Jüdin

Vornamen, Rufnamen unterstreichen

Juname, bei Frauen auch Mädchenname

Beruf

geb. am ........ in ........

wohnhaft in Berlin ........

Gemeinde

Straße, Platz, Nr.

Staatsangehörigkeit        amtlicher Lichtbildausweis

........, wird hiermit die polizeiliche

Erlaubnis zur ........maligen Benutzung des-der ........

Verkehrsmittel

von ........

nach ........

Stadtteil, Straße, Platz

— und zurück —

vom ........ bis ........ erteilt.

Zeitangabe

Im Auftrag

Dienststempel

Unterschrift

Nichtzutreffendes durchstreichen

**Diese polizeiliche Erlaubnis gilt nicht als Fahrausweis**

Normally Jews were not permitted to travel on public transport in Berlin, but in May 1942 Dr Arndt was given a special permit to allow him to use underground trains, trams and buses to call on his patients. He was forty-eight at the time and living in the *Judenhaus* in Oranienstrasse; eight months later the doctor went into hiding with his family.

Klara and Max Köhler before the war. Max hired Erich as a journeyman when he went into hiding; eventually Max sheltered six members of the group in his loft factory.

Anni Gehre and her grandson after the war. She and her husband sheltered Dr Arndt for over two years and arranged hiding places and jobs for the others.

Anni Harm and her daughter Evelyn. Annie hid Charlotte for six months, even though her husband was a German soldier.

Above: Anni and Max Gehre in the USA, where they emigrated to be with their daughter after the war

Right: Uschi Treptow and her husband, Heinz Timm, Berlin, 1947

Uschi's parents, Ernst and Marie Treptow, who hid Bruno for nearly a year

Gretchen Dübler (far right) and her daughter Annalee (far left) with Ellen and Erich in Berlin, 1990. Gretchen sent ration cards to the group for two years.

ann Max Köhler seinen Schalter ohne Furcht öff- der Nazizeit konnte für ihn und seine sieben zlinge jedes Klingeln das Verderben bedeuten.

Noch heute erledigt die 69jährige Klara Köhler im Betriel ihres Gatten alle Büroarbeiten. Auch sie trug durch ihr Ver halten viel dazu bei, das Schicksal von Flüchtlingen zu linder

Max and Klara Köhler in a German newspaper after the war in a feature about their protection of the group.

Purzel Lefèbre (left) and Charlotte with two German soldiers during the war. Purzel hid Lina, Erich, Ruth and Ellen in her bedroom after they went into hiding, until the Germans ordered her to give the room to bombed-out Berliners.

'Schwester' (Nurse) Ruth in the Harz mountains with the Santaella family shortly after D-Day. José Santaella, a diplomat, and his wife, Carmen, employed Ruth as a nurse and Lina as a cook. They hid them in Diedersdorf with another Jewish woman, Gertrud Neumann, from April to September 1944.

José and Carmen Santaella with their Yad Vashem award citing them as Righteous Gentiles in 1991

Charlotte wearing Ellen's wedding suit (they shared it since they had so few clothes), Berlin, 1946

Dr Arndt's passport
photograph, 1946

Lina's 'Victim of Fascism' identity card; everyone in the group received one of these after the war; with these cards they could go straight to the front of food queues and they had priority status for housing when it became available.

Ruth and Bruno in Berlin on their wedding day, 29 September 1945

The portraits of Ellen and Erich (top) and
Ruth and Bruno that the couples gave to
Arthur and Lina Arndt on the occasion of
their silver wedding anniversary in Berlin,
March 1946

On 31 December 1945 Dr and Lina Arndt held a
celebratory New Year's party for friends and survivors.
Front row, from left to right, Werner Lilienthal, Ruth and
Bruno Gumpel, Inge Deutschkron, Ellen's friend Herta
from Schubert; middle row: Günther Gumpel, Ellen and
Erich Arndt; top row: the Arndts' maid, Gertrud
Neumann, Charlotte Lewinsky, Lina and Arthur Arndt,
Martha Maske. All but Günther, Martha and the maid
survived the war in hiding.

On board the *Marine Flasher*; left to right, Ruth, Bruno, Ellen, Erich and Charlotte

The *Marine Flasher* as it approached New York Harbor, 20 May 1946. It was the first ship to carry Jewish war refugees to the USA and carried some eight hundred passengers from Germany, Poland, France, Holland, Belgium and other formerly occupied countries.

Left to right, Ellen, Erich,
Charlotte, Bruno and Ruth on
the pier at New York Harbor,
shortly after disembarking,
20 May 1946

Ellen (far left in right-hand picture) and Ruth (far right), enjoying ice-cream sodas during their first week in New York City. (The newspaper caption wrongly identified Ruth as Mrs Geisenberger.) After this they went up to the top of the Empire State Building.

## Refugees Enjoy Sights and Tastes of N. Y.

Post Photos by Gaston

NEWLY-ARRIVED refugees (left), Mr. and Mrs. Lothar Geisenberger, viewing Our Town from Empire State Bldg. yesterday. Above—Mrs. Geisenberger (right) tastes an American soda with Mrs. Bruno Gumpel (center), another refugee who arrived Monday on S. S. Marine Flasher, and latter's sister-in-law, Mrs. Joachim Arndt. Couples went sightseeing after National Refugee Service, called Jewish Appeal agency, worked to get them settled in their new country. Story appears on Page 14.

# 'Wunderbar, Like a Dream,'
# Say Refugees on Tour of City

By ALVIN ROSENFELD

The young couple stood on the skyscraper observation platform high above the city, held hands and smiled.

It was a dream come true. Rosa Geisenberger, 28, and her husband, Lothar, 36, forgot about the years in concentration camps in Latvia and Germany and thought about their future in the city which lay below them.

"Man glaubt man traumt" (one believes that one is dreaming), said Rosa as she looked uptown from the Empire State Bldg.

Sight Miss Liberty

Then, they stared downtown and Lothar said excitedly, "Look, there's the Freiheit statue (Statue of Liberty). And there," he said, pointing towards the North River docks, "that must be the Marine Flasher"—the ship which brought him and 800 other refugees here in a move which marked resumption of large-scale immigration.

Then the Geisenbergers joined the other two couples and a Post reporter and photographer on a tour of mid-town New York.

The tour was one joyous surprise after another. The couples stared at shop windows jammed with food and clothes. And Ruth Gumpel, 24, told her husband, Bruno, 21, "In Germany there's nothing. But here there is everything."

When they had their first ice-cream soda, they practiced their English. Ruth's brother, Joachim Arndt, 22, turned to his wife, Ellen, 23, held up a long ice-cream soda spoon, and said, "This is a poon, yes?" He was corrected and repeated the word until he had it down pat.

The ice-cream soda episode in the typically-American drug store marked the only disappointing point in the tour. They agreed that they liked ice cream very much and soda too, but they couldn't see the combination. Otherwise, everything was considered "wunderbar."

The tour was taken as the three couples marked time while the National Refugee Service, one of the three constituent agencies of the United Jewish Appeal, worked to get them permanently settled in the U. S.

The couple, already interviewed by trained social workers at NRS headquarters, represent the most difficult task NRS faces at present. They, like many others among the Marine Flasher's former passengers, cannot fall back on friends or relatives here. Both the Gumpels and the Arndts have no relatives in America, while the Geisenbergers have only one relation and he is not able to give them much help.

However, the couples are confident that, with NRS advice and financial aid, they will find not only work but homes to take the place of the hotel rooms they now occupy. The men are all employable—Lothar is a trained leather cutter, and Bruno and Joachim are expert machinists.

Both Mrs. Arndt and Mrs. Geisenberger are happiest about the fact that the children soon to be born to them will be U. S. citizens by birth.

Erich and Ellen Arndt (left) and Ruth and Bruno Gumpel at the Arndts' and Gumpels' fiftieth wedding anniversary celebration in Rochester, New York, 1993

Erich and Ellen (seated left) next to Bruno and Ruth. They are surrounded by their children and grandchildren to celebrate Erich's seventieth birthday.

In 2001 Ellen and Erich Arndt revisited the factory at Oranienstrasse 20 where they hid for over two years; despite the heavy bombing of Berlin the building survived intact.

The Santaellas' daughter, Teti (right), and Teti's daughter visiting the Yad Vashem Museum in Israel in 1999; they are pointing to the monument where the Santaellas are listed as Righteous Gentiles.

Left to right: Ellen Arndt, Erich Arndt and Ruth Gumpel on a trip to Berlin, 1999

fast to them in the mornings. When Frau Wehlen returned home she would often find hair-pins and sometimes even a brassière in her bed. 'Ellen,' she would say, holding up the objects, 'are these yours?'

'No, I don't use hair-pins,' she would reply. 'And I don't have that much on top!'

'Thanks, Ellen. I just wanted to be sure,' she would answer, looking wistfully down at the floor. At least she could trust Ellen and Ruth. She only wished she could trust her husband. But there were more issues to worry about than Wehlen's extramarital affairs; at least he was providing well for the family and, unlike most other Germans, they could regularly eat chocolate, salami and all sorts of cheeses.

Early in December Colonel Wehlen brought home a goose, by now difficult to obtain even on the black market. He planned to host an elaborate Christmas dinner for his partners in crime, and he asked Ellen and Ruth to prepare the meal, since his wife would be in the country with the children.

'But, Herr Wehlen,' said Ellen, 'neither one of us have ever cooked a goose. We would not know what to do.'

'Never?' said Herr Wehlen, who, for all his generosity, had no real appreciation of the deprivation the two young women had experienced for the past five years. How could they be expected to cook a goose when for several years they had not been able to purchase meat or chicken? Ellen could turn cabbages and potatoes into an edible meal; she had no experience of cooking an elaborate, elegant dinner.

'However, my mother is a wonderful cook. She has an excellent recipe for goose.'

'Fine,' said Herr Wehlen, who did not really care who cooked it. 'Ask your mother to come and prepare the dinner. You and Ruth will serve it.'

On the evening of the dinner Charlotte travelled to the Wehlens' on the train, dressed in her best winter coat and wearing a scarf and hat to look as smart as possible. When she arrived Ellen gave her a quick tour. The house was even more elaborate than

Charlotte had imagined. Most important, the kitchen was well equipped with all sorts of roasting pans and a good oven. Charlotte quickly went to work while Ellen and Ruth assisted her. At the appointed hour twelve officers dressed impeccably in uniforms entered the dining-room.

There Ellen and Ruth served them drinks, followed by dinner. As the meal wore on and the officers had more and more to drink, they began flirting with the girls. But Ellen and Ruth were swift on their feet and managed to return to the kitchen without incident. There they would collapse in laughter, and Charlotte would join in.

'Such good help!' they heard one of the officers commenting after the dinner was concluded. 'Where did you find such attractive young helpers in these hard times?'

'They are daughters of friends,' replied Herr Wehlen without hesitation. 'They offered to help out since we could not find anyone else. As you know, all the good help has been recruited to work in the factories.'

'Of course,' said the officer. Then, winking, continued, 'If they are ever free again, I would be happy to hire them. I can think of many uses for them!'

His fellow officers chortled at the innuendo, but Herr Wehlen quickly put an end to this line of thought. 'They are high-class women – not your type.'

The officer stiffened, and the others laughed, holding their glasses high.

The following weekend Co showed up at Köhler's factory with a package of Christmas delicacies he had received from his family in Holland on which the group feasted. On Christmas Day Ruth and Co went to Frau Meier's to celebrate; she had volunteered her tiny kitchen for the holiday. The meal was less elaborate than that they had prepared at Wehlen's, but it was far more meaningful to them.

Then suddenly, just after New Year, Co disappeared. He usually came to visit at weekends. When he did not show up the first weekend they reasoned that he was legitimately detained. But when he failed to show up the next weekend and the weekend after that they began to get worried.

'It's not like him,' said Ruth. 'I know that something's wrong.'

'Maybe he's ill,' said Erich.

'No,' said Ruth. 'I'm sure it's something much more serious.'

Although Erich and Ellen tried to comfort her, Ruth was beside herself with anxiety, but she knew she could not go to his barracks to find out what had happened to him. All sorts of possibilities passed through her mind. Had he been killed in a raid? Was he in danger? And, if he was in danger, were they all in danger? She prayed for him every night and sometimes cried herself to sleep. But she felt deep in her heart that she would never see Co again.

# 8

# CALL ME EISEN

Inside the gas chamber the singing had stopped. Now there was only weeping and sobbing. People, their faces smashed and bleeding, were still streaming through the door, driven by blows and goaded by vicious dogs. All at once a small boy was standing before me. His little face puckered with worry, he asked timidly: 'Do you know where my mummy and my daddy are hiding?' – From Filip Müller's account of his experience at Auschwitz as a Jewish *Sonderkommando* (special unit prisoner selected to transport bodies from the gas chambers to the crematoriums)

The disappearance of Co was soon overshadowed by the American participation in the bombing raids over Berlin. On 1 January 1944 the United States Air Force began bombing the city during the day, while the Royal Air Force continued its raids at night. Clouds of smoke now hung over the city, while firestorms raged. During the last week of the month a series of raids killed almost 2,000 people and seriously wounded about 3,000. Some 200,000 Berliners lost their homes. Germans tried to be stoical about the bombings, but they had had enough of the war, and many wanted it to end before they lost their entire families. The Arndts were also tense and weary from the constant explosions as well as frightened of being caught in a raid; still, they were buoyed up by the hope that the fierce onslaught meant a quicker end to the war.

As the bombing increased in ferocity, Hans Köhler insisted that Erich seek protection in the building's air-raid shelter in the courtyard. He already took shelter there during the day raids, since everyone in the building knew he was working as a journeyman in the factory. Now Hans insisted that Erich shelter there during night raids as well. For the first few nights Hans stayed late at the factory until the warning sirens went off. Then he would accompany Erich to the shelter, telling the other tenants that he had hired him to guard the factory overnight. This meant that Erich could use the shelter at weekends and at night without awkward questions being asked.

One night Hans and Erich returned to the loft inspect it for damage after a bomb had landed in the vicinity. Vibrations from a nearby blast had destabilized some large steel rods propped against the wall, and they had crashed to the floor precariously close to the place where Erich had been sitting out the raids. If Erich had been in the loft when the bomb landed it is likely that he would have been badly injured. Erich wondered what he could ever do to repay Hans for insisting that he take shelter, as it had probably saved his life.

Hans's concern for his welfare was offset, however, by Erich's growing discomfort at being around Helmut, the seventeen-year-old apprentice who supported the Nazis unquestioningly and did not hesitate to let everyone know about his loyalty. Sometimes during their noon break, when the workers all sat around the work table eating sandwiches, Helmut would ask Erich innocent-seeming questions about his home and his family. Where did he live? What did his parents do? Did he have family in the army? Erich tensed up when he had to lie, fearing that Helmut might have suspicions about him. It was relatively easy to lie to a shopkeeper whom you would see once or twice in your life; it was much more stressful to maintain a long-term pretence to a co-worker. He could not tell whether Helmut was simply making small talk or whether he was trying to provoke Erich into betraying himself. Fearful that he might slip up and say something that Helmut could construe as anti-Nazi, Erich decided he would have to make a pre-emptive strike.

One day at lunch Helmut was praising the Führer. 'Of course we'll win. Don't you agree?' he asked, looking first at Uncle Willy and then at Horst and Erich, as though putting them all on trial. Erich knew the time had come. Instead of responding, he stood up and asked Helmut to accompany him to the storage room in the rear of the loft. There he shut the door, and rage surged through him like an electric current. He began pummelling Helmut with his fists, and he found himself choking the boy. Helmut gasped. His eyes bulged. Mild-mannered, gentle Erich, beside himself with fury, released his stranglehold and began punching the apprentice again.

He cast Helmut to the floor.

'You are hurting me,' the boy said weakly, tears running down his face. 'Please stop, you are hurting me.'

Erich, wiry but strong and ferocious with anger, knew he could easily kill him. But now, at the decisive moment, Erich turned coldly rational. What would he do with the body? Where could he hide him? What would he say when his co-workers asked where Helmut was and when his parents showed up? And what if someone reported the mysterious death to the Gestapo? They would certainly investigate the factory, and Erich would be required to show an identity card. As he did not have one he would be arrested, and Max and Hans would also be arrested for concealing a Jew. They could all be imprisoned, tortured and killed.

Erich stood frozen. Helmut dead was more dangerous than Helmut alive. Slowly the boy got up. 'Don't you ever question my loyalty to the Führer again!' Erich spat out. 'Don't you dare, or I'll give you a beating you'll never forget! This time you're getting off lightly!'

Helmut, stunned by the outburst, wiped his hand across his face to see if there was blood on it.

Erich opened the door and went back to work. A few minutes later Helmut left the storage room and contritely approached the lathe where Erich was working.

'I'm sorry,' mumbled Helmut sheepishly.

'Thank you.' said Erich gruffly. 'Just don't provoke me again.'

The next day Helmut showed up with a three-inch solid slab of bacon which he offered Erich. Bacon was a rare treat. Erich drilled a hole through it and gave it to Ellen, who used it to flavour the tasteless gruel she had made for dinner. Then she threaded a string through the middle and hung it up to dry. She used the bacon for many days to flavour their meagre meals. Then, when she had boiled most of the taste out of the bacon, she cut it into three equal pieces and gave one to Erich and one to Ruth and kept the third for herself. That evening they each chewed on their small morsels of meat, as though they were the greatest delicacy, until they were gone.

From then on Erich roughed up Helmut on a regular basis to keep him in line, sometimes punching him on the jaw or slapping him around. And every time he did so the boy – who, like most other Nazis, had learned to respect force and brutality – brought him extra food as a peace offering.

After a brief respite from raids in February, the bombings escalated once again in March. Erich bought himself a small pocket calendar so he could record the times and duration of the raids. Lina was now staying in Burig with Tata and her husband Gustav, since the Allies were not yet bombing the countryside. Ruth often stayed overnight in the factory with Erich and Ellen and worked with the latter during the daytime at the Wehlens'. About this time help came from an unexpected source

Dr José Santaella, the agricultural attaché to the Spanish Embassy in Berlin, and his wife, Carmen, were devout Catholics who were passionately opposed to Hitler's brutal treatment of the Jews. Carmen, whose maiden name was Schrader, came from Halle in Thuringia, an area south-east of Berlin. When José had gone to the university at Halle from Spain to obtain his doctorate in agriculture, he met the Schraders and fell in love with their daughter. They married and moved to Spain, where she she adopted the name 'Carmen'. Later they moved to Berlin. Like most diplomats, they had been evacuated because of the heavy bombing. Indeed, most consulates were no longer standing. The Santaellas and their four children were now living in Diedersdorf, a small town around 100 kilometres (62 miles) east of Berlin where the Axis powers had moved their consulates for safe-keeping. The Santaellas lived in a modest one-storey guesthouse in the grounds of a grand estate which at one time had belonged to German nobility and which was now occupied by Japanese dignitaries. They took with them their valued dressmaker, a Jewish woman named Gertrud Neumann.

When the Nazis had started rounding up the Jews Gertrud sent her only daughter to Holland for safety; then she took refuge with a Gentile woman in Berlin. Carmen, who had hired Gertrud as a seamstress before the outbreak of war, refused to dismiss her when Nazi prohibitions made it illegal for German Christians to employ Jews. They knew that Gertrud was in hiding in Berlin, and when the family moved they took her with them to shelter her in their country home.

In Diedersdorf none of their household staff knew Gertrud's true identity, since the Santaellas gave her a false name. Several months later Carmen decided to find a nanny for her children and asked the seamstress if she could recommend anyone. Gertrud had been a patient of Dr Arndt's, and she knew that Ruth had trained as a nurse.

None of the Arndts recall exactly how Gertrud managed to contact Ruth, but they think that since Gertrud knew both Anni Gehre and the Bachmann sisters she must have written to one of them on the off chance that they would know where Ruth was. It was, in any event, Anni who contacted Ruth and told her about the nanny's job. After Ruth said she would be willing to meet the diplomat, Anni arranged a meeting, but she did not reveal Ruth's last name or whereabouts in case anything went wrong.

Ruth was instructed to meet Dr Santaella in the lobby of the prestigious Adlon Hotel not far from the Brandenburg Gate. Ruth recalls being excited but apprehensive about the meeting, since the Adlon was frequented by high-level Nazis, Gestapo members and Wehrmacht officers. She dressed carefully for the occasion, wearing makeup and donning a hat and coat with a scarf. She asked Ellen to accompany her, more for moral support than anything else. The plan was that Ellen would wait outside while Ruth went into the hotel to look for Dr Santaella. If she did not emerge in half an hour Ellen was to go inside and find out what had happened.

When Ruth walked into the lobby Dr Santaella, a tall, distinguished-looking man with dark hair, immediately spotted her. 'Good day, I am Schwester Neu,' said Ruth cautiously when he approached her. The two immediately got on well, and Dr

Santaella offered Ruth the job, which she was happy to accept. She rejoined Ellen outside the hotel, and together they returned to Tata's by train to tell Lina.

A few days later Dr Santaella met Ruth, now accompanied by her few belongings in a suitcase, in front of the Adlon Hotel. He then drove her in his small black car to the guesthouse at Diedersdorf in which his family was living.

Dr Santaella introduced Ruth to the family and staff as Schwester Ruth and settled her in a room with his three young daughters, Mausi, Vielein and Teti. He and Carmen also had a one-year-old son called Dix.

Several weeks later Carmen asked Ruth if her mother would be willing to work for the family as a cook. When Lina arrived, she was introduced as Frau Lieschen Werner, and she shared a room with Gertrud. Lina ate her meals in the kitchen with the other servants, while Ruth dined with the family.

Ruth and Lina saw each other daily. Sometimes when they passed each other on the stairs or in the hallway they would pull funny faces at one another, but they rarely had a conversation in public. However, being together once more was a great relief, although they worried constantly about the family they had left behind.

During heavy air raids over Berlin they could see clusters of light exploding in the sky, like falling stars. They could not telephone the factory, because it was too dangerous; besides, most telephone lines no longer worked. So they had to send notes through Anni, a process that took several days. They worked hard at their jobs to distract themselves, but Lina betrayed her anxiety about her family in her face. And the lions continued to haunt Ruth's nightmares. She often woke up sweating and frightened.

Every so often one of the children would wake up to see Ruth standing by the window, watching the explosions in the sky. 'What is wrong, Schwester Ruth?' she would say, going over to Ruth and taking her hand. 'You are trembling.'

'Nothing,' said Ruth reassuringly, giving the little girl a hug. 'Go back to bed.'

Ironically, it was in these pleasant surroundings that Ruth became critically ill for the only time during her years underground. It was as though her body had dropped its defences and allowed the enemy to attack. After running a high fever she was barely able to swallow.

The Santaellas insisted on calling a doctor – a Czech who had been forcibly taken by the Nazis to treat Germans. He diagnosed a severe infection in her throat that could be cured only by lancing. He planned to undertake the procedure the next day. Ruth, frightened of having a total stranger treat her, objected so strenuously that Carmen had to call in Lina to persuade her to agree to the operation. At her bedside Lina pretended to be a family friend who knew Ruth's parents in Berlin and who had promised to watch out for their daughter. She managed to persuade Ruth to go through with the operation, which was performed without anaesthesia. Since Ruth was not covered by insurance the Santaellas offered to pay the doctor in cash. But he refused to take their money. He had been conscripted to work as a doctor and possibly realized what was going on at the house. At any rate he offered his services for free.

Ruth recovered slowly, finally able to take the Santaellas' children on walks through the surrounding woods. They always ended up in the kitchen, where 'Frau Werner' would give them treats. Lina also made up stories for them and put on costumes to entertain them, on one occasion dressing up as a witch.

Carmen's mother, Frau Schrader, came to see the family at Diedersdorf, where she was introduced to Ruth and Lina and told their real identity. After she returned to Berlin she started sending ration cards and food packages for the group to Max Köhler via the secretary in the Spanish Embassy.

About six weeks after Ruth left for Diedersdorf Bruno Gumpel, Erich's friend from the Holztmarktstrasse workshop, decided to look Erich up. For the past year Bruno had been living with the Treptow family in Berlin. For reasons he could never explain he decided to find out whether Erich was still alive. Bruno had no idea at all where he might be, but he knew that his friend was resourceful and careful. Hoping for the best, he returned to the Gehres', reasoning that they might be able to tell him what had happened to the family. He remembered only that they lived on the street next to the canal, but he quickly recognized their building and walked boldly up the stairs to their apartment.

As Dr Arndt later told Erich, Anni opened the door a crack to find a gaunt young man standing there with blond hair. She was cautious, since she did not remember meeting him before, and she did not know whether to let him in. So she closed the door and went to consult Dr Arndt who confirmed that Bruno was indeed a friend of Erich's. The doctor was pleased to hear that the young man was all right.

'But how can we be sure he is alone?' asked Anni. 'Maybe the Gestapo is using him to set a trap.'

Dr Arndt assured her that this could not possibly be the case. 'Bruno is a good man,' he said. 'Besides, he has already lost his entire family. There is no way to bribe him. Invite him in. I'd like to see him.'

Anni let Bruno in, who could not believe that he had found Dr Arndt alive and in good spirits – and so quickly.

'And Erich, where is he?' said Bruno, hoping against hope not to hear bad news.

'He is also well. He is with his girlfriend, Ellen.'

Overcome with emotion and relief, tears came to Bruno's eyes and he asked if he could see him.

'I'll see what I can do. Come back next week, and I'll try to arrange something.'

At midnight Dr Arndt went to the factory and told Erich about Bruno's visit. Erich was overjoyed to hear that his friend was still alive. Like his father, he trusted Bruno implicitly. 'Bruno would never give in to the Gestapo,' he told his father. 'He would die first.'

When Bruno returned the following week Dr Arndt gave him directions to Köhler's factory. He told him that Erich would be waiting for him inside the gate at a prearranged time.

When Bruno arrived, Erich let him in and took him upstairs where Ellen was waiting. None of them could believe that they were all still alive. Certainly it was an omen that better times were on the way. They sat down on the benches around the work table, and Bruno told them his story – from early days before the war to what had happened to him since Erich had last seen him..

Bruno and his older brother Günther had grown up on Immanuelkirchstrasse, a lower-middle-class neighbourhood in Prenzlauer Berg, a district in north-eastern Berlin. Their father Gotthold was a textile salesman who often had to travel to East Prussia. Because of the distance involved, he was rarely home. Their mother Ella increased the family income by working as a seamstress. When Bruno was six years old his parents had separated. As Nazism took hold, Ella transferred Bruno to a Jewish middle school in Grosse Hamburger Strasse, the same school where Ruth had been enrolled as a pupil. But since boys and girls attended separate classes Bruno never met her. Even so, he knew about her, since she was a class leader.

As the family's finances spiralled downwards Ella found a job with the Jewish Council of Berlin, mending and sewing for the Jewish Orphanage and the Jewish Old Age Home. She and Bruno also made silk lampshades to earn extra cash. After Kristallnacht Ella paid several hundred marks – a fortune for her – to obtain a visa. The men offering it turned out to be swindlers, and they left Ella and her two boys in more desperate straits than before. Günther, who had finished a course as an electrician's apprentice, decided to apply for a visa to England, hoping to be admitted as he had a valuable work skill. After passing a journeyman's test he received it and left Germany the following April, shortly after his twenty-first birthday. Bruno, then fourteen, cried bitterly when Günther left, fearing that he would never see his brother again. The next year Ella took Bruno out of school and enrolled him in the Holzmarktstrasse locksmith workshop, believing that learning a trade would give Bruno a marketable skill. It was there that he met Erich.

The two apprentices soon became close friends and spent time together every afternoon. During the summer of 1940 the German authorities ordered the shop to send four apprentices to the

Weissensee Cemetery – the large Jewish burial ground – to remove the wrought-iron gates and railings surrounding many of the more elaborate tombs. These the Germans shipped to munitions factories to be melted down and fashioned into weapons. Bruno and Erich were sent, together with two other boys.

The following autumn Bruno's mother gave a party at her home for Jewish teenagers. Bruno invited Erich and told him the gathering would be short of girls. Erich offered to bring Ruth along. Even though she rarely went out with her brother's friends – considering them too young and immature for her – she agreed to attend. Bruno and Ruth barely noticed each other, but Ruth got a chance to talk to Ella. It was the only time they met.

A short time later Bruno's grandmother died. Some months after this Bruno's grandfather, aged eighty-two, was deported to Theresienstadt, the camp where elderly men and women were usually sent before the authorities transported them to Auschwitz. Bruno's grandfather died in Theresienstadt.

In April 1942 Bruno was drafted to work at Siemens in the drill department. Erich was also working at Siemens, but since the boys were in different divisions they rarely saw each other. Blond and good-looking in a typically German way, no one would have guessed that Bruno was Jewish. He was defiant, and he rarely wore his Star of David. When he did, he attached the star to his coat with pins so that he could take it off and walk confidently through the main streets of Berlin.

In October 1942 Ella was notified that she was to be 'resettled'. Her sister Grete volunteered to go with her. Bruno wanted to accompany them. But when he applied for permission his boss, Herr Köhn, an ardent Nazi, refused. 'I do not care what happens to your mother,' he said harshly. 'I need you to work here. Permission denied.'

On 26 October two Gestapo agents arrived to take Ella and Grete to the collection centre. Bruno pleaded with the officers to let him accompany them. As they left the building where Ella had lived for more than twenty years, not one neighbour came out to wish them goodbye. Upon arriving at the Levetzowstrasse Synagogue – the same centre to which Ellen had accompanied her Aunt Johanna – Bruno kissed his mother and aunt goodbye. Then he fled, tears in his eyes, knowing it was unlikely that he would see either of them again.

That night he cried himself to sleep as darkness engulfed him. He was seventeen and totally alone. He had no family and could not see his friends because of his long working hours. At his workplace life grew bleaker as rumours began to circulate about massive numbers of arrests and Jews going underground to avoid deportation. During the last week of December 1942, acting on a premonition, Bruno went to look up his old friend Erich.

'When I saw you moving all those boxes, I had a feeling you were going into hiding,' he told Erich. 'But of course I wouldn't have said anything.'

On 30 January – exactly ten years after Hitler had seized power – a co-worker at Siemens warned Bruno that Gestapo agents were at his home, waiting to pick him up. He knew he could not return there and had to disappear. That evening he walked the streets until dark and then went to the apartment of Günther Plaut, a fellow apprentice and a friend of Bruno's brother. Günther and his wife were Jewish and preparing to go underground the next day. They had secured a hiding place in a small furniture storage loft in west Berlin and invited Bruno to join them. The loft was over a garage, accessible only by a removable ladder. It was fitted out with a bed, a couch and several cartons of tinned food. A pail in a corner served as a toilet. Bruno slept on the couch. Since the entrance to the loft was visible to neighbours through their windows, the trio could enter and leave only at night. Bruno often spent his days in cinemas, hoping to avoid the patrols roaming the streets. As a young man not in uniform he was vulnerable to questioning.

Several days after he went into hiding he returned to his home on Immanuelkirchstrasse late at night and peeled back the paper seal that the Gestapo had used to cover the keyhole. He packed a suitcase with clothing and left, never to return again. He found out later that his home was completely destroyed during an air raid. A week or so later Bruno went to see if another Jewish friend, Joachim

139

Sieburth, was still living in the city. Joachim lived in an affluent section of Berlin. When Bruno showed up, dirty and unkempt,
Joachim's mother immediately offered him a hot bath.

The Sieburths were by then frantically worried that they would
soon be deported. When Bruno offered to take Joachim with him
into hiding, they agreed. The Plauts did not object when Bruno
arrived with his friend; they knew how desperate everyone was.
Bruno and Joachim slept side by side on the couch, gleaning
warmth from each other's bodies.

Within a few weeks, one of the neighbours began noticing
them. It was time to leave. The Plauts went off on their own.
Joachim returned to his parents' home to find out what he had
feared: his parents and his sister had been deported. Joachim, overwhelmed with grief and desperate for options, decided to take a
chance and visit the parents of a non-Jewish friend, Ursula
('Uschi') Treptow. Uschi, he knew, was a passionate anti-Fascist
who had already taken risks by visiting Joachim's sister when it was
dangerous for Christians to be seen socializing with Jews. The Treptows lived in Schöneberg on Kurfürstenstrasse 31 – 1.6 kilometres
(one mile) away from Eichmann's headquarters – in the area where
Charlotte had found temporary refuge with the prostitute. Joachim
had heard through his sister that Uschi's parents were also committed anti-Fascists who might conceivably help them.

When the boys told Uschi about their situation, she asked her
father for permission to hide them. Papa Treptow was somewhat
taciturn, but he had strong opinions and high moral values. He was
not easily persuaded to do things he did not think correct. However, he was extremely fond of his daughter, who could quite often
get what she wanted from him. Mutti Treptow was more lively and
talkative than her husband, compassionate, and fond of jokes. Self-
educated, she was a pragmatic person and a very competent
businesswoman who advised her husband on business matters and
who took charge of all the household expenses.

Papa Treptow ran a scrap-dealing business from the cellar of
their tenement. There he stored pressed bales of wool that he had
bought up before and after the start of the war, planning to sell

them for a profit when the war ended. He agreed to shelter the two young men, directing them to the cellar where they could sleep on the wool bales. The Treptows also volunteered to share their limited food rations. Bruno could not believe his extraordinary good fortune in finding the family.

A few days later Joachim went to see a former neighbour who he knew was opposed to Hitler to enlist his help. The man offered to contact an acquaintance, a wood veneer dealer who required workers. Even though the dealer was a Nazi Party member, he offered to hire the young men on condition that they did not talk in the presence of customers. Instead, they were to conduct their conversations in sign language, thereby giving the impression that they were foreign labourers. They received food for pay.

They worked there for several months and looked for a new sleeping place to take the pressure off the Treptows. Near by they found a veneer storage basement and moved in, sleeping on piles of springy birch veneer. Bruno fixed the padlock so that it could be removed easily. They borrowed blankets and pillows from the Treptows. And they used a tin can for water so that they could shave. This was important, because they had to look well groomed in order not to raise suspicion.

By the end of the summer their employer had been drafted into the army and had to close down his business. Before leaving, he introduced them to the manager of a woodworking factory who was short of labour. They moved back to the Treptows' and went to work in the factory, assembling ammunition cases and caskets for the army, working side by side with forced labourers from occupied countries. One day Bruno noticed a passport loosely stuffed into the pocket of a jacket hanging on a peg in the changing area that belonged to a man from Czechoslovakia. Bruno decided to steal it. He knew that the worker would be upset but that he could easily get a replacement, since he was legally entitled to work in Berlin. Bruno, however, could not get legitimate papers; for him a passport was a matter of life and death. With it, he would have freedom to travel around the city and find other jobs.

After taking the passport, Bruno and Joachim looked up a former classmate, Günther Fleischer, a *Mischling* who had a *Mischling* cousin skilled in drawing. Since both boys were of mixed heritage, they were exempt from deportation. Bruno had a photo taken of himself and took it to Günther. Günther's cousin carefully removed the original photo and replaced it with Bruno's. Since he was roughly the same age and had similar physical characteristics to the original owner, the forgery was extremely successful, and Bruno was transformed into Karel Falta, born in Brüni, Czechoslovakia.

Günther's mother was a Christian, and his father was Jewish. Despite pressures to divorce her Jewish husband, Frau Fleischer – like the majority of German women married to Jewish men – remained faithful to her husband and was sympathetic to Jews who were hiding from the Gestapo. She supplied Bruno with new shirts, socks and underwear from a small shop that she owned and gave him food as well. From now on he would present himself as a Czech worker and speak broken German.

Soon after this he got a part-time job chopping firewood and cleaning up a basement for a friend of his boss. In the basement he found – and stole – tins of liver sausage and asparagus on which he and Joachim feasted. But his employer soon found out, and he was promptly fired from both jobs.

In the meantime, Bruno, Joachim and Uschi went out to the Treptows' cottage in Rangsdorf, a southern suburb with a small military airport. There the three prepared the cottage as a potential refuge in case Berlin was badly bombed. This involved digging an air-raid bunker in the garden and storing tins of food and medical supplies there.

Some time later Frau Fleischer managed to get Bruno a new job with a coal seller, packing pressed briquets into cartons and delivering them to customers. The work was extremely hard and dirty, since Bruno was handling around twenty 45-kilogram (100-pound) cartons a day, often carrying them up several flights of stairs. But at least it was a job.

On the evening of 10 October 1943 Joachim did not return to the Treptows'. Everyone was frantic, fearing that he had been arrested by the Gestapo. They were anxious also that he would be tortured into revealing the names of his protectors. There was no time to grieve for his lost friend; Bruno had to leave immediately.

Again the Fleischers helped out. The Jewish tenants beneath them had recently been deported, and their apartment was vacant. He could stay there. He easily broke the seal on the door, but he had to move around against the walls and always without shoes, for fear of stepping on a loose board that would alert the neighbours. Nor could he flush the toilet: it would make too much noise. Once ensconced in the apartment Bruno decided to eat some of the remaining liver sausage that he had filched. But the food had gone off, and he got violently ill with food poisoning. None the less, he forced himself to go to work, although he spent the day throwing up. He was sure he would not live – or, if he did, he was certain he would be fired.

Several weeks later Uschi persuaded her parents to take Bruno in again, and they agreed since they knew he had no place to live. Uschi went to tell him that the coast was clear. Joachim had never returned: he had undoubtedly been arrested and was probably dead. But at least the Gestapo had not visited their house. What-ever had happened to Joachim, he had not revealed their names or whereabouts. After the war Bruno would learn that Joachim had indeed been arrested that day in a city-wide dragnet and had subse-quently been killed by the Nazis.

So Bruno moved back to the relative safety – and comfort – of the Treptows' cellar. In the evenings, he ate with the family, who shared their food with him. He and Papa Treptow would listen to reports from the BBC with their ears held against the radio, which was set to the lowest volume possible. There was growing antici-pation that the Allies would soon land in France. And that was when Bruno had decided to look up his old friends.

Ellen and Erich sat in the factory, stunned by Bruno's story. They felt that their own experiences paled in comparison; Erich still had both of his parents and his sister. Ellen had her mother – and Erich. Before Bruno left Erich invited him to visit them again.

'When you want to come over, just call up and ask for *Eisen*,'

Erich told him. 'If it's all right to come up, I will answer *"Eisen."* If it's not all right to come up, I will say *"Nein."* '

Bruno appreciated the invitation more than he could say.

After he left Erich and Ellen discussed him for over an hour. 'Have we done the right thing?' said Ellen. 'He won't be caught, will he?'

'No. Don't worry. Bruno is very bright, and he can take care of himself. It'll be all right. Besides, the war is almost over. The Nazis will soon have better things to do than catch Jews.'

Bruno soon looked up Erich and Ellen again and started visiting them at weekends.

In May he asked Erich to ask Max if he could work in the factory, since hauling coal was straining his back. Max promptly employed him and introduced him to the other workers as 'Bruno Gerber'.

As June approached they received a letter via Anni Gehre that the Santaellas had decided to take their family to a resort in the Harz Mountains, a popular holiday resort 210 kilometres (130 miles) west of Berlin. They were closing the house for the month and sending Lina and Gertrud back to Berlin. But they took Ruth along to take care of the children. It was to be a trip that she would never forget.

# 9

# CITY UNDER SIEGE

You are about to embark upon the Great Crusade, toward which we have striven these many months. The eyes of the world are upon you. The hopes and prayers of liberty-loving people everywhere march with you. In company with our brave Allies and brothers-in-arms on other Fronts, you will bring about the destruction of the German war machine, the elimination of Nazi tyranny over the oppressed peoples of Europe, and security for ourselves in a free world. – Order to Allied troops from General Dwight D. Eisenhower, Supreme Allied Commander-in-Chief, 5 June 1944

On the evening of 5 June 1944 several hundred American and British troops parachuted through dense fog and landed inland behind the German lines in Normandy, readying a ground defence so that Allied troops could make it to shore from troop carriers. When Field Marshall Gerd von Rundstedt, commander-in-chief of the German army in Western Europe, heard of men landing in parachutes late at night he dismissed it as another Allied ploy. He considered the weather unsuitable for a mass invasion, and, besides, he believed that such an invasion was going to occur at Calais.

Not until the afternoon of 6 June were Rundstedt and the rest of his staff prepared to admit that they had been hoodwinked. By that time thousands of American, British and Canadian troops had managed to land the largest seaborne force in history on five Normandy beaches – Omaha, Utah, Juno, Gold and Sword. By the end of the day the Allies had cleared the skies of the Luftwaffe, driven back the German navy and overwhelmed the German army, who were caught off guard by the surprise attack. Doing so cost thousands of lives; initial Allied losses at Ohama beach were as high as 90 per cent in

some units, owing to heavy gunfire and land mines, along with usually rough seas that made going ashore even more treacherous. Even
so, the Allies managed to land 130,000 troops. Hitler learned of the
invasion at 10 a.m. but did not believe it to be the main Allied
assault and would not authorize sending his main Panzer divisions
to Normandy. Then he went to bed and refused to be disturbed until
3 p.m., by which time it was too late to retaliate with full force.

On 7 June Ruth was sitting in the back of the Santaellas' car,
playing games with the children and singing to them. It was early
afternoon, and Dr Santaella had stopped to refuel at a petrol
station near the Harz Mountains. The attendant told Dr Santaella
of the Normandy invasion, which he had just heard about on the
radio. When the Spanish attaché gave Ruth and his wife the information they were speechless. They had been waiting for such news
for so long that it seemed like a miracle.

We might be free; we might be free before long, Ruth thought
over and over, hugging and kissing the children, who did not
understand why everyone was so excited. As they travelled on,
Ruth tried to concentrate on the children's games, but all she could
think of was victory.

Ellen, meanwhile, was serving coffee to Colonel Wehlen and a
guest on the afternoon of 7 June. When she heard the report of the
Normandy invasion on the radio her hands began shaking so badly
that she nearly spilled coffee on to the lap of the German officer sitting next to Wehlen. 'That will be all,' said the colonel calmly,
dismissing Ellen quickly for fear that her excitement would endán-
ger both of them. After hurrying to the kitchen she closed the door
and flung her arms into the air. Then she rushed to the landing
overlooking the back courtyard. where she hurled metal dustbin
lids down the concrete stairs so that the noise would cover her
whoops of joy. Barely able to contain herself, she returned to the
kitchen and waited impatiently. An hour later she heard Wehlen
call her into the library. When she arrived he stood up and shook
her hand. 'It won't be long now. You and your family will be free. As
for us' – he paused – 'we will not be. But that is not your concern.'

*

Wehlen was not the only German who knew that the arrival of Allied troops on European soil would make German victory improbable. Many high-level Nazis urged Hitler to give up the fight, hoping to preserve what they could of the German nation. But the Führer, increasingly prone now to frequent fits of rage, would not entertain such a course of action. Nor would he cease his persecution of the Jews. Even while Allied troops were battling their way through the French countryside German officers were gassing some 400,000 Hungarian Jews who had recently been deported to Auschwitz.

There is no evidence to suggest that any high-level German officer ever made an attempt to question Hitler's brutal campaign to exterminate the Jewish nation. But, faced with the prospect of losing the war, some top-ranking Nazis began to develop an ambitious plan to assassinate Hitler and salvage Germany before it was bombed to annihilation. Thus was born the July plot.

On the morning of 20 July 1944 Colonel Klaus Graf Schenk von Stauffenberg – a count and chief of staff who had access to Hitler's headquarters – travelled to Hitler's underground bunker in Wolfsschanze, intending to plant a bomb in the concrete bunker where Hitler used to meet his officers. At the last minute the meeting was changed to a wooden barracks. A co-conspirator, Freyend, helped Stauffenberg plant a briefcase containing the bomb near the table where Hitler would sit. Stauffenberg planned to move it closer to Hitler, but he had to leave the meeting and did not get a chance to move the case to a more strategic position. The bomb went off at 12.42 p.m. Stauffenberg, assuming the mission had been successful, flew to Rangsdorf to initiate a coup d'état. In fact Hitler survived, because the bomb was too far away to prove fatal.

Bruno was queuing at a barbers' that evening to get his hair cut, as he and Erich did once a month. Around 6.30 the radio blared forth: a certain Count von Stauffenberg had attempted to murder the Führer, but Providence had spared the great leader. Hitler was slightly injured, but he would address the nation at midnight.

As the announcement went out Bruno noticed the strange

silence. No one in the shop said a word; no one even looked up. The barber kept trimming his customer's hair as though the radio message had been entirely inconsequential. Bruno calmly stayed in line until his turn in the barber's chair came. After the haircut he walked calmly to the loft, deliberately not running to avert suspicion.

'They've tried to kill Hitler,' he exploded, when he finally reached the loft. 'Turn on the radio. A bomb exploded in the bunker.' He told Ellen and Erich excitedly about the silence in the barbershop after the report came through. 'You know that's the end. I think they all want him dead. That's why no one said a word. It can't last much longer. The Germans might kill him before the Americans get to him.'

'I don't believe it,' Erich responded. 'Hitler still has too much power. I think it's going to get worse before it gets better.'

'How much worse *can* it get?' asked Bruno.

But Erich's instincts were sound. Even though most Germans acknowledged that the war had taken a decisive turn in favour of the Allies, Hitler continued his campaign to rid the world of the Jews before they could be saved. The day after the failed assassination Germans rounded up 2,000 Jews on the island of Rhodes and sent them to Auschwitz; the next week they raided children's homes in France and sent 300 Jewish children to the same concentration camp. And to prevent the Soviets from liberating Jews from the ghettos and concentration camps in the east, SS officers rounded up Jewish inmates and sent them on hazardous death marches to the west, assuming that most of them would die *en route* from exhaustion or starvation. On 28 July the first of these major death marches took place. After evacuating the Gesia Street Ghetto in Warsaw, Nazi officials sent 3,600 underfed and scantily dressed prisoners on an 130-kilometre (80-mile) march to Kutno. A thousand prisoners either died or were killed by German soldiers on the arduous journey.

Hitler, now verging on insanity, also turned his tactics against all those Germans who were directly or indirectly involved in the Stauffenberg fiasco. Gestapo were ordered to scour the city of

Berlin, searching for relatives and friends of the saboteurs. Thousands of innocent Germans were arrested in the process; many were imprisoned and deported to concentration camps. The eight ringleaders of the plot were imprisoned and savagely tortured in Plötzensee prison, as they awaited trial in the People's Court. On the day of reckoning they were stripped to the waist and hung by piano wire that was attached to meathooks on the ceiling. As they slowly dangled, their beltless trousers falling to the floor, a film camera recorded their last moments so that Hitler could watch their deaths..

As the witch hunts for traitors continued, it became even more dangerous for the Köhlers and the Gehres to protect the Arndts. Nevertheless they continued to shelter them. Bruno had been introduced to Max and Hans, and he was now welcome as a regular visitor at the factory. Uschi, who was taking courses at the university to prepare for a career as a bookseller, often accompanied him.

On Saturdays Bruno would often help Erich wring out the wet clothes that Ellen boiled and washed, since they needed to be dry by Sunday evening. Occasionally he brought in ration stamps that he had managed to steal from a shop, since food was becoming more and more difficult to procure. Around this time Bruno and Erich made themselves a chess set, cutting small pieces of metal from a pipe into different sizes to be used as chessmen, and creating a board out of brown packing paper. They would sometimes play the game for hours.

By mid-August the Allies were preparing to liberate Paris. As air strikes on Berlin escalated, it became more and more difficult for the Arndts to find food. Ellen and Bruno, with their blond hair and fair complexions, would sometimes go out and steal ration cards from local grocery stores while the shopkeeper's back was turned. Bruno's speciality was canvassing neighbourhoods where a bombing had occurred and memorizing the address of a demolished house. As soon as field kitchens were set up for bombed-out residents, he would stand in a food queue and give the address to the officer in charge to get a hot meal. Then he would move on to the next queue to get emergency ration stamps.

Charlotte, too, used considerable ingenuity to obtain food, one day remembering an uncle who was married to a non-Jewish woman. Her uncle's wife had two sisters in Berlin, both of whom had been kind to Charlotte. She therefore decided to write to the sisters on the off chance that they might be able to help. Amazingly, the sisters responded. Overjoyed to hear that Charlotte and Ellen were still alive, they informed her that they were working in a large restaurant near the Friedrichstrasse train station. They invited Charlotte to visit and told her that they could give her some food from the kitchen. She gladly accepted the invitation.

Charlotte, wearing her silken dress and elaborately feathered hat, took Ellen with her to see her cousins. As they headed for the kitchen, located in the rear of the dining-room, Ellen spotted a slim, very attractive woman with blonde hair. She was wearing a green felt hat with a green feather and standing near the back wall with a tall, dark man dressed in a suit. Ellen gasped. She recognized the woman at once: it was Stella Goldschlag, her classmate from art school – the feared Jew-catcher – whom Tannenbaum had warned Erich about at the opera the previous autumn.

Stella was now working full-time for the Nazis as a spy, mainly in partnership with her accomplice, Rolf Isaaksohn. Unbeknownst to Ellen, Stella had already managed to discover more than two hundred Jews in hiding – many of them unsuspecting co-workers from Siemens – and lure them to places where the Gestapo was waiting to arrest them. By an awful coincidence Stella and Rolf had decided to visit the restaurant that day.

For a few seconds, Ellen froze. When she recovered, she placed both hands firmly on her mother's shoulders, turned her around and pushed her firmly outside. 'Quick,' Ellen whispered. 'We have to leave.'

'What's wrong?' Charlotte asked, surprised to see her daughter so agitated.

'Come on, we have to get out now!' Ellen hissed. 'I'll explain later.' Grabbing her mother's hand, Ellen ran towards the nearest tram and, pushing her mother ahead of her, they jumped on to it as soon as it stopped. When they were both safely inside, Ellen walked quickly with her mother to the rear of the car and sat down, her face flushed and her voice shaking.

'I saw Stella Goldschlag,' she whispered. 'The blonde traitor from art school. Tannenbaum told us she's been working as a spy for the Nazis. She was there with her partner. I saw her. She could be on our trail. She turns in Jews to the Gestapo.'

'My God,' said Charlotte. 'Are you sure?'

'Yes. I'm positive.'

'Do you think she saw us?'

'I don't know,' said Ellen. 'But we can't take a chance. We have to outwit her.'

They changed from the tram to a bus and then ducked into the subway. There they hoped to lose Stella if she had managed to follow them out of the restaurant. Mingling with a group of pedestrians waiting for the next train, they boarded with them and travelled for a few stations. From there they caught another train; and then another.

They rode trains and trams all afternoon, determined to lose Stella and prevent her from tracing them to the factory. After sunset they returned to Kreuzberg. When they finally arrived at the loft it was late and Bruno was there, waiting anxiously with Erich for Ellen to return. They entered, exhausted and out of breath.

'What on earth happened?' asked Erich.

'We saw Stella Goldschlag,' Ellen gasped, still shaking with fright. 'We were almost spotted.' She took several deep breaths to regain her composure, then told them what had happened at the restaurant. 'Stella is blonde and beautiful,' she told Bruno. 'She wears a green felt hat with a green feather, and sometimes she is accompanied by a tall man with dark hair. If you spot her, do not let her see you. It could be the end of us all.'

On 23 August Paris was liberated. Thousands of French civilians marched triumphantly down the Champs-Elysées, waving flags and sobbing with joy. Meanwhile Allied troops pushed their way through the dense forests of the Ardennes, intent on gaining access to Germany through the west.

As it became more dangerous for representatives of pro-Nazi governments to remain in Germany, the Spanish Embassy in Berlin transferred Dr Santaella and his family to Switzerland. He wanted to take Ruth with him, but it was too complicated to apply for a visa for her, since doing so would have involved obtaining false papers, a dangerous and time-consuming process.

So, reluctantly and with great sadness, Ruth, Lina and Gertrud Neumann returned to Berlin. Gertrud returned to her former protector, while Ruth and Lina once again moved into Tata's apartment in the city. Tata and Gustav were still in the country, but they came to Berlin once a week to bring food to Lina and Ruth. Since the apartment was crowded with all four of them there, Ruth tried to find other places to sleep. Sometimes she travelled around with a change of clothes and a toothbrush in her bag, not knowing until the end of the day where she would sleep that night. Sometimes she slept at the Wehlens'; other times she stayed at the factory, sleeping on the work table; or else she would stay with Charlotte while Frau Meier was out of town visiting her husband. Always on the run, she rarely stayed in the same place more than two nights during that autumn.

Meanwhile Lina was growing nervous about staying at Tata's apartment, since some of the neighbours were becoming nosy – asking questions and even occasionally peering into the windows during the daytime. Why was Lina there again? Always on the look-out for new hiding places, Ellen returned to the madam on Prinzenstrasse. Did she know of anyone who could take in her mother-in-law? The woman referred Ellen to two middle-aged prostitutes who lived in a dingy, cockroach-infested basement apartment near by. They agreed to shelter Lina. At least this place was relatively safe from neighbours and from bombs, thought Ellen.

Through the prostitutes she also heard of another possible hiding place – an empty tower located alongside the elevated train on Prinzenstrasse. If she could find a mattress she and Charlotte could stay there. Ruth and Lina, meanwhile, could move in with Frau Meier. Around this time Ellen ran into Herr Bukin, Aunt Johanna's tenant, in the street. When he asked about her and Charlotte Ellen told them they were still in hiding and planning to move into an empty tower on Prinzenstrasse if they could find a mattress. Herr Bukin offered to send her to a friend in the country who had a spare one.

On Saturday 16 September Ellen and Erich went to fetch the mattress. Herr Bukin's friend insisted that they come in and plied them with homemade wine and biscuits. Ellen and Erich drank the wine – a rare treat – and left with the huge mattress stuffed with horsehair. On the way to the train station Ellen grew dizzy and threw up. She felt she could not go on, but Erich encouraged her.

'We can't waste any time,' he said. 'You can rest when we get home.'

Ellen knew he was right. She forced herself to continue. When they reached the tram they had to plead with the conductor to let them carry the bulky mattress on board.

'We've been bombed out,' said Ellen, now crying – mostly because she still felt so sick. 'Please, we need to take the mattress to a new room to have something to sleep on.'

'Everyone's been bombed,' said the conductor sternly. 'But I'm not allowed to let people bring furniture on. There'll be no room for passengers.'

'*Please*,' begged Ellen, tears running down her face. '*Please*, you must help us.'

Finally the conductor relented, and they managed to lift the huge mattress on to the tram. When they got to the tower they dragged the mattress up the narrow wooden stairs to the room. Ellen, despite still feeling queasy, spent the day getting rid of the dirt and cobwebs. At sunset Erich went back to the factory and Ellen walked to Frau Meier's to spend the night with Charlotte and Ruth, who was also staying there since Frau Meier was visiting her husband.

Shortly after midnight the three women woke up suddenly,

alerted by the loud wailing of an air-raid siren. Overhead they heard the engines of B-17s. Grabbing their suitcases, they rushed to the hallway, stood their suitcases on end and crouched down behind them against the wall. Suddenly there was an ear-splitting crash. The house had taken a direct hit. They could hear flames crackling on the roof as smoke filled the doorway. With their suit-cases they made their way with difficulty to the door on the ground floor, pushing past the other tenants who were gasping for breath and also trying to escape into the fresh air.

Once outside, they ran across the street as fast as possible and threw themselves to the ground, placing their cases over their heads to shield them from the pieces of burning wood and broken glass now flying through the air. As they lay there, listening to the roar of the fire and the cries of people near by, they feared for their lives. They had been living as *U-boote* for eighteen months, yet they felt that this was the closest they had been to death.

The bombs ravaged the entire area; the overground train and the tower with the vacant room that Ellen had cleaned came crash-ing down. Erich heard the explosion from the factory, which, miraculously, was not touched. Fearful that Ellen, Ruth and Char-lotte had been caught in the bombing, he jumped on his bicycle and rode at top speed towards Prinzenstrasse. But as he approached, the streets were covered with so much broken glass that he had to pick up his bike and carry it over his head. Covering his face with a scarf to protect it from the smoke and cinders now thick in the air, he carefully made his way to Frau Meier's, dreading what he was going to find.

As he made his way down Prinzenstrasse he suddenly caught a glimpse of Ellen, Ruth and Charlotte weaving unsteadily on their feet. As he got closer he saw that they were bleeding from cuts and scratches. Their faces were covered with soot, dirt and tears.

'It's a miracle,' said Erich. 'You're alive. Come on. Let's go to the factory.'

He led them back in silence, trying to avoid burning debris and staying as far as possible from collapsing houses. As they continued walking, the sun came up, casting a reddish beam through the thick smoke. When they finally made their way into the courtyard, Frau Jaeger, the building supervisor, was standing there.

'They've been bombed out,' Erich told him. 'I'm going to put them up in the factory. They have no other place to stay.'

'Of course,' said Frau Jaeger. 'I'll make everyone a hot drink.'

After drinking the ersatz coffee the four climbed the stairs to the loft. There Erich fetched blankets and they sat together, still too stunned to say anything or think clearly.

Eventually Erich found some towels and soaked them in water; Ruth then took charge, cleaning the wounds and checking everyone for fractures. Shortly after they found out that the entire area had been badly bombed. When Max and Hans arrived early the next morning Erich told them that Frau Meier's house had been bombed. Max immediately agreed to take in Charlotte. Ellen volunteered to bring over the other cot from Blesen that was still stored at the Gehres'. Charlotte could sleep on it in Max's office, where there was a large stove, and Ruth would sleep on the work table. Ellen and Erich could move to Hans's workroom which had another stove. They would store both cots during the daytime in the cabinets in the hallway. Charlotte and Ruth would have to leave with Ellen early in the morning and stay away until 5 p.m.

After Ruth and Charlotte moved into the loft, 'organizing' ration cards – a euphemism for stealing – became their chief priority. By this time they had all become adept at shoplifting ration cards, but Bruno was particularly good at it. He would go into a shop armed with enough ration cards for a few bread rolls. Then, when the clerk's back was turned to find the rolls, he would quickly reach behind the glass partition on the counter and grab a handful of loose coupons out of the box where they were stored and stuff them into his pocket. When the clerk turned around Bruno paid for the rolls, raised his hand, saluted 'Heil Hitler' and calmly left the store.

Once he was able to filch a chunk of salami from the counter of a butcher's shop at the same time. Salami was a rare treat. When he brought it back to the factory everyone celebrated. Ellen used the sausage to flavour their meals for days, then she finally threw it into a pile with vegetable peel and other discarded food and left the room. Ruth walked in soon after and spotted the dried-out piece of salami lying on the table. She put it into her mouth thinking it was too good to throw out. After chewing it for a while until it had lost its flavour, she spat it out and put it back in the pile of garbage. After that she left.

Some time later she walked back into the dining area and could not believe her eyes: the pile was still on the table, but the chewed-up piece of salami was nowhere to be seen. 'Where's that salami? she asked Ellen.

'I ate it,' she replied, with a sheepish smile.

'But I ate it already!' exclaimed Ruth. 'What could you possibly have found left?'

Not knowing whether to laugh or cry at the ludicrousness of their behaviour they laughed. They still laugh when they retell the incident.

Most of their meals, however, were no fun. The group usually dined on watery, flavourless soup, sometimes accompanied by a morsel of turnip and, on even rarer occasions, a small piece of cauliflower. Even so, Ellen would formally set the work table for dinner, laying down brown packing paper as a tablecloth and setting each place with plates and cutlery lent to them by Max. It was more important than ever to maintain their routine; it was the only way they could transcend the daily grind and hang on to their dignity.

Afterwards Bruno and Erich would sometimes enjoy a cigarette, also a rare treat, since these were available only with ration cards. They would collect cigarette ends that they found on the streets and in ashtrays in public places. Then Erich rerolled them in a small, flat metal cigarette-rolling box, a prized possession that he had managed to take with him into hiding. (To this day, he still keeps the box as a souvenir.)

Dr Arndt continued to visit the group about once every ten days – always formally dressed in a jacket and a tie – to check on their health, to bring them bits of soap and any food that Anni could spare. When he asked how they were managing to get enough food to eat, they explained that they had 'organized' ration cards. It did not take long for Dr Arndt to understand what the euphemism meant. True to form, he lectured them about this. '*Kinder, kinder,*' he would say, 'I hope that after this war is over you will not continue stealing. I know it's necessary now, but you must promise me it will not continue. I did not raise you to be thieves.'

# 10
# IN THE INFERNO

Fellow students, the day of reckoning has come, the day when German youth will settle accounts with the vilest tyranny ever endured by our nation. In the name of German youth, we demand from Adolf Hitler's state the restoration of personal freedom, a German's most precious possession, which it took from us by base deceit . . . Each of us must join in the fight for our future, for a life in freedom and in honour in a state that is aware of its moral obligations. – From a pamphlet dated 18 February 1943, distributed by Hans Scholl, leader of the White Rose, a student resistance group based in Munich; all members of the group were arrested, tried for treason and executed by the Gestapo

One evening, soon after Charlotte and Ruth had moved into the factory, Max Gehre rode on his bicycle to a farm outside Berlin and rustled a very small calf. He killed it by hitting it over the head and stuffed it into a large leather bag that he used for newspapers and deliveries. When he arrived home, the large sack slung over his shoulder, Max asked Anni and Dr Arndt to join him in the bathroom. 'Arthur, bring your medical tools,' he added slyly. Once they were assembled he opened the bag over the large tub. Out tumbled the dead calf.

'Excellent!' said Anni. 'Enough meat for several meals.'

Dr Arndt stood there dumbfounded for several minutes. 'Well, Max, is this a legal calf?' he asked finally.

'It's legal for hungry people to eat,' said Max. 'Do your job!'

Dr Arndt went to work, skinning the calf and quartering it, using his medical instruments for the task. Anni immediately roasted the meat in the oven. When it was cooked, she cut it into even smaller portions and wrapped each one in wax paper. She put some aside for her family. Later that evening Dr Arndt took the remaining portions to the factory where Ellen placed them in the large bag she used to store the group's food. The next evening she heated up some of the meat and served it with porridge. They all ate with relish. It was the first hearty meal they had enjoyed in months, and they badly needed the protein.

Weekdays were now more and more of a scramble, particularly for Charlotte, who had to leave the loft before 7 a.m. with Ellen and Ruth, both of whom were still working for the Wehlens several days a week. Ellen also continued working for the Mattuls and the Bachmanns. When Ruth did not have work she spent the day with her mother. But Charlotte could not get a job, so she had to occupy herself during the day. When the weather was mild she would walk for hours and hours, stopping sometimes in a restaurant and ordering whatever 'free' food was being served – usually thin, tasteless bouillon. There she would read a newspaper over and over. Sometimes she spent the day going from one cinema to another. Or she would ride the trains from one end of the line to the other. Occasionally she would visit some trusted people for a couple of hours, such as Anni Harm's sister Martha, whom she had befriended while staying at Anni's, or Martha Maske. During air raids she would go to the nearest shelter.

The frequent bombings, combined with the stresses of not having enough to eat and always being on guard, made everyone tense and anxious. But they managed to hang on, sure that victory would come soon, and living for the weekends, when they could move around freely and say what they wanted without the fear of being overheard. On Saturdays Ruth helped Ellen do the washing. Their clothes, worn and threadbare, needed constant attention, and with the addition of Charlotte and Ruth there were now four sets of underwear and a mounting pile of socks, shirts, skirts, trousers and dresses to mend and patch. Sometimes in the afternoons Erich would find time for a game of chess with Bruno when he stopped by. Or everyone would sit around the work table and play gin rummy, Charlotte's favourite card game, while they listened intently to war reports on Hans's radio.

Sundays were devoted to bathing. Eveyone got two basins of warm water that had been heated in the large oil drum used for washing clothes. A blanket was hung over the beam by the sink to provide privacy. While people took turns bathing, Ellen cut new tablecloths and floor mats from brown packing paper to lay under the mattresses. Ruth ironed clothes, gave manicures and groomed people's hair. It was critical for their protection – and their self-esteem – to look neat and well groomed and to do whatever housekeeping they could.

By November everyone had adjusted to their new quarters. Then a phosphorous bomb landed on the Treptows' roof. Bruno and the Treptows were safely in the train station when the bomb landed, but when they emerged they knew that the house was doomed. Phosphorous bombs – neither as heavy nor as large as regular bombs – could start fires that were impossible to extinguish.

When the all-clear siren sounded, Bruno, Uschi and Papa Treptow went cautiously into the house, the top of which was alight, and salvaged whatever food, clothing and valuables they could carry out. Then they spent the night in the station, which was crammed with people carrying whatever valuables they had been able to rescue from their homes. At the first signs of smoke-filled dawn Bruno and the Treptows found a train and travelled to their small cottage in Rangsdorf with their possessions.

Once they were settled in, the stress of being bombed out made itself felt. Papa Treptow, traumatized by the simultaneous loss of his house and his business, began taking things out on Bruno, who, for the first time, felt unwelcome. Uschi did her best to defuse the tension, but Bruno knew he could not stay. To add to the strains inside the cottage, Mutti Treptow had to field questions from curious neighbours. Bruno was young and strong: why was he not in the army?

Around ten days later Mutti Treptow told Bruno he had to move. She felt that his presence was endangering them all. He did not think of challenging her. The Treptows had been exceedingly good to him for almost a year, and he did not want to put them in jeopardy. That night he packed his small suitcase and set off for

Köhler's factory. He stayed there overnight, sleeping on the work table. In the morning he told Max that he had lost his hiding place.

'I suppose you want to move in here with the others,' said Max nonchalantly.

Bruno nodded.

'All right,' said Max, and waved Bruno away before he had a chance to thank him. 'Now get to work. There is nothing more to say and a lot to do.'

Bruno had barely settled in when Uschi stopped by one evening to tell him that she had seen an advertisement for an air-raid warden to work at a nearby factory on Ritter Strasse. The street, which ran parallel to Oranienstrasse, was less than fifteen minutes' walk from the factory. Bruno applied immediately for the position, showing his Czech passport, and he was hired on the spot. He was given a small room with a bed and a sink, so he could stay there overnight, examining the building after air raids and making sure there were no fires. During the day he continued working at Max's factory.

A few weeks later Uschi stopped by again. She had been drafted into the German army, and she was leaving in a few days for Bavaria.

It was during the next few months that Ruth and Bruno got to know one other. After dinner – or what passed as dinner – they would sit together in a corner of the loft, talking quietly and laughing. Ruth had barely spoken to him before, although she did remember his mother, Ella. Bruno still carried a small photo of her in his pocket. When he showed the worn and cherished memento to Ruth, his eyes filled with sadness. Since the deportation of his aunt and mother he had not heard from them and doubted that he would ever see them again. Nor did he have any idea whether his brother was safe in England.

Ruth was deeply moved when Bruno opened up to her; in listening to him her own troubles seemed to dissipate as she realized how lucky she was to have Erich and her parents. She did not think she could bear it if she lost any of them, yet she knew that the prospect of their all surviving was exceedingly slim. Ruth tried to comfort Bruno, but there was little she could do or say. Sometimes she just let him talk; sometimes she tried to steer the conversation to a lighter topic, discovering as she did so that Bruno had a sharp wit and sarcastic sense of humour that he often used to mask his true feelings. When Ruth recited poems that she had memorized in school, Bruno gently poked fun at her erudition. But then he admitted his great love of opera and would impersonate some of the great tenors for her benefit.

Ruth began looking forward to the evenings when they could spend time together. On Saturdays, when she was helping with the weekly washing, she found herself taking particular care to ensure that Bruno's shirts were clean. Then on Sundays, when Ellen repaired Erich's socks, Ruth – who was abysmal at sewing – started darning Bruno's socks and cutting frayed threads from his shirts and trousers. Bruno, who had been attracted to Ruth almost immediately, spent as much time as possible with the group at weekends. As Ritter Strasse was just a short walk away he could always get there after an air raid to inspect the factory for damage.

As December approached and the freezing winter set in, Charlotte could no longer spend hours walking aimlessly on city streets. Instead, she spent more and more time riding the underground trains from one end of the line to the other just to keep warm. Occasionally Ellen joined Charlotte to keep her company. She did so on one memorable day around Christmas. After riding the same train from one end to the other, they decided to walk outside. When the train arrived at the Potsdamer Platz station, they trudged upstairs. The air was crisp and chilly, and the sky was blue and sunny with few clouds. Ellen thought to herself how beautiful Berlin looked. Even ravaged by bombs, the city still retained a certain splendour in the sunshine.

Around her hair Ellen had wrapped a green and pink paisley scarf, on top of which she wore her favourite fur hat, attached to the scarf with a hatpin; she was wearing her dark maroon coat with fur-trimmed pockets and high boots. Charlotte, meanwhile, was dressed in her black winter coat; over her shoulders she had draped her favourite silver foxes. They looked well groomed and happy.

The only glances they got were ones of admiration.

As they walked across Potsdamer Platz Ellen saw a large poster on a building: SS *Weihnachtsfeier* (SS Christmas Party). 'Let's go,' she said, jabbing her mother gently with her elbow and pointing to the poster.

'Are you crazy?' retorted Charlotte. 'We can't go to a party with Nazis. I refuse!'

'But we'll be safe there and warm. No one will suspect we are Jews in hiding. Not there.'

'No!' repeated Charlotte firmly.

Finally Ellen prevailed. Together they entered the building in which the party was taking place and asked the guard at the door if it was open to everyone.

'Of course,' he replied. 'Please, come in.'

Inside, the large room was filled with German officers and civilians. On the stage were performers, singing and dancing to the music of a small band, trying hard to maintain a spirit of revelry. As Ellen and Charlotte sat on their chairs, a waiter came by offering them brandy and biscuits. They thanked him and helped themselves to a handful of biscuits and a glass each of the amber liquor, which quickly warmed their insides. They were both too cold and hungry to be frightened.

After several hours the party wound down and the crowd began to walk outside. As they tried to wander casually out, an officer came up and tapped Ellen on the shoulder. She tensed up but tried to stay calm.

'Excuse me,' he said politely, "I would very much like to see you home.'

Ellen looked at his face. He was clean-shaven and young.

'That is not possible,' said Charlotte quickly. 'Ellen's husband has just returned from the Eastern Front. He is on leave and sleeping. He would be very upset if my daughter returned with another man, even if he was an officer.'

'Of course,' said the officer. 'I understand. Lucky man to have such a beautiful wife!'

'Thank you,' said Ellen pleasantly. 'Goodbye.'

'Yes, goodbye,' he replied, and then, snapping his heels together, as if he had suddenly remembered that he might be reported for forgetting his duty, he saluted them. 'Heil Hitler.'

By mid-January life in Berlin was turning into a nightmare dominated by round-the-clock air raids and fires in the streets. People fled the city for any refuge in the country they could find. Food was now harder and harder to come by as many groceries, bakeries and butchers' shops had been hit by bombs. Those still functioning ran out of food supplies before they could serve the long queues of tired, hungry people waiting outside. Refugees from eastern Germany also began pouring into Berlin, hoping to avoid the approaching Soviet army.

On 16 January Hitler moved his headquarters into the so-called *Führerbunker* – an underground bunker situated next to the Chancellery that was safe from bombs. There he continued to insist to his chief officers that the Eastern Front was secure, even though 180 Soviet divisions had just rammed through Poland and East Prussia. When anyone tried to challenge him, he lost his temper and flew into blind and uncontrollable fits of rage. Meanwhile, he ordered the SS to recruit teenage boys and elderly men for the Volkssturm, a makeshift last-ditch army intended to defend Berlin from the approaching Soviet troops.

Everyone was now frightened of being trapped in a shelter. Erich and Bruno volunteered to dig a passage through the back wall of the shelter used by the tenants in the building so that people could escape through another exit in case the front entrance was sealed off by falling debris. In the course of digging the passage, two women who ran a small grocery shop in front of the building, repaid the two boys by giving them a plate filled with open-topped sandwiches. When Bruno and Erich brought the platter back to the factory everyone rejoiced at the sight of the food.

'But there are only three and a half sandwiches,' pointed out Ellen. 'Where is the other half? Who ate it?'

'No one,' said Bruno. 'It must have fallen on the ground.'

'We can't waste half a sandwich!' exclaimed Ellen, racing down the stairs to the yard to find the missing half, ravenous with hunger. It was there, in plain view. She grabbed it off the ground, raced back upstairs, rinsed it off with clean water and slowly consumed it there and then, savouring every soggy crumb and morsel.

On 1 February Goebbels declared Berlin *Verteidigungsbereich* (a Zone of Defence); every male – young and old – was required to defend the city with his life. Policemen were ordered to wear steel helmets and carry carbines. Much to everyone's relief, Helmut, the Nazi apprentice, went off to join the German navy. Most other German males who had so far managed to avoid military duty were not so inclined: many hid in cellars or with friends, often feigning illness or handicaps to avoid being drafted. Others desperately sought ways out of the city. Since money was now useless, they bartered whatever valuables they had – jewellery, furs, coffee, whisky and cigarettes – for a private car and fuel.

Two days later, on the morning of Saturday 3 February, Erich heard sirens. Erich and Bruno went to the window to see if they could spot any planes. As the sirens wailed louder and louder, they ran down to the factory shelter. Meanwhile Charlotte and Ellen walked briskly to the large shelter on Oranienstrasse. Everyone made it just in time: hundreds of planes flew over the area. A hit in the neighbourhood seemed imminent; people clasped hands in the shelter and took in gulps of air, so as to be able to exhale when the bombs fell, a precautionary measure needed to equalize the air pressure and protect their lungs. Seconds later the sky seemed to explode with a series of deafening noises, like claps of thunder, one after the other. The shelter shook from the vibrations. Smoke wafted into the shelter through crevices around the door. When the all-clear siren finally rang two hours later Erich and Bruno took the lead in cautiously venturing outside. 'Thank God,' said Erich. 'The factory is still standing.'

He relayed the information to the others in the shelter. As relief flooded through them, some of the women cried. When they walked outside their mood changed. A huge black cloud hung over the area; heavy smoke was everywhere, stinging their eyes. Wrapping their faces in the scarves and towels they had brought with them to protect them from inhaling noxious fumes, the tenants walked solemnly back to their apartments and lofts.

Bruno and Erich decided to inspect the area and see whether the factory where Bruno had been staying on Ritter Strasse was still intact. Wearing their warm winter coats, helmets and high boots, they walked slowly up Oranienstrasse, turned down Prinzenstrasse and then prepared to turn into Ritter Strasse. The air became increasingly warm, and they saw that the houses on both sides of the street were burning. Eventually they stopped, unable to go further because of the intense heat and huge flames. They turned back to Köhler's factory.

As they walked past the burning buildings, many still collapsing as fires burned through their floors, a man ran up to them and grabbed them by their sleeves. Erich and Bruno pretended not to speak German, but the man refused to let them go. Using sign language, he insisted that they go into a house with him to help carry out the injured and the dead. In front of the door was one stretcher, with a badly burned corpse on it. Erich and Bruno dumped the body unceremoniously on the ground and took the stretcher into the house to rescue someone else.

After managing to recover a wounded man, they laid the stretcher on the ground and briskly walked on, fearing that they would be enlisted as rescuers by the police who were beginning to fill the area. Keeping their heads bowed slightly toward the ground and covering their mouths with cloth to keep from inhaling fumes and acrid smoke, they passed charred bodies with their clothing burned off; in many cases the corpses' arms were stretched out imploringly and their eyes were wide open. The raging fire was so strong that it seemed to have changed the weather, causing a thick pall of cloud to appear on a sunny day.

Ruth was working at Colonel Wehlen's that day, scrubbing floors. As soon as the air-raid alarm went off, she ran into a nearby shelter. Once inside, she could hear the fierce explosion, but she could tell from the noise that the bombs were dropping far away. Even so, the walls of the shelter shook. When the all-clear siren sounded, she set out to return to Köhler's factory, intending to use the underground train – normally a twenty-minute ride.

When she reached the entrance to the subway she found it was closed. She decided to walk, even though she knew it would take several hours. At first, walking was not difficult, since the temperature was above freezing and there was no rain. But as she approached Kreuzberg she began to see houses burning. Others had been completely levelled. She stepped carefully through mounds of debris and around dead horses that were lying in the street, their legs twisted and their eyes still open. Streams of filthy water from melting snow mixed with dirt and mud flowed through the streets. The smoke and the stench from burned bodies were nauseating. Above, iron girders that had supported the elevated train hung twisted in the air like giant sculptured spiders. The devastation was the worst she had witnessed. But more upsetting than this was the fear that she would find the factory destroyed and her family injured – or dead.

As she approached Oranienstrasse and saw that the building was intact, relief flooded her. Smeared with ashes and dirt, she raced through the courtyard and ran upstairs into the loft. 'Thank God you're all right!' she exclaimed. 'I can't believe it!' They were just as overwhelmed with relief to see Ruth standing in front of them, unharmed

That evening they had a meagre dinner of soup. Bruno had managed to steal several sheets of grain coupons that previously could have purchased a more than 45 kilograms (100 pounds) of rice, flour and noodles and other grains. But these were no longer available in the shops. Therefore Ellen and Bruno used the coupons to purchase the only available grain they could find – an inferior form of broken grain used mainly to feed chickens. They purchased just a kilogram or so a day – fearful that buying large quantities at one time would make shopkeepers suspicious. Despite its awful consistency and lack of taste, Ellen did what she could with it, making it into thick gruel and seasoning it with salt. It was horrible, but it was their only reliable source of food and remained so until the end of the war.

Bruno slept in the factory that night, since the streets were totally unnavigable. The following morning he and Erich dressed warmly in their winter jackets and, with scarves over their noses to keep out the smoke, they once again set out to find out whether the factory on Ritter Strasse was still standing. When they arrived at the site they found the building completely gone; Bruno's small suitcase – containing all his possessions – had vanished. They shivered with apprehension as they stood there contemplating the wreckage. The bombing had come perilously close this time.

On the way back they passed a bombed-out bakery. 'Food!' yelled Bruno. 'Let's go!' Without hesitating, he climbed into the charred remains of the building and dragged out a heavy sack weighing at least nine kilograms (twenty pounds). Erich took one end and, carrying the sack between them, they negotiated their way back to the factory through the debris and rubble. They also found two jars filled with what appeared to be honey; these they took as well.

When they arrived at the loft they opened the sack to find dozens of burned *Salzbrötchen* – small salted rolls covered with flour. When they opened the jars to put honey on the rolls they had another shock: the jars were filled with floor wax. They tried to chew the badly burned rolls, but they were so hard that they could not break them open with their teeth. The boys, desperate to consume them, took a sledgehammer and pounded the rolls into the tiniest pieces possible. Eating the hard crumbs made their gums bleed, but they eventually managed to swallow them.

That night Ellen tried to make bread soup from the crumbs. But the concoction tasted so strongly of charred ash and smoke that, despite their desperate hunger, everyone spat it out. Then they listened to the German newscast: more than a thousand Allied bombers had flown over Berlin the previous day, destroying major sections of the central area as well as the south-east districts. The Adlon shelter, located across from the Brandenburg Gate, was a foot deep in water that had leaked through from melting snow above it. The streets were impassable owing to huge puddles or floods caused by burst water mains and the danger that an unexploded bomb lying in the street would go off.

Deadly firestorms were now raging through the city streets, set off by phosphorous bombs. Hundreds of civilians were trapped inside shelters and cellars, unable to dig their way out of the piles of debris that blocked the exits. Many suffocated from heat and deadly gases. Others died when the tops of shelters collapsed on top of them. It was the most deadly air attack that Berlin had suffered – a portentous warning of the fires that would soon consume Dresden. The official German data collected after the raid reported that 2,541 people died in the blast, including Roland Freisler, the notorious chief of the People's Court; 1,688 had been injured; 714 were missing; and 119,057 lost their homes.

When Max managed to get through the rubble to the factory, he told the group that his home on Reichenberger Strasse had been destroyed in the raid and the violin he had been guarding for Lina was gone. Luckily he and his wife and Hans had been in their country cottages when the raid had occurred. They would be able to remain there through the coming months, since their city apartments were no longer habitable. Then Erich told Max that Bruno had been bombed out of Ritter Strasse and would be moving back to the factor to sleep. 'Fine,' said Max without hesitation. 'Where else would he go?'

Soon after the raid Hans brought in a large Swiss cowbell and gave it to Erich so that he could ring it outside the window when he heard on his wireless that bombers were headed towards Berlin. Having advance notice would give the building's tenants time to prepare for the oncoming raid. The strategy made Erich so popular with residents that they wanted to elect him to the position of official air-raid warden. Erich declined, fearing that the job would focus too much attention on him. Max meanwhile informed the tenants that Bruno was joining 'Walter' as a guard and that he would be staying in the factory in the evenings and at weekends.

Shortly after Bruno moved in, he and Ruth went for a ride on the S-Bahn. They sat across from one another so that if one were detained by the police the other could escape without detection. Of course neither thought this was likely – they had lived with danger for so long that they felt immune from it. But their confidence was to be tested. At the first stop two military police entered the train and headed straight for Bruno who, not being in uniform, looked suspicious. They immediately asked to see his identity papers.

As Ruth watched she began trembling with fear. She knew nothing of Bruno's forged Czech passport and was sure that this signalled the end of their freedom. But he confidently brought out his papers and, speaking in the broken German he had cultivated to hide his true identity, he showed the passport to the officers who scrutinized it and held the photograph up to his face. Finally, after what seemed like an eternity, they said brusquely, 'It's expired. Get a new one quick or you'll be arrested.'

As soon as they left the carriage relief flooded through Ruth. She resisted the temptation to embrace Bruno, instead sat still and maintained her composure. When the trained pulled into the next station they got out. Once outside, they turned round and, not speaking, began walking together back to the factory. Only when they reached the safety of the loft did she allow herself to break down in tears: the prospect of losing Bruno had made her realize how vulnerable they all were as well as how much she cared about him.

However, the incident soon faded from her mind as she and Erich began worrying about Lina's safety in Burig. After the Prinzenstrasse bombing she had moved there to stay with Tata and Gustav, thinking the countryside would be safer from bombs than the city. But now, as the Soviet army approached, Germans were fleeing from eastern Germany. In Berlin you could die from the bombs; in the east you could be killed by Russians. After discussing where Lina would be safest, Erich and Ruth decided that Lina would be better off staying with them in the factory, where they at least could watch out for her. Erich asked Max if it was all right if Lina moved in with them.

Max immediately consented. 'Where else would she go?' he asked with a shake of his head.

It was decided that Ruth would go to Burig to fetch her on a Friday, so that when she returned there would be no workers around. Meanwhile Hans, Erich and Bruno decided to put bunk beds in the rear storage room. Hans found some long slats of wood and brought them upstairs into the loft. Then the three men nailed the slats to a wall of the room. On top of the slats they put straw and feather beds. Then they lined the walls of the storage room with black-out paper to prevent light from escaping through cracks in the walls. Lina, Ruth and Charlotte would have to hide in the tiny room during factory hours without detection by the other workers. In the corner they placed a large pail that would serve as a toilet during the day. Hans, meanwhile, would tell the workers that they could no longer enter the storage room, as Bruno and Walter had been exempted from military service to work on a special project and would need access to the room where they were keeping secret documents and weapons.

Once the storage room was set up, Ruth travelled to Erkner on one of the few trains still operating. From there it was a two-hour walk to Burig along snow-covered lanes. She arrived exhausted and freezing. Tata and Gustav were still there, but they were were preparing to leave for the city to stay with friends. After drinking some hot broth and resting, Ruth set off with Lina for Berlin.

When they arrived at the factory Erich and Ellen had already moved their cot into Max's office, so that Lina could share the room with Charlotte. Each mother would have her own bed. Ellen and Erich would sleep on the floor in Hans's workroom on the thin blue mattresses that Bruno and Ruth had been sleeping on, while Ruth and Bruno would sleep on the bunk beds in the rear storage room. Lina was not exactly thrilled about this aspect of the new arrangement, but in the circumstances there was little that she could do.

Food was now very scarce, and starvation was a real threat. To make their limited provisions last as long as possible and to prevent anyone consumed with hunger from raiding the food supply, Ellen was made responsible for locking up their rations in a safe place and doling them out in daily portions. Erich and Bruno would each have two slices of bread a day, since they needed more calories to survive than the women. The women would each have one slice.

Everyone was supposed to eat the bread during the daytime, but since there were constant air raids – sometimes two or three a night – sleeping more than three or four hours at a stretch was usually impossible. Hunger gnawed at them all, causing some of them to break out in hives from malnutrition.

Starving and tired, Erich and Bruno would sometimes eat their bread rations during the night. Then they would be ravenous during the day. As tensions mounted, Bruno and Erich would argue about petty issues and at one point got into a serious fight. Even Lina, typically good-humoured and practical, began to be affected by the stress. Soon after she moved into the loft she woke up one Saturday morning and walked into the main room. There, she saw Ellen preparing to do the weekly washing. After collecting everyone's dirty underwear, shirts and socks, Ellen dumped them as usual into the oil drum filled with water.

Lina immediately ran over and scolded her. 'Ellen, you can't wash clothes that way! They have not been properly soaked!'

'What do you mean?' asked Ellen, not understanding why Lina was objecting.

'The clothes, they have not been soaked with washing soda!'

'But we do not have any soda or time to soak the clothes,' replied Ellen. 'They must be washed today so they can dry by Sunday night.'

'This is not the proper way,' insisted Lina. 'We cannot wear dirty clothes, particularly in these surroundings.'

'Mutti Arndt,' said Ellen, 'we are being bombed every day. We are lucky to have any clothes at all, clean or dirty. I am washing them this way, and that's that.'

Lina was not the only one who found mental refuge by fixating on mundane daily chores. Dr Arndt shared his wife's passion for decorum, and he hung on to these values throughout the war, refusing to surrender the customs that gave him comfort and moral strength.

One evening Ellen decided to make noodles with an egg she had managed to 'organize' from a neighbourhood store. An egg was a rarity; she would use it to make noodles with some rye flour she still had. The evening she set aside for making noodles Dr Arndt visited the loft. When he arrived Ellen was mixing dough with her hands, scraping every crumb off her fingers and putting it back into the bowl so as not to waste a scrap.

'Ellen,' said Dr Arndt sternly, when he saw her doing this. 'Cooking with your fingers is not right! It is unhygienic.'

'But, Vati Arndt, we need every morsel of dough. We will boil the noodles and they will be fine.'

'It's not right,' repeated the doctor. 'We cannot risk swallowing germs and dirt. We have to stay healthy.'

'We need whatever food we can get,' said Ellen boldly, knowing that she was right and that she had to stand her ground. 'I will boil any germs and dirt out of the noodles. And that's that!'

Ellen proceeded to roll the dough and cut it into small vertical strips. Then she laid the strips on brown packing paper near one of the front windows, intending to dry the dough overnight.

That midnight the shrill air-raid sirens went off, and they all ran downstairs to their shelters. An hour or so passed, and the all-clear siren wailed. They returned to bed and fell into a restless sleep. Several hours later a huge explosion shook the factory, breaking the front windows and causing glass to shatter. Black-out paper hung in shreds as the moon threw a white sliver of light on the floor.

'What on earth was that?' shouted Bruno, who had fallen out of bed from the vibration.

'Quiet!' said Erich. 'Stay put. There might be another explosion.'

'What about the shelter?' asked Ellen. 'Should we go down?'

'No time,' replied Erich. 'We will be in more danger on the stairs.'

After waiting several minutes Erich and Bruno got up to repair the damage. With the help of a hoist they lifted the window frames back into place, then they glued and patched black-out paper over the windows. When the black-out paper was back in place they turned on the lights and Ellen ran over to inspect the noodles she had left to dry.

'The noodles!' she screamed. 'They are full of glass.'

'Never mind,' said Erich. 'At least we're alive.'

As Ellen scooped up the noodles to carry them to the sink, Ruth exclaimed, 'We can't throw them out!'

'No,' agreed Ellen. 'We must wash them.'

Ruth went over to the precious noodles and starting picking the glass out of them.

The next morning Erich and Bruno went downstairs to see what had caused the explosion. They found out it was a bomb that had gone off belatedly. Early that evening Dr Arndt arrived to check on everyone's safety, having heard the nearby explosion the previous night. Ellen and Ruth were once more washing the noodles to make sure they had removed all the glass splinters.

'What on earth are you doing?' he asked, alarmed by the sight of Ellen and Ruth picking tiny splinters of glass out of the strips before dropping them in a pot of boiling water. 'You cannot eat noodles full of glass!'

'No, of course,' said Ellen unperturbed. 'We have picked out all the glass, and we are washing them again to make sure. We *have* to eat them.'

'But you'll hurt yourselves!'

'We don't have any other food. Don't worry. The noodles will be fine. We need them.'

Dr Arndt knew that he was not going to win this argument, so he left after checking to see that the other members of the group were all right.

Afterwards everyone devoured the noodles ravenously. Not even the prospect of eating glass could restrain them. As for the explosion, they agreed that it had been a close call. But worse was still to come. The grain on which they had been depending for many more meals began to move. Ellen saw at once that it had become infested with meal worms. They could not get by without it, so she did not tell anyone and boiled the grain thoroughly. Then she served it up in the dark so that they could not what they were eating. She knew that they would starve to death without it.

# 11
# ICH BIN JUDE!

If the war is lost, the nation [Germany] will also perish. This fate is inevitable. It will be better to destroy those things ourselves because this nation will have proved to be the weaker one and the future will belong solely to the stronger eastern nation [Soviet Union]. Besides, those who will remain after the battle are only the inferior ones, for the good ones have been killed. – Adolf Hitler's remarks to Albert Speer, 18 March 1945, before the Führer ordered that Germany be destroyed by its own army

By late February the Russian offensive was stalling, as ice floes on the River Oder made it impassable. Factories, hospitals and bakeries in Berlin resumed whatever activities they were capable of performing. Köhler's factory started up again, and workers came in when they could. But now Lina, Charlotte and Ruth were forced to spend their days confined to the airless storage room in the rear of the factory, a situation that all three would for ever remember as unbearable. The space was tiny and stuffy, it was dangerous to cough or even to whisper, and they had to urinate in a bucket in the corner. They were so weak and hungry that they spent the day either sleeping on their bunks or lying there listlessly.

Within a short time illness attacked their systems. Charlotte developed a hacking cough, and Ruth came down with cystitis. When Anni Gehre came by early one evening to check on them, she was alarmed by the state of their health. She said she would send Dr Arndt over immediately.

The doctor rarely went out now, fearing that he might be seen on the streets by German officers and recruited immediately for duty in the Volkssturm. None the less, he came to the loft with his medical kit as soon as Anni relayed her message. Charlotte, he diagnosed, was in danger of coming down with pneumonia. He gave her cough syrup with codeine to ease her condition, while he gave Ruth sulpha tablets for hers. Even after taking the medicine Charlotte continued to cough constantly and had to cover her mouth with a pillow to muffle the sound. Ruth also continued to experience great discomfort; she had to control her urge to relieve herself, since she knew the sound of urinating in the metal bucket could arouse suspicion.

Power cuts were now frequent, and during these the machines on the factory floor came to a halt. In the silence that enveloped the loft, any noise was a potential death sentence. To provide some relief, Erich would enter the room at regular intervals and clatter his tools loudly, giving Charlotte an opportunity to cough without inhibition and Ruth a chance to use the bucket.

Day air raids were a scramble for everyone, since the women could not use the building's official shelter. To solve the problem, Bruno would hustle the remaining workers – Uncle Willy, Horst and Manfred – down the front stairs to the shelter in the courtyard. Erich would then unlock the storage room so that Charlotte, Lina and Ruth could go down the back circular stairs to the Naunyn-strasse shelter located on the street across from the back of the factory. When the all-clear siren rang Bruno would detain the factory workers downstairs, sometimes ordering them to check the yard for unexploded bombs, thus giving the women a chance to return. When they were safely inside, Erich would run down the front stairs and give Bruno an all-clear sign. The latter would then order the workers upstairs. Meanwhile, Ellen, who had managed at this point to find odd jobs working for other tenants in the building, sewing for Frau Hopfgarten and cleaning floors for the Kleists, would sit out the air raids in the official building shelter.

Early in March a huge air raid took place near Kreuzberg. Köhler's factory was not hit, but all work came to a standstill. Erich and Bruno decided to go outside and investigate the damage. They wanted to gloat at the harm done to the Nazis.

'Come on,' Erich said, leading the way. 'It's our turn to celebrate.'

'Let's go,' said Bruno.

The two young men, still dressed in their work clothes, headed for the bomb site. As they followed the trail of devastation, they arrived at a schoolyard on Mariannenstrasse. The entrance to the yard's air-raid shelter was piled high with debris and rubble. As they heard the muffled screams of women and children trapped inside, they stopped in their tracks, overcome by feelings of shame and remorse. These were not the cries of trapped German soldiers. Mothers such as Anni Harm and her young child could be inside. Several people were standing near the mounds of debris. Some were parents, traumatized by the thought of their children being buried alive inside the shelter. Without saying a word, Erich and Bruno began trying to clear the entrance, trying to enlarge a small opening to rescue the victims.

After digging with their hands for what seemed like hours, they managed to make a small hole and rescued seven children: seven out of hundreds. When they could do no more, Erich and Bruno quietly returned to the factory. The cries of those children would haunt them for ever, causing their eyes to fill with tears whenever they recalled the incident.

By mid-April Berlin was a wasteland. Industry all over the city had come to a standstill. The streets were virtually deserted of civilians. As German males lurked within buildings, some lying in bed to feign illness, SS men and Gestapo agents began raiding homes and workplaces for recruits of all ages for the Volkssturm. Bombers no longer flew overhead; instead, one could hear artillery fire and rocket launchers as the Soviet troops – now 25 kilometres (15 miles) from the outer edge of the city – approached from the east.

Herr Hopfgarten and his wife, anticipating that the end was near, took all the tinned food and bread out of their grocery shop and distributed it to tenants in the building. During an air raid Erich drew Herr Hopfgarten aside and told him that he and Bruno were planning to hide from the SS in a small unused storage cellar on the tenants' side of the building. Herr Hopfgarten asked if he could join them, and Erich agreed. After the Hopfgartens left, Erich and Bruno quickly packed some clothes and tinned food into their small suitcases and filled their canteens with water. As they walked down the front stairs, they told any other tenants they passed that they had decided to enlist in the army: they would do their duty and defend Berlin in its darkest hour.

In the courtyard they looked around to make sure no one from the building was watching, then they ran into the small, musty cellar. Herr Hopfgarten joined them soon after, bringing with him some tins of food and bread from his grocery shop.

On 16 April American troops reached Nuremberg and Zhukov's Soviet Army crossed the Oder River. By 21 April the army had entered Berlin from the east, and the Arndts could hear artillery. They knew that troops might enter Kreuzberg at any time; there could be serious fighting in the streets and the building might receive a direct hit.

Ruth and Ellen, who were still upstairs in the factory loft, hastily packed some bread and tins of food in their bags, while Charlotte and Lina collected blankets and towels to take into the factory shelter for warmth. Lina and Ruth packed their winter coats as well, because they still had their Jewish identity cards hidden in the seams. They reasoned that if the Russians should discover them they might be able to gain their freedom by showing their cards.

Then the four women walked down the front stairs and crossed the courtyard to descend into the shelter, no longer caring if they were recognized by the other tenants. The shelter was already crowded with people from the building, mostly middle-aged women and elderly men. Some of the women were weeping. Others were silent and stony-faced. One elderly woman was seated on a wooden chair, holding a feather pillow on her head. Some others stood in the dank corridor, nervously smoking cigarettes. That evening nobody slept.

Since Ellen and Ruth were the youngest and fittest people in the shelter, they took turns fetching water from a pump located in back of Oranienstrasse near Oranien Platz. One of them would don the French army helmet that Hans had given to Erich, and she would take two empty pails, one in each hand. Then she would carefully make her way to the pump, threading a path through shells and gunfire. Ellen usually crawled on her elbows to the pump, keeping her body close to the ground, while Ruth walked upright, staying close to the buildings for protection.

By 23 April the Soviet troops were in the streets of Tempelhof, Steglitz and Zehlendorf, districts in the southern part of Berlin. The next day they moved through Neukölln and Treptow, approaching Kreuzberg from the south. Troops were also closing in on north Berlin through Spandau and Reinickendorf.

On the morning of 26 April it was Ruth's turn to go to the pump. It was now extremely dangerous, but everyone inside the shelter needed water. Ellen walked up the cellar stairs with Ruth to make sure that no soldiers were in view. 'Be careful, Ruthchen,' she cautioned, as Ruth tucked her hair under the helmet and clutched a pail in each hand, preparing to make a run to the well. 'Stay down. Keep low. The shells are coming.'

'Of course,' replied Ruth, making a dash for the street. There she walked carefully along the pavements, staying close to the sides of the buildings; if she saw troops approaching she could quickly duck inside a doorway. As she slowly edged her way toward the pump, she saw in the distance two uniformed men. She stopped abruptly, not knowing whether to run or to speak. The men's uniforms were dirty brown, with a red insignia on each lapel. One of them was smoking a cigarette. The other was eating a pickle from a large barrel on the ground beside him.

Suddenly it occurred to Ruth that they might think she was a soldier, since she was wearing a helmet. She quickly removed it and dropped it in the street, then she began running back to the shelter.

When Ellen spotted her, she yelled, 'Get down, Ruthchen, get down. You'll get hit.'

But Ruth shook her head and laughed. 'No, no!' she yelled back. 'It's over!' When she reached the shelter she raced down the stairs shouting 'The Russians are here! The Russians are here! They are eating pickles from a barrel! The soldiers, I saw them at the pump. It's over! The war, it's over!'

'Are you sure, Ruthchen?' asked Lina, embracing her daughter. 'I can't believe it.'

'Yes, yes, I saw them.'

'Thank God!' exclaimed Ellen. 'We're safe. We're made it.'

As the women shouted and laughed with relief, the occupants of the shelter watched them apprehensively, not understanding why the four women were so jubilant. For them, the end of the war meant the beginning of more terrors.

After several minutes of rejoicing, Lina took the lead. 'We are *Juden*,' she explained to the others. '*Juden*. We are free.'

'*Juden?*' replied one of the tenants. 'How could that be? *Juden* are no more.'

Lina, who by this time had ripped open the seam of her coat, pulled out her Jewish identity card and held it up.

'I cannot believe it,' said the woman.

'Ah yes. I suspected it all along,' said Frau Kleist, who owned the leather factory on the floors above and below Max's loft. Then, walking over to Ellen, she said, 'God bless you. We recognized Erich some time ago, but we did not want to say anything. We were afraid you would be frightened if you knew we knew. So we left a turnip or a cabbage on the stairs for you to find.'

'So you were the ones!' said Ellen smiling. 'We could never work out how they got there. Thank you very much,' she said, shaking Frau Kleist's hands, 'Thank you. We are now all safe.'

'Maybe, maybe not,' said Frau Jäger, the superintendent who lived on the ground floor, who had also suspected the truth. 'They are angry, undisciplined Russian soldiers, and we're female. Who is safe under these circumstances?'

'Yes indeed,' agreed another woman, staring straight ahead with fear in her eyes. 'Who can feel safe now?'

'We must go and tell Erich and Bruno,' said Ellen, moving toward the stairs. 'They won't know what's happened.'

Ellen bounded up the stairs with Ruth following her. Then, hearing footsteps and noise in the street, they walked cautiously into the courtyard entrance and, shielding themselves behind the large door that opened on to the street, watched a stream of soldiers proceeding through Oranienstrasse on foot, on horseback, in small, rickety horse-drawn wagons and on large trucks. It was the most welcome sight they had ever seen.

Ruth returned to the shelter to tell the other tenants that Russian troops were outside in the streets, while Ellen rushed to the small cellar where Erich and Bruno were still hiding.

'Erich, Bruno,' she shouted, running down the stairs. 'The Russians are here! We saw soldiers in the street.'

Erich immediately put on his leather coat and raced upstairs with Ellen to see for himself what was happening. Then Ellen returned to the shelter where her mother and the others were waiting. Erich, curious to see for himself what was going on, began walking through the courtyard towards the street. A soldier with a machine-gun walked into his path and pointed the rifle at him, mistaking him for a German officer.

'*Nein*,' said Erich, waving his hand in front of the soldier. '*Ich bin Jude! Ich bin Jude!*'

Miraculously, the soldier seemed to understand and put his weapon at his side. But when Erich returned to his cellar the soldier followed him. Bruno and Herr Hopfgarten froze when Erich entered, followed by a sinister-looking soldier with a machine-gun pointed at his back. No one said a word. Once inside, the soldier pointed his gun at Erich's coat, gesturing for him to take it off. Erich immediately removed it. The soldier could take anything he wanted, Erich thought at that moment. He simply wanted his life. The soldier nodded and, holding the gun securely between his legs, he took the leather coat and a small case that was sitting on the floor. Then he left.

'Close call,' said Bruno, overcome with relief. 'At least you still have your other jacket.'

'More important, I have my life!' replied Erich, putting on a pair of work trousers and a shirt.

The next moment they heard a tremendous crash in the yard. Bruno climbed cautiously up the stairs to investigate. Peering outside, he saw a Soviet Army truck trying to drive into the passageway from the street. Determined to enter at all costs, the driver accelerated and got the truck partly inside the courtyard.

'A Russian truck!' exclaimed Bruno. 'Let's go!'

'No,' said Erich, pulling him back. 'Not yet. There may be more fighting. Besides, no one knows we are Jewish. We were lucky that the soldier I ran into spoke German. Most Russians don't. And I don't have any more leather coats to give them.'

Herr Hopfgarten sat there mutely, nodding his head, grateful that the soldier had ignored him. But he later told Erich that he had been filled with dread. He was not Jewish, so he had no reason to expect any leniency from the Russians. Rumours were rife that the Russians would do to the Germans what the Germans had done to their countrymen. And, frankly, who could blame them?

The three men remained in the shelter, listening to the rumble of tanks rolling through the streets, punctuated by artillery fire. Several hours passed. When the streets seemed quiet, they cautiously ascended the stairs and walked over to the large shelter where the women were still gathered.

'It's over. We're free,' said Erich, hugging his mother.

'I cannot believe it,' said Bruno, embracing Ruth, Charlotte and Lina.

They went into the building. 'Upstairs,' said Erich. 'Quick, we have no time to waste.'

Once inside, Bruno and Erich bolted the factory door. They all washed their faces and ate whatever food they could find. Ruth meanwhile ripped open the seam of her coat to make sure her identity card was still safely inside. Taking it out, she looked at it. At one time it had been her passport to hell; now it was her passport to freedom.

Within a week or so, the Soviet Army had taken over a small shop on Oranienstrasse and were using it as a local headquarters. On the other side of the street – directly in front of Köhler's factory – they installed a rocket launcher, intending to launch missiles into the inner city which was still being defended by Germans. Each day they would set off over a hundred rockets, creating such intense vibrations that the factory shook. During one of these launches

Charlotte was in the ground-floor WC. The blast stunned her so badly that she fell off the toilet seat and, as she tumbled on to the floor, she cried out. Ellen heard her cries and ran downstairs, expecting to find her mother pinioned under a Russian soldier. When she found Charlotte on the floor, her bloomers halfway down her legs, she burst out laughing and asked her mother what had happened.

'The rocket blast threw me off the seat,' said Charlotte. 'I thought the factory had been hit!'

Ellen walked outside into the passageway. A soldier with an old machine-gun slung over his shoulder on a string, walked over to her. 'Coffee,' he said in broken German. 'Coffee.'

Ellen ran to Frau Jäger and told her to make some ersatz coffee for the soldier. When the water had boiled Ellen gave a large mug to the soldier. Motioning with his hand, he made Ellen drink from the mug first to make sure it was not poisoned. Then he took the mug from her and drank from it. 'Good,' he said, waving her away.

As the street fighting and rocket blasts continued throughout the week, everyone stayed inside for safety, moving only between the loft and the shelter. Now, indeed, the women were more vulnerable than the men. The Russians would not know whether the women they attacked were Jewish or Christian. And they may not have cared even if they did.

By 29 April the Soviet Army reached the eastern end of the Tiergarten and were about to enter Potsdamer Platz, a block away from Hitler's bunker. When Hitler learned of the advance, he reputedly went into another rage. This truly was the end. But he would not suffer the fate of Mussolini. He would not allow his German enemies or the Allies to mutilate his body and hang it up so that the jeering crowds could desecrate it. Nor would he allow anyone to control his departure from the world. Early in the morning he poisoned his favourite dog, Blondi, and married his mistress Eva Braun. Then he assembled his staff and gave them vials of poison as a farewell gift.

At exactly 3.30 on the following afternoon Goebbels, Martin

Bormann, Hitler's trusted colleague and executor, and several other Germans who had not fled the bunker heard a shot in Hitler's bedroom. They went inside to find the Führer's corpse sprawled on the sofa. He had shot himself in the mouth and blood was dripping on to the floor. Eva Braun lay beside him. On the floor were two revolvers, but only one of them had been used. Eva had chosen death by poison. Their corpses were taken to the garden, doused with petrol and burned.

On 1 May Goebbels sent a telegram to Admiral Doenitz – commander-in-chief of the German navy and the highest-ranking officer whom Hitler had continued to trust – notifying him that Hitler was no longer alive. Doenitz was now in charge. Then Goebbels poisoned his six children and commanded two orderlies to shoot him and his wife in the back of their heads and burn their bodies. The following day General Helmuth Weidling, commander-in-chief of the defence zone of Berlin, signed a document of unconditional surrender that ended the war in Berlin and effectively ended the war in Europe.

When the Arndts heard the news on Hans's radio they ran down to the streets. There, small subdued groups of Germans were beginning to assemble as trucks with loudspeakers rumbled through the city, announcing the fall of Berlin. Dr Arndt and the Gehres were overjoyed when they heard the news. The following morning the doctor walked outside in full daylight, for the first time in two and a half years.

Outdoors he breathed deeply, relief flooding his body. The chestnut trees were beginning to bloom; the water in the Landwehrkanal sparkled with light. There were few clouds in the blue sky. The air was warm. It was exactly the kind of day that he had cherished before the grim horrors of the Third Reich had turned his beloved city into hell. But now it was good to be alive. The fighting had stopped, and even though an official surrender was yet to be signed, the war in Europe was over. The agony, the misery, the fear and the terror were suddenly lifted from him.

He could not wait to enjoy the pleasure of seeing his family again, for once without the threat of imminent arrest or death. But when he reached the large intersection of Skalitzer Strasse and Oranienstrasse the reality of war came home to him. Here the streets were littered with debris and rubble; some buildings had been completely destroyed; others were just skeletons. Now and again he had to step over the body of a dead soldier.

When he arrived at the factory yard he found Erich, Ruth, Bruno and Ellen outside enjoying the sunshine that was now embracing the ruined city like a warm blanket. 'Father, we made it. We made it,' said Erich.

'I can't believe it,' replied Dr Arndt, still trying to absorb the fact that he and his family were alive. But there was little time for reflection. They were not yet out of danger. 'Now,' he said sternly, taking Ruth and Ellen by the hand, 'go upstairs. And stay inside until the soldiers are gone. That is an order! The war may be over, but the city is still not safe.'

Max and Hans Köhler arrived soon afterwards, to check on the safety of the Arndts and to make sure the the factory was all right.

'We're free!' said Ellen. 'Free! We can never thank you enough. Never.'

Max nodded, a hint of a smile lighting up his face. 'You've made it! I knew you would.'

Hans stood next to his father, nodding his head in satisfaction and shaking Erich's hand. 'A good job,' he said. 'We can all sleep now. The bastards have had their day.'

'Will it be all right if we stay here a little while longer, until we find somewhere else to live?' asked Erich.

'Of course,' replied Max without hesitation. 'Where else would you go?'

# 12

# BITTERSWEET VICTORY

In a score of great cities of Germany scarcely a building stands intact; the Russian armies have swept like an avenging hurricane over the shattered avenues and places of Berlin. In the factories . . . the wheels of industry have stopped. Famine and pestilence lower over Germany; only by the efforts of her conquerors can she hope to escape or moderate their ravages. – VE editorial, *The Times*, 8 May 1945

Within a week Soviet officers began inspecting factories in Berlin, intending to strip them of all machinery and materials to send to the Soviet Union. When they arrived at the Köhlers', Hans answered the door.

'We have come to inspect the factory,' said the officer. 'We are taking it over.'

As soon as Erich heard the conversation, he came to the door. 'We are Jewish,' he explained, showing the officer his identity card. 'The Köhlers sheltered us in their factory throughout the war. They are good people and they deserve to be protected.'

'Jews?' said the officer. 'I did not think there were any Jews still in Berlin.' He took Erich's identity card and looked at it carefully. Lina and Ruth also brought their cards for the officer to inspect. 'A miracle,' he said. 'A miracle.'

The officer agreed to leave the factory in the hands of Max and Hans, and he offered to speak to his commanding officer to place an order for air-brushes; the army would pay for them and send them to their homeland. Two days later the officer returned with the order and a large sign in Cyrillic script meaning 'Jewish Quarters'. Erich placed the sign over the heavy wooden front door of the building so that all the tenants would benefit.

The worst was now over. The Arndts would be out of danger.

A few days later, in the early evening, Erich heard a loud banging on the wooden front door. Erich and the others tried to ignore
it. The sign was there; they were safe. But the banging persisted, so
Erich went downstairs. Cautiously he opened the door, to find a
short, dark-haired Russian soldier standing there with a bayonet.

Where are the *Juden*?' said the soldier in broken German and
Yiddish, pointing to the sign. 'I want to see the *Juden*! I do not
believe there are any Jews in Berlin. It is impossible.'

'*Ich bin Jude*,' replied Erich in German, who could understand
some Yiddish even though he could only speak German.

'*Nein, nein*,' said the soldier emphatically, gesturing with his
hand as if to slash his throat, 'All *Juden* caput.'

'*Ich bin Jude*,' repeated Erich.

'Proof, where is proof,' challenged the soldier.

'My papers are upstairs,' said Erich, pointing upstairs and hoping that the soldier would understand him. 'I will get them.'

'*Nein*,' said the soldier, poking him with the bayonet. 'The
Shema, recite the Shema.' By this he meant the Hebrew prayer.

'*Shema Yisroel, Adonah Elihaynu*,' began Erich, intoning the
words slowly, words he had not uttered in public since his bar mitzvah. As he continued, the soldier stood quietly, then grabbed Erich
by the shoulders and embraced him, kissing him on both cheeks,
tears filling his eyes.

'*Ich bin Jude*,' he said, hugging Erich tightly. 'I can't believe it.
You are the only living Jew I have seen since I left Moscow!'

Erich, stunned and shaken, could not grasp the implications of
this statement. The only living Jew? Still dazed by the soldier's
response, he began to recount his story to the soldier, speaking
slowly so he would be understood. As he talked, the soldier cried
openly, shaking his head from side to side in disbelief. When he finished, the soldier hugged him again and said he would return with
a bag of food.

After this Ellen and Ruth felt more confident about walking in
the streets. They hoped that they would be protected from the less
disciplined Russian soldiers, but their optimism was short-lived.
One afternoon Ellen walked into the courtyard and a soldier

approached her. He pointed to her wristwatch and said one word: '*Uhr*'. She gave him the watch without hesitation. He put it on his arm, already bearing several watches confiscated from Germans, and walked away grinning.

When she returned to the loft and told Ruth what had happened, she was outraged. 'We must get it back!' she said. 'He has no right to take your watch! We are Jews!'

'No, it's too dangerous. I'll survive without the watch. They could hurt us if we try to argue with them.'

'You'll see,' said Ruth, determined to sort things out. 'We'll go and get it back!' Ruth took Ellen's hand and they went across the road to the makeshift command post occupying an empty shop. Inside, the room was filled with Russian soldiers in varying stages of inebriation.

'I want the watch that someone just took off my friend,' said Ruth boldly. '*Uhr, Uhr*,' she added, pointing to Ellen's wrist.

None of the soldiers understood what Ruth was saying, and they laughed at the two girls.

'Call the commandant!' Ruth insisted. 'Commandant! Commandant!' she repeated over and over.

At last one of the soldiers got up and went to find an officer who could speak German.

'We are Jews,' she explained to him. 'Jews! The soldier had no right to take my friend's watch. We must have it back!'

The commandant spoke briefly to the soldiers. One of them reluctantly stood up and pushed up his sleeve, revealing an arm covered with watches. 'Find it,' the officer told Ruth.

'There,' Ellen said, pointing to a small rectangular watch with a slim grey leather strap. 'That's it!'

The soldier removed the watch and handed it over to Ellen with a sheepish grin. The soldiers also gave the girls two bottles of wine. Then, with their heads held high, they left and walked back across the street to the factory, trying not to break into a run. Once inside the courtyard they ran up the stairs to Köhler's loft and told everyone what had happened.

Erich and Bruno were impressed by their pluckiness, but Dr

Arndt was appalled. 'My God,' he exclaimed. 'How could you put yourselves in such danger! You could have been attacked.'

'No,' replied Ruth. 'They were all too drunk to be dangerous. Besides, we got Ellen's watch back.'

At exactly 2.41 on the morning of 7 May 1945 General Alfred Jodl and Admiral Hans-Georg von Friedeburg, acting on an order sent by Doenitz, signed a document of unconditional surrender in a small red schoolhouse in Reims where Eisenhower was headquartered. The following day the ceremony was repeated in Berlin, so that Zhukov could sign for the Soviet Union. The war in Europe was now officially over.

As the city slowly filled with refugees, concentration-camp victims, soldiers and homeless Germans, Nikolai Bersarin, a representative from the Soviet Union, was put in charge of the city. He tried to restore some sort of order, but it was impossible to stop the Red Army soldiers from raping women and looting German homes and shops. Unlike the first troops of war-weary soldiers, most of them from Mongolia, who had liberated Berlin, these new Russian troops were bent on ravaging and destroying whatever they came across. Bands of drunken soldiers roamed the streets, plundering shops and carrying away furniture and appliances on their shoulders. Some ripped faucets from walls and seats from toilets, planning to take them back to their families as booty.

At night German snipers known as Werewolves were active on streets and rooftops, seeking Russian soldiers to shoot. The Arndts decided to aid the Russians and to keep guard at the factory windows in round-the-clock teams, looking out for Germans who might try to enter the courtyard and climb on the roof. Ellen and Erich stood duty for a four-hour shift; Ruth and Bruno took the next four-hour shift, looking for snipers so that they could run downstairs and warn the soldiers.

Soon Berlin became a jungle as the Soviets turned the tables on the Germans, forcing them to clean the streets with shovels or even by getting down on their hands and knees. It reminded the Arndts of how the Germans had once forced the Jews to scrub the streets and latrines on their hands and knees. Food was now almost impossible to come by. Most Germans were living on the tinned food they had managed to hide in their cellars and the small rations of flour and potatoes that the Soviets were providing for the population to prevent massive starvation. Cash had no value, giving rise to a thriving black market where cigarettes and valuables and sometimes sex were traded for food.

As most bakeries and groceries had been demolished in the bombings, Germans frequently fought each other for a stale crust of bread or a can of peas. Erich and Bruno watched one day as a soldier in Oranienstrasse removed the harness from a horse that had died. As soon as the soldier left, Germans, armed with axes and knives, ran into the street and began cutting the horse into small pieces. Frenzy took over as men stood ankle-deep in blood, hacking away at the carcass with their axes. Then they grabbed what they could, clutching the bloody meat to their bodies to stop anyone else taking it. One man carried a whole horse leg over his shoulder.

In the chaos that prevailed, Bruno and Erich decided to go out and see what food and clothing they could salvage. Ellen was suffering from malnutrition and the others were near this state, as everyone had lost enormous amounts of weight. Ellen and Ruth each weighed about 40 kilograms (less than 90 pounds); Erich and Bruno had each scaled down to 45 kilograms (100 pounds). They were also badly in need of new clothing and shoes; they had not been able to buy underwear, socks or soles for their shoes in more than six years.

But their trials in the underground had made them fearless. Bruno and Erich had few qualms about charging into the lawless mobs in the streets. For the first time since 1933 they were free men. Walking along Oranienstrasse, they watched Berliners as they looted stores, carrying out chairs and small tables on their backs and stuffing bags and satchels with appliances, fabric and boxes. As they stepped over rubble and ashes, they stopped to watch a crowd of Germans shoving and pushing to enter a fabric shop. Bruno noticed a grate on the pavement next to the shop. He had become something of an expert in the art of spotting hidden entrances to cellars, so he went up to the grate, pried it open and looked down.

'Aha!' he said, peering inside. 'There's a warehouse in the basement. I'm going in!' He pushed his way into the shop and located the stairs to the basement. No one noticed him as he descended: people were too preoccupied with stealing rolls of fabric from the shelves and fighting with each other. A few minutes later Erich, still waiting outside the shop, lifted the grating off. Getting down on his knees, he whistled to Bruno through the open hole, whereupon his friend began passing him bolts of material: several bales of black velvet, one of white-and-brown checked wool and, finally, a large bolt of heavy brown velveteen. Finally Erich told Bruno to stop and rejoin him outside.

Erich replaced the grating, and Bruno emerged from the building. They quickly gathered up the rolls of material and took off for the factory. When they arrived, everyone was overjoyed with their booty. Ellen, with her sewing skills, realized that the brown-and-white fabric, in particular, would be perfect for dresses and that the velveteen would make excellent curtains and upholstery.

Several days later Erich went off on another expedition, this time for food and shoes. He came across a group of good-natured Soviet soldiers celebrating the defeat of Germany. They were drinking vodka and singing and dancing to the strains of a badly played accordion. Erich, a natural musician, offered to help out by playing for them, using a combination of German and gestures to make himself understood. As soon as they handed over the accordion, he began playing folk songs that delighted the rowdy group. As their voices soared, they plied Erich with vodka. Not much of a drinker, he found it hard to swallow the strong spirit. But he got it down and, within a couple of hours, he was totally drunk. When he stood up to go home he swayed on his feet. The soldiers laughed and applauded.

When he reached the factory loft, he collapsed on a cot. 'My God!' said Ellen smelling his breath. 'You have been at some party!'

A few days later Dr Arndt came by again. As he approached the entrance, a group of Soviet soldiers appeared with shovels. They had been ordered to dig up a soldier who had been shot and buried in the street, so he could be reburied properly in a military cemetery. After uncovering the body, the officer in charge reached down and took a cigar out of the dead man's breast pocket. He turned to Dr Arndt and stuck the cigar between his lips. The doctor kept the cigar in his mouth while the Russian soldier completed the task of exhuming the soldier. Then, as soon as the soldier left, he threw the cigar on the ground and squashed it with his foot.

A few days later Bruno and Ruth set off for Rangsdorf, concerned about the safety of the Treptows. A few surface trains were running, but the main underground lines were not functioning, having been blown up when retreating German troops had bombed the tunnels under the River Spree to prevent the Soviet Army from advancing through them. (In the process, they had drowned hundreds of German civilians who had taken shelter in the tunnel.) To find an operating train, Ruth and Bruno had to walk through rubble-filled streets where many dead German soldiers still lay unburied, mostly SS troops who had defended Berlin until the very end. Some bodies were burned or mutilated; others looked as if they were asleep. Smashed Soviet tanks with bodies hanging out of them littered the roads.

Ruth and Bruno arrived at the Treptows' home to find that they were in sound health and reasonably good spirits. They welcomed Bruno and Ruth, but they still had no news of Uschi, who had been conscripted into the German Army. As far as they knew, she was still in Bavaria. Later it turned out that she had been captured by the liberating American forces and was serving as a translator, helping them communicate with German prisoners-of-war. She returned unharmed to Berlin several months later.

By late May the behaviour of the marauding troops improved, as their leaders became stricter about imposing discipline. Even so, the city was still in chaos as neighbours competed with each other for loaves of bread and tape to seal up broken windows. Dr Arndt continued to sleep at the Gehres', but he spent most days with his family, who continued to live in the factory loft until they could find shelter elsewhere.

Everyone now had ration cards supplied by the Soviet commanders to obtain food and other basic supplies. But groceries and bakeries almost always ran out of provisions before they could provide rations for everyone standing in line. So Lina went to the butchers and bakers she had bought goods from before the war, armed with money that Dr Arndt had taken with him into hiding. With her Jewish ID card, she could go to the front of the queues and obtain food before the merchants ran out of supplies.

Gretchen Dübler, who had been sending Ellen and Charlotte ration cards from Schwerin, arrived unexpectedly at the loft with sandwiches for the group. Her husband, Karl, had been drafted into the Volkssturm in the final months of the war, leaving her and her two small daughters alone in Schwerin. Fearing attack from the advancing Soviet troops, Gretchen hastily packed a bag and put her daughters into the family's small car, hoping to find refuge with her sister, who lived in Berlin. She managed to make it to the outskirts of the city where German soldiers confiscated her car. Gretchen none the less got safely to her sister's house and waited there through the last days of the war. When it seemed safe to venture out into the streets, Gretchen went to the factory to see if the Arndts were still alive.

'Thank God, you are all right. It's a miracle,' said Charlotte when Gretchen arrived. 'We feared the worst when the ration cards stopped coming.'

'We had to flee from the army,' explained Gretchen. 'We have not yet heard from Karl, but we hope that he's still alive.'

Some time later Erich managed to rescue more food. As he stood one day on the pavement of Oranienstrasse, he saw a group of Germans walking by, each of them carrying a large box.

'Excuse me,' said Erich to one of the men. 'What's in the boxes?'

'Lard,' the man answered, nodding his head in the direction from which he had come. 'A warehouse of lard.'

Erich immediately ran down the street. Anything cooked with lard tasted 100 per cent better, as far as he was concerned. As he walked inside the building he saw a crowd of people near a stack of boxes, all of them pushing and shoving one other to get at them. In another corner Erich spied a smaller pile of boxes that no one seemed to have noticed. Quietly he made his way over to them, placed a box on his shoulder and walked out. When he returned to the loft and showed the group his booty, Ruth and Bruno decided to try their luck and immediately went off with a small handcart. But by the time they arrived, there was little left and they could only rescue half a box of lard. Now the group had over 33 kilograms (74 pounds) of lard – more cooking fat than they could ever possibly use.

They decided to share it with other tenants in the building. Erich went to the window, opened it and rang his well-known cowbell, shouting, 'Come and get some lard. Bring a container. We have enough for everyone!'

Within minutes tenants began lining up outside the factory door, while Ruth and Ellen rolled up their sleeves to hand it out. Then Erich fired up the wood stove they used for cooking and Charlotte fried a large number of *Spritzkuchen*, a kind of doughnut. Soon everyone feasted on cake and ersatz coffee, their first high tea in many a year.

Gradually a fledgeling Jewish community developed in Wedding, a district in north Berlin where the Jewish hospital was located, and in Oranienburger Strasse. As offices opened in both districts, Jewish war survivors went to register and apply for the special cards called *Opfer des Faschismus* (Victims of Fascism). These cards entitled them not only to go to the front of food queues but to have priority in housing and receive first choice of furniture from Nazi warehouses, most of which had been stolen before the war from Jewish homes. As soon as survivors from the concentration camps returned to Berlin or were shepherded to camps for displaced persons, their names were posted on lists drawn up by Red Cross workers.

By the end of March 1945 the number of Jews living legally in Berlin had shrunk to a minuscule 5,990. Almost all were Jews married to Christians or *Mischlinge* children. There were also 800 Jewish prisoners, patients, doctors and nurses who had managed to survive in the Jewish Hospital. Now, as word quietly spread that a Jewish agency was in operation, Jews began emerging slowly from the shadows in which they had hidden during the war. Eventually some 1,400 hidden Jews would register at the office, about one-quarter of the 6,000 or so Jews who had gone into hiding during 1942 and 1943. Most of those who had survived in this fashion were single survivors or, sometimes, couples. Although many Jews had gone into hiding with other family members or colleagues, almost all these groups suffered attrition of some members. Often they were arrested by the Gestapo when they went out on the street to look for food. Sometimes a report from a neighbour led to the arrest of everyone in the hiding place, often the back room of a shop. Even when no arrests occurred, some Jews died from starvation or disease or in bombing raids. A few became so depressed by the difficulties and seeming futility of their furtive lives that they committed suicide.

The Arndts remain the largest group known to have survived in hiding intact. Miraculously, no one was arrested and everyone had managed to withstand the hunger and stresses of life underground. They were not aware of their unique status at the time and, as the truth about the concentration camps emerged, their relief at having survived was tempered by their growing awareness of the horrors experienced by fellow Jews and others.

As lists of survivors were posted and the Arndts went to look up relatives and friends, Ellen realized she would never again see her aunt Johanna Kroner or her father David Lewinsky or her cousin Meta or many of her other relatives. Bruno would never again see his mother Ella or his aunt Grete or his grandparents or any of the rest of his family who had remained in Germany. Lina would never again see her sister Paula Arnoldi. Ruth would never see the babies she had taken care of in the Niederschönhausen orphanage. And there were countless other friends and co-workers that had met their ends at the hands of the Nazis. Eventually Ellen would learn that her aunt and her father were killed in the Riga work camp in Latvia. Her other deported relatives all died in Auschwitz.

While Ellen, Erich, Ruth and Bruno had been certain from

early on that they would not survive if they were sent to the camps, they had assumed that they would die from abuse or starvation. They did not know about the gas chambers until they began hearing stories from survivors who returned to Berlin and read the reports that started to appear in the newspapers. And when they did learn of these devastating crimes against humanity, crimes so huge as to be almost unimaginable, they could not find words to express the depth of their grief.

Eventually they determined that they would honour their relatives and friends by remembering them as they lived and not linger on the gruesome details of their deaths. And they would continue to focus upon the daily challenges they faced. They had vowed not to allow Hitler to ruin their lives or control their destiny. Now was not the time to renege on this vow by obsessively focusing on the terrors of his reign. Living courageously and fighting to create a better world, a world where such brutality could never again occur, this was their only choice.

As for the vast majority of non-Jewish Germans, they, too, said little when radio and newspapers began reporting that nearly six million Jews had been senselessly and viciously killed in concentration camps. After all, they had not protested when in 1938 Nazi stormtroopers had swept through Berlin, burning synagogues, smashing Jewish stores and looting Jewish homes. They had not protested when vans had rumbled through the city streets, carrying away men and women and children to unknown destinations. They had turned deaf ears to reports of mass genocide in Auschwitz, Dachau and Treblinka. Why should they listen now? Now, when they had lost sons and husbands and fathers in the war, when they were penniless and hungry and homeless, why should they be held accountable for sins they had not personally committed?

Besides, as they said to one another privately, what could they have done? Could they have stopped Hitler and the SS? Could they have gone to the concentration camps and reported to the outside world what was going on? Could they have marched in the streets? Or sat in protest outside the Reichstag? Or refused to shoot Jews in the back? And, if they had refused, would Hitler have killed them all, as well?

As for those other Germans – the Gehres, the Köhlers, the Treptows, Tata, Purzel, Anni Harm, the Bachmann sisters and the others who had managed to protect the Arndts throughout those years – what was so special about them? What impelled *them* to risk their lives and the lives of their families when the vast majority of Germans either supported the Nazis or did nothing? The Arndts could never answer these questions, but they would be for ever indebted to these fifty extraordinary people who chose to defy evil and behave with courage, honour and dignity.

# 13

# A NEW LIFE

Humanity will not be cast down. We are going on – swinging
bravely forward – along the grand high road – and already behind
the distant mountains is the promise of the sun. – Winston
Churchill

Early in June Ellen and Erich assembled everyone in the loft and
told them they had set a date for their wedding: 16 June. There
were shouts of jubilation: this was the moment they had all been
waiting for. In the midst of the celebrating, Bruno and Ruth found
themselves looking at one another. They, too, had formed a deep
bond during the war. Ellen's and Erich's announcement crystallized
Bruno's feelings about Ruth. He realized that he did not want to
face a future without her.

That evening he asked her to take a walk with him. The air was
clear and warm. Holding her hand as they walked along the street
filled with debris and rubble, Bruno proposed to her. Ruth immediately accepted.

Later that week Bruno went to Dr Arndt to ask him formally for
Ruth's hand in marriage. The doctor was less enthusiastic than
either Bruno or Ruth had anticipated. He prefaced his remarks by
telling Bruno that he and Lina were extremely fond of him. 'But
you have only known each other for six months,' he pointed out.
'And being together in these kinds of circumstances can play tricks
with our emotions. I think the decision to marry now is premature.'

Dr Arndt, like most other German men of his generation,
believed that it was the responsibility of men to support their families. Bruno had not even finished his secondary education. 'How
will you support a family?' he asked. 'You need time to prepare
yourself for a career. *Then* you can think of marrying.'

'I'll get a job and be a good provider,' insisted Bruno, who had been prepared for this kind of response. 'After all, if I managed to survive the Third Reich I can get along well enough in ordinary times. I love Ruth and she loves me. We want to spend the rest of our lives together.'

Dr Arndt could tell that he was not going to win. Bruno was as stubborn and headstrong as his son and his daughter and Ellen. Finally he and Lina finally managed to persuade the couple to wait until the autumn. Then, if they still wanted to marry, they could have a proper wedding.

When Bruno told Ruth what the doctor had said she laughed. 'Father has not changed a bit,' said Ruth. 'He is just as stubborn as ever.'

During the next week Lina and Ellen set about inviting all the protectors who were still in Berlin to the wedding party. The Kleists offered to host the celebration in one of their lofts, which was more spacious than Max's factory. Charlotte set about making *crüllers* – spiral-shaped biscuits sprinkled with sugar and fried in fat. After all, they still had many kilograms of lard.

Gertrud Neumann, the seamstress who had shared a room with Lina, had managed to find the Arndts through the Jewish Office in Wedding. When, on her first visit, she heard about Ellen's plans, she offered to make a wedding suit for her from the bolt of black velvet that Bruno and Erich had liberated. Everyone was touched by her offer. When Lina asked about Gertrud's daughter, whom she had sent to Holland for safekeeping, she shook her head. She could barely speak. 'We think she went to Bergen-Belsen,' she admitted quietly. 'We have no more information.'

Lina tried to reassure her. 'Let us hope for the best. Survivors are still returning. She may be all right.'

The subject was then changed. Gertrud started planning the wedding suit. She also offered to make a chiffon insert that Ellen could wear under the velvet jacket and promised to return the next day to take measurements and create a pattern.

A few days later Charlotte managed to get in touch with Anni Harm's sister, Martha Hübl, whom she had met while she was staying with Anni. Martha was delighted to find out that the families were alive and well, and she offered to provide a wedding veil for Ellen. But she had sad news. Anni had died during the last year of the war owing to complications from a heart ailment.

Charlotte was shaken. 'How terrible. I had no idea.'

'That is not all,' continued Martha. 'Evelyn went to stay with Oma [Anni's mother] when Anni was taken ill. On the last day of the street fighting, Evelyn and Oma were both asleep in Oma's large bed. A bullet flew through the window and struck Oma in the neck while she was asleep. She died instantly.'

'What about Evelyn?'

'Evelyn ran to our house immediately. She was hysterical and frightened. Of course we took her in right away and she is still with us.'

As for Herr Harm, he had not yet returned from the army, and no one had any information about him. Charlotte did not know what to say, so she simply put her arm around Martha to comfort her.

Dr Arndt asked Max Köhler if he would act as a witness for Erich. Max said he would be honoured. Lina asked her closest friend in Berlin, Martha Maske, to stand up as a witness for Ellen. Shortly before the wedding day Frau Liebold found out from neighbours that the two 'Nazi spies' she had hidden in her apartment in the spring of 1943 were not spies after all but Jews in disguise. The widow managed to get the address of the Arndts and immediately went to see them.

'I knew all along you were Jewish,' she told Ellen when she opened the door. 'I am so happy to see that you are safe.'

She asked them to sign a document verifying that a German had protected a Jew or an anti-Fascist during the war. The documents became known informally as *Persilschein* (Persil was and is a well-known brand of washing powder) since they would 'cleanse' Germans of all Nazi associations. Having such a document made it easier for Nazi Party members and high-level German administrators to go through the 'de-Nazification' procedure required by the Allies.

The Arndts had signed such documents for all their protectors, but they refused to sign one for Frau Liebold. And she was not the only one who came to the Arndts hoping to receive absolution. The day before Ellen and Erich's wedding Helmut, the seventeen-year-old apprentice who had gone off to fight for the Germans, knocked on the factory door. He had just returned from the navy; his ship had been torpedoed – several times – but he had managed to survive the icy waters.

'I have just heard the good news!' he said brazenly when Erich opened the door. 'I want to offer you my congratulations and celebrate with you.'

Neither Erich nor Ellen could believe his nerve.

Erich recovered his composure first. 'No way! You were a Nazi then and you are a Nazi now. We do not want to have anything to do with you, not now, not ever!'

Then, since they did not have old dishes to throw down the stairs – a tradition known as *Polterabend*, which typically occurs on the night before a wedding – they gleefully threw Helmut down the factory stairs.

The following day Erich and Ellen were married at the Registrar's Office in Kreuzberg. Afterwards the newly married couple and the tiny wedding party, consisting of the Arndts, Charlotte, Max Köhler and Martha Maske, went to the Kleists' loft for the reception. There they joined the Gehres, Hans and Klara Köhler, Tata, Manfred (the young apprentice who had accompanied Erich and Ellen to the opera), Martha Hübl, Gertrud Neumann and Gretchen Dübler. Many of the other Germans who had protected them had left the city; a few others, like Frau Meier, had died in bombing raids.

Ellen and Erich planned to spend their wedding night in a room that had become available in the residential part of the factory building. Bruno, meanwhile, had found another small, vacant room on the floor beneath them. Ruth was supposed to have another small room, but the party went on so late that Tata could not return to Burig that evening. Lina suggested that Tata stay overnight in Ruth's room, while Ruth could share her that of her brother.

Ruth had no intention of sharing her brother's bridal chamber, particularly when Bruno had his own room. But in deference to her parents, who now that the war was over were intent on re-establishing old-style propriety, Erich and Bruno worked out a strategy so that Ruth could sleep in Bruno's room without letting on to the senior Arndts. Erich nailed a string to the windowsill of his room and dropped it outside, so that Bruno could catch it from his window. Bruno then attached the string to his pillow. When it was safe for Ruth to return in the morning, Erich was to jerk the string. Ruth would then go up the back stairs to Erich's room where she would be when their parents arrived in the morning.

As the Red Cross workers continued posting lists of survivors throughout the summer, someone told Bruno that a man named 'Gotthold Gumpel' was on a list of returnees from Auschwitz. Bruno had not seen his father since he was six and his parents had divorced. Could this Gotthold Gumpel possibly be his father? Summoning up all his courage, Bruno decided to go to the address he had been given, Fehrbelliner Strasse 13, a street in Prenzlauer Berg, a district north of Kreuzberg. When he arrived, a woman let him into a tiny basement apartment.

'Gus,' she called out. 'You have a visitor.'

An elderly, sad-looking man walked into the room. Bruno introduced himself. 'I am Bruno Gumpel, the son of Gotthold Gumpel.'

Tears filled the man's eyes and he walked over to Bruno and embraced him. He was, indeed, Bruno's father.

The reconciliation, Bruno later told Ruth, was incredibly emotional. Bruno cried like a child in his father's arms. And Käte, the woman who had opened the door, cried, too. She told Bruno that she was a Christian who had lived with Gotthold in Berlin for many years before he was arrested and deported to Auschwitz. She then took Bruno aside and told him that in the concentration camp his father had been used by the Nazi doctors as a guinea-pig for surgical experiments. Somehow he had managed to survive them, but he would not talk about his experiences. Not even Käte knew the details. But, she said, he had returned from the camps a changed man: sad, broken and old beyond his years. They had married after he returned. Eventually, she told Bruno, Gotthold planned to emigrate to Palestine. But first he needed to regain his strength. Finding Bruno, she knew, would do much to revive his spirits. Bruno agreed to return the following week. He, too, wanted to renew the relationship; after all, his estranged father was now his only living relative in Berlin.

As there was no longer any work to be done in Max's factory Erich and Bruno began to explore Berlin. The Soviet soldiers had stolen both of Erich's bikes, so he managed to purloin another, better one that he found on the street. Soon after this he spotted an old car without a top in Skalitzer Strasse that had been abandoned. Erich went to fetch Bruno. Between them they managed to hotwire the ignition and drive to the factory. Several days later they spied another abandoned car in even worse shape, but this one had a top and four reasonably good tyres. They returned with their tools and cut off the top, removed the tyres and some other parts and used them to refurbish the original car. The resulting vehicle was good enough to get them around the city. For the first time in two and a half years they could drive through the rubble-filled streets as free men.

In mid-June Dr Arndt received a letter from the Russians, now controlling the city, notifying him that a large apartment in Kreuzberg was available for him to rent. As Victims of Fascism, the Arndts received priority in receiving apartments when they became available. The doctor immediately accepted. So at the beginning of July Lina and the doctor took possession of a nine-room apartment, which had been vacated by a German doctor who had fled the city to escape the approaching Soviet Army, at Schlesische Strasse 31, a small street in the south-eastern part of Kreuzberg near the banks of the River Spree. Ruth and Bruno also moved in, but with the resumption of the pre-war moral code they had to sleep in separate rooms.

When Dr Arndt reopened his medical practice Ruth worked

with him as his nurse and receptionist. Since there were few physicians in Berlin the stairs leading to his office on the third floor were always lined with patients, many of them clients from his previous practice but a great number of them new patients. After hours the doctor would make home visits to patients who were bedridden, doing his rounds on an old reconditioned bicycle.

About this time Allied troops began pouring into the city and Berlin was divided into three zones. The Russian sector was largely in the east; the British were to govern the western part of the city, where Charlottenburg was located; the Americans were to control the southern part of the city. Early in August a fourth – French – sector was created from the British and American zone. Köhler's factory and the Arndts' new home were located in the American sector. Soon after this the Americans made Dr Arndt the director of the Board of Health for Kreuzberg. There he found a job for the Gehres' daughter who had selflessly given up her tiny bedroom so that he could live with the family.

Later in July Ellen and Erich were offered their own apartment at Friedelstrasse 10 in Neukölln, the district just south of Kreuzberg where Anni Harm had lived. Charlotte moved in with them. Ellen proceeded to upholster a couch and make curtains from the brown velveteen fabric that Erich and Bruno had acquired. Ellen also made dresses and skirts for herself and Ruth from the brown-and-white checked wool material.

But life outside their apartment was still harsh, as Berliners continued to fight with each other for food, shelter and jobs. Across the road there was a bakery, but bread was only available for a few hours each day, since flour was still rationed. When Ellen went there to shop for bread one day, she went, as was her right, to the front of the long queue. But the women in the line screamed at her and would not allow her to take her place.

'But I have an ID card,' Ellen pleaded, almost in tears.

'Go to the back of the queue. We are *all* hungry,' said the women.

Just then Erich came along on his bicycle. Ellen told him what was going on. Without saying a word, he rode his bike up to the corner of the street. There he stopped, turned around and accelerated towards the shop and the queue. As he headed at top speed towards the women they scrambled to get out of his way. Before they could reassemble Erich placed his bike at the front of the line to block them.

'Now,' he said to his wife, waving her into the store, 'you have your place in the queue.' After she had entered the shop he hopped back on his bike and rode off.

Bruno found a job as a caretaker at the Fasanenstrasse Synagogue, located in Charlottenburg near the Zoo underground station. At one time the synagogue had been one of the largest and most fashionable in the city, but it had been burned during Kristallnacht and suffered bomb damage during the Allied raids. It needed major restoration work, and Bruno was hired mainly to guard whatever artefacts and fixtures still remained. It was around this time that he decided to find out what had happened to his older brother, Günther, who had emigrated to England in 1939. Bruno had only one address for him – the Kitchener Refugee Camp near London – and he sent a letter to him there via an American soldier that he met by chance on the street. The soldier was a cautious man. He said he would have to have the letter read by someone who understood German to make sure the contents were harmless before he passed on the message.

In August Bruno and Ruth decided to travel out to Burig, taking a large cart and several shovels with them, to see whether the possessions they had buried in Tata's garden had survived the war. The digging took several hours, but almost all the boxes were unharmed. Dr Arndt's medical instruments and his textbooks had survived without damage, and the family's silver was still in good shape, even though it was badly tarnished. Ruth's best leather handbag and a similar one belonging to her mother were, however, so mildewed that they had to throw them away. Under the circumstances these were trivial casualties.

When Ellen went to retrieve her possessions she was less fortunate. She had stored several boxes at the Bukins' home, but when she went to recover them Frau Bukin told her that her husband had died. The widow was so angry about this that she refused to return Ellen's and Charlotte's clothing or their camel-hair blankets; she said she was keeping them as a 'reward' for having helped the family. Ellen had a similar experience when she went out to the Haydens' to recover the large basket of goods she had stored with them. Frau Hayden met her and told her that Herr Hayden had died in the Volkssturm. She insisted that she and her daughter needed the clothing and other articles in the basket, since they no longer had a source of income.

By the end of August Bruno and Ruth were still intent on marrying, and by this time Dr Arndt and Lina had grown extremely fond of Bruno and welcomed him enthusiastically into the family. Bruno and Ruth planned to wed on 29 September in a civil ceremony at the nearby City Hall. Gertrud Neumann, who had found a temporary apartment in the building where Max's factory was located, offered to make a wedding suit for Ruth from the black velvet material. It would be similar in design to the one she had created for Ellen, but Ruth's jacket was to be fitted whereas Ellen's had been more flowing.

On the day of the wedding Ruth wore her suit with a white scarf around her neck and a matching black velvet turban, and she carried a bunch of pink roses. The bride and groom had double wedding rings fashioned from the wide gold band that Lina's sister, Paula, had given Lina for safekeeping before she was deported to Auschwitz. After the ceremony they had a small party for about twenty people in the Arndts' spacious apartment. Since housing was still scarce, Bruno and Ruth continued living in her parents' apartment. But now that they were married they could at last share a room.

More celebrations were to follow. Although the main sanctuary of the synagogue on Kottbusser Ufer, where Erich had been bar mitzvahed, had been burned during Kristallnacht, the small annexe next to the sanctuary had been restored and repainted with financial aid from the US Army. The synagogue's Torah scrolls had

209

been hidden from the Nazis in an underground safe. On 7 September Rosh Hashanah services were held to celebrate the Jewish New Year for the first time since 1938. Among the five hundred worshippers who attended were a small number of Berlin Jews, as well as many American and Russian soldiers who were stationed in Berlin. *Life* magazine photographed the event for its readers.

Soon after these festivities Lina went to see the cantor, Martin Riesenburger who had been assigned by the Nazis to take care of the Weissensee cemetery during the war. He was now taking on the duties of the congregation's rabbi, who had been killed by the Nazis. Lina wanted to arrange a Jewish double wedding so that her children's marriage could be consecrated in a synagogue.

The double wedding ceremony took place on 7 October. Ruth wore a long dress that Gertrud Neumann made from black silk that Lina had stored with a friend during the war, while Ellen borrowed a long black evening gown from the daughter of a friend and Martha Hübl's veil. Ruth wore the veil from her mother's wedding trousseau. Erich wore a dark-blue suit that he had worn when he was a teenager; since he had lost so much weight he could still get into it. Bruno wore a dark pinstriped suit.

It was the first Jewish wedding held in that synagogue after the war and only the second Jewish wedding to take place in post-war Berlin. The temple was crowded with many high-ranking American military officials, city officials, many of the Arndts' protectors as well as a few friends who had also survived in hiding. Afterwards the newly-weds were driven to Ellen's and Erich's new home in an US Army staff car. There, everyone assembled for a party.

The following month, on 15 November, Bruno had more good fortune. He returned home from work to find Ruth standing in the foyer, her face flushed with excitement. She pointed to a man in the next room dressed in a British Army uniform. It was Bruno's brother Günther. They shouted with joy when they saw one another, embraced and wept.

Günther told Bruno that when war had broken out in September 1939 he had enlisted in the British Army, determined to do whatever he could to defeat the Nazis. Soon afterwards he met a Jewish refugee from Vienna, Herta Rosenkranz, who was also living in London. They married a year later and had a son, Peter. During the London Blitz Herta and Peter were evacuated to Cookstown in Ireland.

When Bruno's letter reached authorities at the Kitchener Refugee camp officials forwarded it to Herta in Cookstown. She contacted Günther, who was then a staff sergeant with the Royal Army Service Corps. He immediately requested a transfer to Berlin so that he could find Bruno.

As soon as he arrived in Berlin Günther went to the address given on Bruno's letter. When Ruth opened the door and found a man who looked like her new husband's double standing there, she could not believe her eyes. 'My God!' she exclaimed, when Günther told her that he was her husband's brother. 'We never thought we would see you again. I am Ruth, Bruno's wife. Do come in.'

The brothers spent the evening talking and laughing and crying, and they did not fall asleep until early morning.

The next day Bruno took Günther to visit their father for another emotional reunion. Günther was billeted at a sergeants' mess in the British sector of Berlin. He stayed there until the following March, visiting Bruno and his father, often on his motor cycle, and bringing them extra food from the army headquarters.

Erich, meanwhile, found a job as driver of a small Tempo three-wheeled truck, delivering bags of coal and potatoes to households in Berlin. He largely took the job so that he could surreptitiously skim a few potatoes and some coal from the tops of each of the bags, as the family needed all the food and fuel they could get. His experience in the underground would not go to waste.

Soon they heard that Siemens had reopened. 'Let's go and find our Nazi supervisor,' suggested Bruno.

'Let's kill him if he's still there, the Nazi bastard,' said Erich, eager for revenge. They intended to give the man a beating he would never forget.

Arriving at the entrance of the building, they flashed their identity cards and the guard let them in. They found the right office, where, seated behind the desk, was their former supervisor. Wearing an ordinary suit without any party insignia on it, he looked less menacing and not at all impressive. But he recognized the young men at once and sensed their hostility. Cringing in fear, he protested, 'I didn't want to mistreat you and the others. I was forced to do it to save my life. I have a family. A wife. Children. What else could I do?'

Erich almost blacked out with rage. He and Bruno began beating the man, who continued to protest his innocence. 'They would have killed me if I had not obeyed. Please, please, have some mercy.'

'You do not deserve mercy!' Erich shouted at him.

'You deserve to die!' added Bruno.

Finally they left the man in a heap on the floor, his face bloody and bruised. They could easily have killed him; there were no guards in the vicinity and they would have got away with the crime. No one these days would investigate the murder of a former Nazi. But Bruno and Erich could not bring themselves to murder the man. They, after all, were not Nazis.

In February 1946 the newly reorganized Jewish Council of Berlin arranged to hold a festive ball for the tiny band of surviving Jews in Berlin to celebrate Purim, a Jewish holiday consecrating the liberation of the ancient Jews from massacre by the tyrannical Haman. Organizers recruited a popular singer and band to entertain the group with American songs. The Arndts attended with about four hundred other Jews who had lived out the war in hiding in Berlin. On 29 March the younger Arndts celebrated their parents' Silver Wedding Anniversary. Ellen, Erich, Ruth and Bruno went to a professional photographer and had their pictures taken, and these they gave to their parents. Afterwards they had a gala party at the elder Arndts' apartment.

In April the Arndt and Gumpel families celebrated Passover, the eight-day holiday that commemorates the flight of the Jews from ancient Egypt where the Pharaoh had held them as slaves.

This Passover seemed particularly symbolic. Once again Jews were celebrating their freedom from a terrifying oppressor.

Boxes of *matzoth*, unleavened bread, arrived from the USA. Günther, now in England, also sent the group a package of food. A care package also arrived from Lina's cousin, Claire Josephson, who had emigrated to the USA in 1938. As the Red Cross posted lists of survivors throughout the world and postal service was restored in Berlin, letters arrived from Lina's oldest sister, Johanna Paul, who had emigrated to Johannesburg, from Lina's youngest brother, Max Arnoldi, who had fled to Santo Domingo, from Arthur and Lina's close family friends, the Rosenmanns, who had resettled in Peru, and from the Rachmanns, who had made it to New York City.

In mid-April 1946 Erich heard a rumour. Displaced persons, he found out, could apply for emigration to the USA. But émigrés had to leave within two weeks. It did not take long for Erich to persuade Ellen and Charlotte to leave.

'Think, Ellen,' he said, 'a new life, in a new land, where there is plenty of food, work and accommodation and where we won't be persecuted for being Jews. I promised you when we met that we would move to America. Now I want to keep the promise.'

Ellen, who was five months pregnant with her first child, immediately agreed, and Charlotte would go with them. When Bruno and Ruth heard the news Bruno was very enthusiastic about applying. Ruth, however, was hesitant, since she was considering signing up for the newly reopened medical school in Berlin and did not want to leave her parents. But she finally agreed that it would be best for her and Bruno to leave. While neither the Arndts nor the Gumpels would ever blame every member of the German race for the Holocaust, Berlin would always be filled with painful memories, memories of suffering and cruelty and terror that would haunt them for ever. Why remain in a city where they could never truly escape the past?

In America they could have a fresh start. As skilled toolmakers Bruno and Erich would both have increased professional opportunities. Moreover, both families could bring up their children in an environment where they would not have to explain their past or apologize for their religious beliefs. Dr Arndt and Lina planned to remain in Berlin for another six months. Since the doctor was employed in Berlin and earning a substantial income, he wanted to know as much as possible about life in America before emigrating. Once he was in the USA he knew that he would have to go without an income for many months while he studied for the American medical boards. And, even then, he knew it would be difficult to find a good position, since he would be competing with doctors trained in US medical schools, doctors who did not have a German accent.

As the date for their departure approached, the group packed their meagre possessions and prepared to take a train north to Bremerhaven. Bruno and Erich each had Homburg hats made for the journey, since they could not find any new clothing to buy in the stores. They would have to make do with their worn shoes and threadbare, patched trousers.

In Bremerhaven they stayed at the United Nations Relief and Rehabilitation Administration Camp for two weeks with some eight hundred other Jewish refugees from Germany, Poland, Belgium, France and other countries, the majority of whom were concentration camp survivors. The group also included sixty-seven orphaned children, most of whom had no recollections of their parents or their birthplace. On 11 May 1946 the refugees boarded the *Marine Flasher*, an 11,000-ton former troop carrier. It was the first ship to carry Jewish refugees to the USA, and the immigrants got a rousing send-off from an American military band stationed on the pier.

Since Ellen was pregnant she was assigned a room on an upper deck with two other pregnant women. The rest of the group stayed below in more crowded quarters. From the voyage's beginning the waters were choppy, and most of the people on board became violently seasick. Ruth volunteered to take care of the young children on board, but as soon as the ship headed out to sea she became too ill to assist them. Bruno also suffered from severe bouts of seasickness. Ellen, Erich and Charlotte were among the few passengers on board who never got ill. They ate their fill of breakfast and lunch and dinner and tended to the other passengers, most of whom were suffering badly.

On 20 May the ship sailed past the Statue of Liberty. Everyone was on deck, cheering and waving and sobbing with joy. It was a warm, sunny day, the skies were blue and cloudless and the air smelled fresh and clean. As the ship prepared to dock at Pier 64 in New York Harbor, 1,500 relatives, reporters, customs officials, welfare workers and representatives from Jewish agencies were there to greet the new immigrants. On board Charlotte had sent a wire to her cousins, Werner and Margot Gurau, who lived in Queens, New York. They travelled into the city with their two teenage children so that they could meet the new arrivals.

As the group disembarked, Erich and Bruno wearing their heavy Homburg hats under the warm sun, Ellen, Ruth and Charlotte clomping along the dock in their worn shoes with wooden soles, they managed to find Charlotte's relatives. A few days later a reporter from the *New York Post* took them across town to see the Empire State Building. Charlotte stayed with her relatives while the two couples bundled into two taxis, along with another refugee couple.

The reporter took them to a soda fountain located on the ground floor, bought them ice-cream sodas and interviewed them while a photographer snapped their pictures. Erich held up a utensil and was quoted in the newspaper the next day as saying that he ate ice cream with a 'poon'. After the photo session and the ice cream the reporter took them up to the top of the building. When they emerged from the elevator they took a deep breath and walked over to the guardrails. Holding tightly on to the rails, they looked down at the city gleaming in the sunlight with possibilities and challenges. It was a sight they would never forget.

# Appendix 1

## America the Beautiful by Ellen Arndt

On the pier the US Army band plays 'Don't Fence Me In!' and I am standing at the railing of a small army transport ship in the harbour of Bremerhaven. I am leaving Germany. Life is beginning again this day, 10 May 1946. I share a petty officer's cabin with two other pregnant women. It has a shower just for us, and everybody gets two bars of Palmolive soap. The rest of my family – my mother, husband, sister-in-law and her husband – are down in the hold, stacked three high in bunks. Everyone is happy and excited.

Still at anchor, supper is served. Women over sixty-five and mothers-to-be are in the dining-room; everyone else eats army-style with trays, queueing down below. God, all this food for each person! Potatoes and sausage, vegetables, bread and butter and oranges are on the table. I can hardly believe the fabulous spread.

On my mother's birthday Ruth and I wrap up two bars of marvellous soap and write a poem for her. She is thrilled with the gift.

At sea I feel great – no seasickness whatsoever – and I spend the days with my family. My mother is busy caring for seasick passengers, but Erich and I sit on the uppermost deck (no chairs on an army transport) and watch the sea – sunken ships and war debris in the English Channel, endless ocean past the British Isles. A storm! I am up on deck looking down from the height of a big wave into a deep canyon of water, the spray flying over me. It is wonderful, exciting, exhilarating.

The crew is very good to us. Seasickness keeps many others in their bunks, so I find myself almost alone at breakfast. The steward tells me that I can have as many breakfasts as I want. I cannot eat like this. It is amazing to know that there is food, lots of it, always available!

One day a member of the crew, a young man of Italian origin, hands me a piece of paper with his mother's New York address. He tells me, 'In America, with all the freedom and opportunities waiting, your husband might be overcome by it all and leave you. If that should happen, go to my mother, and when I return from the sea I will marry you and take care of

217

you and your baby.' I assure him that this will not happen, but I am touched – and very flattered – by his gesture. After all, I am six months pregnant – and look it!

At nightfall ten days later our ship stops outside New York Harbor. New York and New Jersey are all lit up; we realize that the thousands of moving lights are vehicles on the highways. Everybody remains on deck until very late, just drinking the sights in. In the morning we sail by the Statue of Liberty. Cheers go up, and most of us are in tears – tears of happiness.

We had bought a loaf of bread on the black market in Bremerhaven and carried it all the way into the harbour. Now, with great ceremony, we throw it in the water, knowing that we will never be hungry again.

Out on the pier are reporters. The first question, five minutes after disembarking, is: 'How do you like America?' We laugh. We are loaded on to buses and driven through New York City. There are endless cries of 'Isn't it big!' 'Look at the apples in front of the store!' Look here, there!' We finally arrive at some grimy old hotels around Times Square, where women from relief agencies help us. Up in our rooms we don't care if the plumbing spews forth rusty water and the place is not as clean as our little ship. We have arrived!

There are reporters at the hotel, and soon a newspaper man asks to take six of us up to the top of the Empire State Building. We are so dazzled, so overcome by it all that we hardly knew where to look first.

The next day our husbands shave off their moustaches: Americans are clean-shaven. They then jump off the beds on to their Homburgs, flattening them. 'Destroy them!' they yell. 'Let's go bareheaded.' I comb my hair differently – American-style. Later my mother's cousin from Queens arrives with a brand-new maternity dress, my first store-bought dress in eight years. The process of assimilation has begun.

As we walk along the streets of New York, we are constantly stopped by people stunned by our strange appearance. We make our way uptown to Washington Heights to the address of some family friends, the Rachmanns, who emigrated from Berlin before the war began. We ring the bell, the door opens, and there is pandemonium. By the evening the five of us have been taken in and snowed under with gifts of beautiful clothes and shoes. The dresses do not fit me in my pregnant state, but I get to choose my share for later.

Soon, however, we get into trouble with the refugee agency. We are informed that we are to be settled in Alabama. No way! As far as we know, Alabama and the American south is an oppressive society filled with racial tension and discrimination, and, thank you, we have had enough of that! We refuse to leave New York, so no more help from the relief agency for us. After that we go it alone. But that is another story.

# Appendix 2

## Arriving in America by Ruth Arndt Gumpel

We each received five dollars and a carton of cigarettes before our arrival in New York Harbor on 20 May 1946. Disembarkation took hours. The weather was warm and sunny, and cousins of Ellen's mother had come to greet us. Then we were taken by bus to a small and rather dingy hotel in the garment district on West 36th Street, where the five of us shared a 'suite' with another refugee couple. We were given meal vouchers for certain restaurants, one of which was Siegel, a small Kosher restaurant near by. How impressed we were when the piece of *flanken* meat turned out to be just the appetizer! Then came chicken soup (I had seconds) and more meat with potatoes and vegetables and dessert! Unbelievable – and even better than what we had been served aboard ship.

We must have looked a sorry sight. People on the street turned round to get a better look at us in our patched clothes that were much too heavy for the time of year; our strange-looking shoes and at Erich and Bruno wearing their Homburgs. Unfortunately nobody took a picture of them. The next morning they discarded their hats and got haircuts for fifty cents.

On our second or third day in the city we pooled all our money and took a taxi to the Rachmanns' house in Washington Heights in upper Manhattan. Dr Rachmann, who was from Berlin, had trained with my father. He and his family had emigrated to New York City in 1938. They had found out through newspapers that we were among the survivors, but they had no inkling of our impending arrival in the USA.

When we rang the bell Tante Carola, Dr Rachmann's wife, opened the door. 'The medical practice is over for the day,' she told us. She did not recognize Erich or me, and she had never met Ellen, Charlotte or Bruno. We still looked thin and undernourished. I will never forget the expression of surprise on her face when I said, in German, 'It is us, Ruth and Erich.' She screamed for her husband, Onkel Emil, and her daughter, my childhood friend Steffie, to come and see who had just arrived.

They did not know what to ask first. They brought out food and more food. Tante Carola's sister, Edith Bergman, who lived near by, went to get her family. They brought clothes for us – heaps of clothes. Ellen had a hard time fitting into anything, being six months pregnant, but Charlotte and I had a field day! The Rachmanns would not let us stay in the hotel a day longer and for the next week or so Bruno, Charlotte and I enjoyed the Rachmanns' hospitality, while Erich and Ellen slept at the Bergmans'. The next day the two families took Bruno and Erich off to buy suits and shoes for them. It seemed like a non-stop celebration.

A few days later I telephoned my mother's cousin, Claire Josephson. She and her husband and son lived in a private house in Forest Hills, New York. Claire was besides herself when she heard my voice and immediately offered Bruno and me a room in their house, even though her elderly in-laws, her brother and the family dog Tibby, an adorable German Shepherd crossbreed, were also living there at the time.

Bruno found a job working as a tool and die maker earning $60 a week and I did some part-time work as a baby nurse. It took quite a while to get used to the idea that we could buy almost anything we wanted. It seemed as though we bought shoes every weekend. We slowly gained weight and started to look, we hoped, more American, thanks to better clothing and different hairstyles. In October Bruno and I moved into a furnished room with access to a kitchen in Brooklyn, and on 20 December my parents arrived on a bitterly cold and snowy day. They were still thin and had not yet recovered physically, but they were overjoyed to meet Ellen's and Erich's daughter, their first grandchild Marion, born 11 August, and to see us all in good health and spirits.

In April Bruno and I moved to an apartment in central Manhattan in an area known as 'Hell's Kitchen', where many German Jewish refugees then lived. Our living-room overlooked the roof of the next building and was furnished with a lumpy sleeping couch, an old easy chair, a big wooden table, a dresser, a mirror and a closet with doors that would not close. The kitchen had a four-legged cast-iron stove, a table and chairs and by the door a bathtub with a folding cover. We had another very small room with a window facing an airshaft. I was pregnant and expecting our first child that August, so this was to become the nursery. Our toilet was in the hallway next to a pay phone.

We had made it to America!

# Appendix 3

## Dramatis Personae

### The principals

Arthur Arndt: physician and First World War veteran who lived in Kreuzberg

Lina Arndt: Arthur's wife

Erich Arndt: the Arndts' son

Ruth Arndt: the Arndts' daughter

Charlotte Lewinsky: divorced mother from Blesen

Ellen Lewinsky: Charlotte's daughter

Bruno Gumpel: schoolfriend of Erich Arndt

### The main rescuers

The Bachmann sisters: patients of Dr Arndt who ran a dressmaking salon on Prinzenstrasse

A brothel owner on Prinzenstrasse who knew the Bachmann sisters

Herr Bukin: tenant of Ellen's aunt, Johanna Kroner

Gretchen and Karl Dübler: Charlotte Lewinsky's neighbours from Blesen

Ida Forbeck: elderly patient of Dr Arndt who lived on Prinzenstrasse

Max and Anni Gehre: patients of Dr Arndt who lived in Kreuzberg

Greta: neighbour of Ida Forbeck who befriended Co Spyker

Anni Harm: a mother in Neukölln who worked with Herr Bukin

Herr Hayden: Ellen's foreman from Schubert

Max Köhler: patient of Dr Arndt who ran a small factory in Kreuzberg with his son Hans

Klara Köhler: Max's wife and friend of Anni Gehre

Frieda ('Purzel') Lefèbre: patient of Dr Arndt's and Anni Gehre's neighbour

Frau Liebold: cleaning woman at the German Opera and Anni Gehre's neighbour

Martha Maske: seamstress who worked for Lina Arndt

Herr Mattul: tailor in Spittelmarkt who knew the Bachmann sisters

Frau Meier: elderly woman who lived on Prinzenstrasse and who befriended Co Spyker

Gertrud Neumann: Jewish seamstress and patient of Dr Arndt's who knew Anni Gehre

José Santaella: agricultural attaché in Berlin for the Spanish consulate who sheltered Gertrud Neumann with the help of his wife, Carmen

Anni ('Tata') Schulz: the Arndts' first nanny

Co Spyker: Dutch slave labourer who worked near Prinzenstrasse

Ernst (Papa) Treptow: scrap-metal dealer whose daughter, Uschi, went to school with a friend of Bruno Gumpel

Colonel Wehlen: German Army officer who knew Herr Mattul's son, Bruno

Marie Wüstrach: owner of a small delicatessen who knew Anni Gehre and Lina Arndt

# Appendix 4

## Postscript

**Arthur and Lina Arndt** emigrated to the USA in December 1946 and settled in New York City. Dr Arndt joined the staff of the Hebrew Home for the Aged as a physician and worked there until he retired in the 1960s. Lina worked privately taking care of newborn infants. Dr Arndt died in 1973 at the age of eighty-one. Lina died in 1980 at the age of ninety-four.

**Ellen Lewinsky and Erich Arndt** married in June 1945 and emigrated to the USA in May 1946. They settled in Hempstead, New York, and had two daughters, Marion and Renée. In 1957 Erich was offered a management job with the Alliance Tool and Dye Company in Rochester, New York, and they moved there. Erich retired in 1983. The Arndts have six grandchildren and two great-granddaughters. Their younger daughter, Renée, lives in Rochester, as does their granddaughter, Timna, and her two daughters, Sarah and Sophie. Marion and her husband live in Kalamazoo, Michigan.

**Bruno Gumpel and Ruth Arndt** married in September 1946 and emigrated to the USA in May 1946. They settled in Queens, New York. Ruth worked as a paediatric nurse and Bruno took a job with CBS, eventually becoming an audio supervisor. They had two sons, Larry and Stanley. After Bruno retired from CBS in 1991, the Gumpels moved to Petaluma, California, to be near Stanley and their grandson Alex. Bruno died in 1996 from cancer. Ruth still lives in Petulama where she works as a volunteer at a local hospital and an animal shelter.

**Gretchen and Karl Dübler** died in Berlin. Their twin daughters still live there and see Ellen, Erich and Ruth whenever they visit.

**Max and Anni Gehre** emigrated to the USA in the 1950s to join their daughter, who had settled in upstate New York after marrying an American serviceman she met in Berlin. They were honoured as

Righteous Gentiles by Yad Vashem in 1991 after their deaths. Their daughter speaks regularly to Ellen and Ruth on the phone.

**Gotthold Gumpel**, Bruno's father, and his wife emigrated from Berlin to Israel. They later returned to Berlin, where they died.

**Günther Gumpel**, Bruno's brother, who served in the British Army, emigrated to New York City in 1947 with his wife Herta and his son Peter. Günther died in 1994. Peter, an architect, still lives in New York City; his younger brother, Julian, born in the USA, lives on Long Island.

**Anni Harm** died during the war from a heart ailment; her husband never returned from the front. Anni's daughter, Evelyn, was brought up by her mother's sister, Martha Hübl. Evelyn became a nurse and married a British soldier. They live in Germany.

**Herr Hayden**, Ellen's foreman from Schubert, was drafted into the Volkssturm and died in battle.

**Hans Köhler** got married after the war, and he continued to run the shop in Berlin with his father. After Max and Klara died, Erich arranged for Hans to get a job working in his employ in Rochester, New York, where he and his wife could have an easier life. They emigrated in 1958 and found an apartment near the Arndts. When Hans retired in 1968 he returned to Berlin, managing to draw Social Security from both the USA and Germany, which Erich helped arrange to repay Hans to some extent for his role in protecting them during the war. Hans and his wife died in Berlin in the 1970s. They had no children.

**Max and Klara Köhler** continued to live in Berlin and run the shop after the war. After their deaths they were honoured as Righteous Gentiles by Yad Vashem in 1991.

**Frieda ('Purzel') Lefèbre** died a natural death in Berlin. Her daughter, Ilse, lives in Germany.

**Charlotte Lewinsky** moved to Hempstead, New York, to be near Ellen and Erich and found a job there acting as housekeeper for an elderly man in exchange for a room. In the mid-1960s Erich and Ellen invited Charlotte to live with them in Rochester. She was ill at the time and died in 1970 from cancer at the age of seventy-one.

**Heinz Lewinsky**, Ellen's uncle, remained in Brazil until his death in the early 1970s. He was in his sixties.

**José and Carmen Santaella** had three more children after they moved to Switzerland. Eventually they moved to Córdoba in southern Spain and retired there on a ranch. Ruth and Bruno visited them in 1972. Carmen, now widowed, still lives in Córdoba. Most of her seven children live in Madrid. The Santaellas were honoured as Righteous Gentiles by Yad Vashem in 1991. Carmen and Ruth still correspond every year.

**Gustav and Anni ('Tata') Schulz** remained in Berlin after the war. When Tata went into a nursing home the Arndts sent money from the USA to help support her. Gustav and Anni were honoured as Righteous Gentiles by Yad Vashem in 1991.

**Jacobus ('Co') Spyker**, the Dutch forced labourer who befriended the Arndts in Berlin, left Berlin hastily in January 1944 owing to interrogation from his supervisor about his frequent absences from the barracks. Fearing that he would endanger the Arndts, he fled east to Odessa on foot and by train and remained there until the war ended. After rejoining his family in Holland, he married, had three children and became a successful businessman in Harderwyk. In 1959 a colleague looked up Hans Köhler in Berlin and brought Co news of the Arndts. Each had thought the other to be dead and were overjoyed to find out they had independently survived. Co subsequently visited the family in New York in 1961. Three years later the Gumpel family visited the Spyker family in Holland. The two families visited each other several more times, until Co died in 1972 of a heart attack.

**Ernst and Maria Treptow** were posthumously honoured as Righteous Gentiles by Yad Vashem in 1991. Their daughter Ursula ('Uschi') Treptow accepted the award on behalf of her parents. When Uschi returned to Berlin after the war she met and married Heinz Timm, a German journalist who had been a prisoner-of-war in Texas. They had two sons. In 1954 Bruno found a job for Heinz in his company in Corona, New York, so that they could emigrate. When they arrived the Timm family lived with Ruth and Bruno until Heinz could afford to rent an apartment. The two families became close friends. When Heinz retired they returned to Germany. Uschi, recently widowed, now lives in Berlin, while her sons live in Munich and Vienna. She speaks to Ruth and Ellen frequently on the telephone and they visit each other whenever possible.

# Bibliography

Andreas-Friedrich, Ruth, *Berlin Underground, 1938–1945*, tr. Barrows Mussey, New York: Henry Holt, 1947

Anonymous, 'Jewish New Year: American Army Helps Berlin Jews Restore Their Sacred Services', *Life* magazine, September 1945, p. 49

Bauer, Yehuda, *A History of the Holocaust*, Danbury, Connecticut: Franklin Watts, 1982

Benz, Wolfgang (ed.), *Die Juden in Deutschland 1933–1945*, Munich: C.H. Beck, 1988

Berliner Geschichtswerkstatt (ed.), *Juden in Kreuzberg: Fundstücke, Fragmente, Erinnerungen*, Berlin: Hentrich, 1991

Brothers, Eric, 'On the Anti-Fascist Resistance of German Jews', in *Leo Baeck International Yearbook 13*, London: Secker and Warburg, 1987

Deutschkron, Inge, *Outcast: A Jewish Girl in Wartime Berlin*, tr. Jean Steinberg, New York: Fromm, 1989

Dörner, Bernward, 'Heimtücke', *Das Gesetz als Waffe, Kontrolle: Abschreckung und Verfolgung in Deutschland 1933–1945*, Munich: Paderborn, 1998

Elkin, Rivka, *Das Jüdische Krankenhaus in Berlin Zwischen 1938 und 1945*, Berlin: Hentrich, 1993

Erpel, Simone, 'Struggle and Survival: Jewish Women in the Anti-Fascist Resistance in Germany', in *Leo Baeck International Yearbook 18*, London: Secker and Warburg, 1992

Gay, Peter, *My German Question*, New Haven, Connecticut: Yale University Press, 1998

Gross, Leonard, *The Last Jews in Berlin*, New York: Simon and Schuster, 1982

Hartung von Doetinchem, Dagmar and Rolf Winau (eds), *Zerstörte Fortschritt: Das Jüdische Krankenhaus in Berlin 1756, 1861, 1914, 1989*, Berlin: Hentrich, 1989

Kaplan, Marion A., *Between Dignity and Despair: Jewish Life in Nazi Germany*, New York: Oxford University Press, 1998

Kwiet, Konrad, 'Forced Labour of German Jews in Nazi Germany', in *Leo Baeck International Yearbook 17*, London: Secker and Warburg, 1991

Landesbildstelle Berlin (ed.), *Die Grunewaldrampe: Die Deportation der Berliner Juden*, Berlin: Colloquium, 1993

Mark, Bernard, 'The Herbert Baum Group', in *They Fought Back*, ed. Yuri Suhl, New York: Crown, 1967

Meyer, Beate, 'Jüdische Mischlinge', in *Rassenpolitik und Verfolgungserfahrung 1933–1945: Studien zur Jüdischen Geschichte*, Volume 6, ed. Monika Richarz and Ina Lorenz, Hamburg: Dölling und Galitz, 1999

Meyer, Beate and Hermann Simon (eds), *Juden in Berlin 1938–1945*, Berlin: Philo-Verlagsgesellschaft, 2000

Anon, 'First Jewish Refugees Dock in New York Harbor', *New York Times*, 21 May 1946, p. 1

Paul, Gerhard and Klaus-Michael Mallmann, *Die Gestapo: Mythos und Realität*, Darmstadt: Wissenschaftliche Buchgesellschaft, 1995

Rosenfeld, Alvin, '"Wunderbar, Like a Dream," Say Refugees on Tour of City', *New York Post*, 23 May 1946, p. 14

Rürup, Reinhard (ed.), *Berlin 1945: Eine Dokumentation*, Berlin: Willmuth Arenhövel, 1995

Rürup, Reinhard (ed.), *Jüdische Geschichte in Berlin: Bilder und Dokumente*, Berlin: Hentrich, 1995

Rürup, Reinhard (ed.), *Topography of Terror*, tr. Werner T. Angress, Berlin: Willmuth Arenhovel, 1987
Sandvord, Hans Rainer, *Widerstand in Kreuzberg*, Berlin: Gedenkstätte

Deutscher Widerstand, 1996

Schneider, Peter, 'The Good Germans', *New York Times Magazine*, 13 February 2000, p. 52

Shirer, William L., *Berlin Diary*, New York: Galahad, 1940

Shirer, William L., *The Rise and Fall of the Third Reich*, New York: Simon and Schuster, 1960

Steinberg, Lucien, *Not as a Lamb*, London: D.C. Heath, 1974

Studnitz, Hans-Georg von, *While Berlin Burns: Diaries 1943–45*, London: Weidenfeld and Nicolson, 1963

Sulzberger, C.L., *History of World War II*, revised by Stephen Ambrose, New York: Viking, 1997

Walk, Joseph (ed.), *Das Sonderrecht für die Juden im NS-Staat: Eine Sammlung der gesetzlichen Maßnahmen und Richtlinien – Inhalt und Bedeutung*, Heidelberg: C.F. Müller, 1996

Vassiltchikov, Marie, *Berlin Diaries 1940–1945*, New York: Vintage, 1988
Wyden, Peter, *Stella: One Woman's True Tale of Evil, Betrayal and Survival in Hitler's Germany*, New York: Simon and Schuster, 1992

# STREET MAP OF KREUZBERG, THE AREA WHERE THE GROUP MAINLY LIVED AND WORKED DURING THEIR TIME IN HIDING

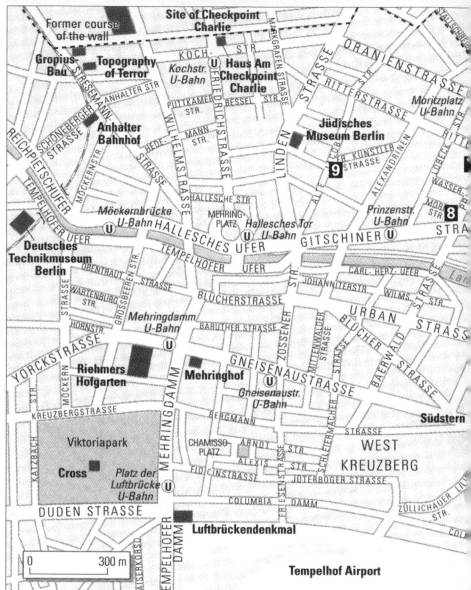

1 Max Köhler's factory at Oranienstrasse 20 where Erich worked: six members of the group were living here by the end of the war.

2 Anni and Max Gehre lived here and sheltered Dr Arndt for over two years. Purzel Lefèbre, Anni's neighbour, hid Erich, Lina, Ruth and Ellen in her bedroom for a time. Frau Liebold, another neighbour – and a Nazi – hid Ellen and Ruth not knowing they were Jews. Marie Wrustrach owned a small delicatessen here and took in Lina, Ruth and Ellen for several days.

3 Ruth hid here initially with the parents of a *Mischling* friend.

4 Anni Harm lived here and took in Charlotte, although her husband was fighting in the Wehrmacht.